5280 TIPS
for INNOVATORS &
ENTREPRENEURS

From Startup to Stable ...

JIM JINDRICK

5280 TIPS for INNOVATORS and ENTREPRENEURS

Copyright

Wencil Research, LLC
120 S Houghton, Suite 138-130
Tucson, Arizona 85748 USA

www.5280TIPS.com

1.04

5280 TIPS for INNOVATORS and ENTREPRENEURS

What, Why, When, and How?

Question: What is in this book?

As an engineer, inventor, entrepreneur, and mentor, I've had the distinct pleasure of working with and learning from many really wonderful, smart people ... mentors, teachers, colleagues, students, family, and friends. I got lots of good advice, how to and not to do things, what works and what doesn't. I took a lot of notes.

I particularly liked the short, sweet, right-to-the-point words of wisdom, tools, and rules of thumb. So, I went searching for more, particularly from those I would probably never meet (they're all over the world!) or could never meet (they're dead!). In the process, I collected several thousand "tips" that I know would be useful for innovators and entrepreneurs. I share those with you in this book.

When I compiled the tips in this book, I didn't set a word limit per se. Rather I had a goal of keeping each tip a "reasonable" length so that it could be assimilated quickly and easily by the reader, a diverse, balanced, inclusive collection of useful information.

Some of the tips are "light" ... a few quick words of encouragement, emboldenment, and insight. Other tips are more detailed, informative, micro-checklists, reminders of things to do, recommendations of things not to do, educational tweaks of things you already know, or stimulators to learn about new things you don't know.

Many tips, by design, may not have anywhere near enough detail ... use them as triggers for further investigation. This book is not a substitute for detailed information about business, entrepreneurship, engineering, creativity, marketing, or any of the many topics that innovators and entrepreneurs must have a reasonable understanding. Rather, this book is a checklist of those elements, a snapshot review, an outline for further investigation and learning.

Question: Why should I read this book?

All the tips in this book are intended to help innovators and entrepreneurs create something new and better (the role of an innovator), and to put that something to work (the role of an entrepreneur). In some way or another, we are all innovators, we are all entrepreneurs. We have all found new and better ways of doing things, be it big or little. We have all gone out on a limb, one time or another, to try something new, something better, something with more value than whatever came before. We've done it before, we will do it again.

While some of the tips are direct quotations, most I have edited to make them more relevant to current times, to make them more focused, to make the intent of the message clear and succinct. I have tried to be very diligent about the source of the words, to do my best to give credit where credit is due. In many cases, I give my thanks to the person from whom I believe I first received a particular nugget of wisdom. My apologizes for any misconnections or misperceptions or undue credits.

I firmly believe that everyone, regardless of profession or calling in life, should have at least a basic knowledge of core business principles. We are all in business in one way or another. We have inherent value in what we know, what we can do, how we can earn a living. We are, like it or not, all in business. Innovators and entrepreneurs are simply more proactive at creating new value and putting that new value to work solving customer problems.

Question: When should I read this book?

First, if you're truly an innovator and entrepreneur, don't just sit around reading books about innovation and entrepreneurship! Go do it! But when you have a little spare time, when your brain needs a little diversion (and it will and should), that's a good time to pick up this book. This book is short and sweet and can be read bits and pieces at a time. A minute here, 10 minutes there.

This is not a book that can't be put down. This is a book you should put down and go do something productive. But productivity tends to come in bursts (there's Tip 5281!). Our brain needs a little diversion now and then to help it think better. So don't leave this book in the down position! Rather, pick it up when you need a little lift, a little encouragement, some little smarts to start your motor running again.

I'd suggest you leave it lying around, pick it up every now and then as a little refresher. Let your colleagues pick it up, too.

Question: How should I read this book?

You could certainly start at the beginning and read to the end. But wouldn't you think a book about innovation and entrepreneurship might also provide some alternatives to the reader.

Consider these: read the book in reverse, from back to front; jump in anywhere and see what you find; take pen to the pages and use the checkboxes to mark the items you like (or don't like!); leave the book lying around where you'll see it every now and then, and when you do, pick it up and just flip to a random page and see what you find; share what you read with your colleagues, ask them what they think; argue with the book, you may well have a much better idea; take an idea from the book and look it up on the internet, see what you find. Have some fun, learn some things, take some things to heart, reject things you don't like. Most important, please use this book as a stimulus to trigger learning and doing and making things new and better! That's what you do, Mr/s Innovator and Entrepreneur ... you learn and do and do and learn. Have at it!

5280+ Tips

[ ] "... and away we go" ... innovators and entrepreneurs can't sit around and do nothing, they are always up and running ... [Thank you, Jackie Gleason]

[X] what you like in this book!

[ ] Jim Jindrick Rule of Thumb: Innovators create something new and better, entrepreneurs put that something new and better to work ...

[ ] Venture: an enterprise involving risk but with a significant reward for success ... a venture could be a business, a company, an organization, a not-for-profit enterprise ...

[ ] Venture Adventure: the process of discovering a new opportunity, defining a new venture that can capitalize on the opportunity, designing and developing the details of the new venture, and deploying the venture plan ...

[ ] To create a new venture, product, service, process, go on a DXpedition: Discover, Define, Design, Develop, Deploy ... 1] Discover what is needed, wanted, desired ... 2] Define what is required to meet those needs, wants, and desires ... 3] Design a solution to meet the defined requirements ... 4] Develop the solution from prototype to production-ready ... 5] Deploy the solution to customers: measure the results, learn what does and doesn't work, then refine the solution to be even better ...

[ ] Key question for our venture: what's the worst thing that could happen to us? ... what will we do if it does? ...

[ ] There is no right way to do the wrong thing ... [Thank you, Waylon Jennings]

[ ] We always have a choice ... and so do our customers! Let us make the right decisions ... [Thank you, Alicia Morga]

[ ] Everyone has their own personal vested interest ... if our business doesn't serve their need, they won't buy in ... [Thank you, Ralph Blazek]

[ ] Don't underestimate our competition ... some of them are geniuses ...

[ ] Persistence pays ... [Thank you, Amber Feller]

[ ] Character will win us respect ...

[ ] Start at the ending, then figure out how to get there ...

[ ] Trust our gut ... unless it's just telling us to eat more!

[ ] Manage transitions ... change is inevitable!

[ ] A source of opportunity for innovation is new knowledge, both scientific and nonscientific ... [Thank you, Peter F Drucker]

[ ] There are three types of people ... those with wishbones, those with funny bones, and those with backbones ... [Thank you, Barbara Ann Kipfer]

[ ] Change can be chaotic ... it's the nature of the beast ...

[ ] When in doubt, panic ... [Thank you, George Jonas]

[ ] Skilled innovators and entrepreneurs are looking for opportunities in problems ...

[ ] Beware: pseudo-investors ... big egos, little money ...

[ ] Govern the clock, not be governed by it ...

[ ] Crank it out ... don't stop until the deed is done!

[ ] Everyone we know is a potential door opener to a new opportunity ... [Thank you, Nelson Wang]

[ ] Value equals Benefits divided by Price (V = B / P) ... to increase Value, we can decrease our Price, we can increase our Benefits, or we can do both ... better Benefits at a lower Price is "the killer deal" for our customers!

[ ] Don't micromanage and interfere with an employee's work ... help, but don't hinder ... it can be a fine line ...

[ ] Don't discriminate ... it's just not right ... not because of age, sexual preference, race, religion, gender, ethnic background ...

[ ] Customers are the stars of our show ... let's do all we can to keep them happy and shining bright ...

[ ] Big corporations increasingly turn to small companies for new ideas ... part of our strategy should include positioning our venture to complement and collaborate with the big players in our industry ... don't be annoying like a gnat, be a purring comfort like a cat ...

[ ] If you want to keep it a secret, keep it a secret ...

[ ] Entrepreneurship is a mashup of many different perspectives, experiences, skills, talents ...

[ ] How should we start tomorrow? ...

[ ] Unhappy customers are our greatest source of learning ... of course, if they're too unhappy they're not going to be customers for very long ... [Thank you, Bill Gates]

[ ] It could be a good opportunity if our team can find the resources needed to pursue it properly ...

[ ] Figure rarely lie; liars frequently figure ... [Thank you, Dennis Kozlowski]

[ ] The most frequent reason for unsuccessful advertising is advertisers who are so full of their own accomplishments (the world's best seed!) that they forget to tell us why we should buy (the world's best lawn!) ... [Thank you, John Caples]

[ ] If we're not part of the solution, we're the precipitate ... [Thank you, Henry J Tillman]

[ ] Never let our emotions take control ...

[ ] Skilled innovators and entrepreneurs are looking for problems to solve ...

[ ] Understand why ... and why not!

[ ] We live in a world of unprecedented change, increasing global competitiveness, and the very real threat of commoditization ... innovation in this world is the best way to win, arguably the only way to really win ... innovation is not a separate, discrete activity but the job of everyone in a leadership position and the integral, central driving force for any business that wants to grow organically and succeed on a sustained basis ... [Thank you, A G Lafley]

[ ] Charm: giving delight, arrousing admiration ...

[ ] The hardest part is getting started ...

[ ] Radical innovation never originates with the market leader ... [Thank you, Jim Utterback]

[ ] Failure isn't fatal ... unless we make it so ...

[ ] Work smart ... work hard, too, and we've really got something going!

[ ] Skilled innovators and entrepreneurs are continuously curious ...

[ ] Promote our venture with newspaper insert ...

[ ] Be passionate about everything we do ...

[ ] The truth is sometimes hard to hear ...

[ ] When in doubt, deduct ... referring to filing income tax returns ...

[ ] Help others on their path ...

[ ] Always look our best ...

[ ] Beware of zombies ...

[ ] Potential business model: Sell and deliver services ...

[ ] Luck has a lot to do with it ... the more we prepare, the luckier we get ...

[ ] We can do it if we have the passion to do it ... if we don't, we won't ...

[ ] Build-Measure-Learn (B-M-L): the process of creating a new product, service, process, or method through continual incremental change and improvement ... with B-M-L, speed is a critical ingredient to product development where a prototype product is built, tested with customer interaction, and feedback recorded and used to learn more about serving customer needs, wants, and desires ... build rapid prototypes, measure customer satisfaction, learn what does and does not work, and have successes and failures as we go ... we'll know more about what we're doing as we're doing it, instead of guessing before we do it ...

[ ] Beachhead: focusing resources on one key area, usually a smaller market segment or product category, and winning that market first, even dominating that market, before moving into larger markets ... it's a holdover from World War II when the allies stormed Normandy, the beachhead from which they moved forward ...

[ ] Forget a wrong, remember a kindness ... think good thoughts ...

[ ] Something: a product, service, process, marketing position, paradigm, or combination of some or all ...

[ ] How to kill creativity: "Our customers wouldn't like it ..."

[ ] No speech was ever too short ...

[ ] When someone does something good, applaud ... we will make two people happy! ... [Thank you, Samuel Goldwyn]

[ ] The safe way to double our money is to fold it over once and put it in our pocket ... [Thank you, Frank Hubbard]

[ ] Winning is a habit ... unfortunately, so is losing ... [Thank you, Vince Lombardi]

[ ] Respond to negative feedback ...

[ ] Limitation is the severest storm of fattery ... dieting made simple!

[ ] Key question for our venture: Can we show that "the dogs will eat the dog food"? ... that our prospective customers will buy our products and services? ...

[ ] Fate laughs at probabilities ... [Thank you, Edward George Bulwer-Lytton]

[ ] Like a child plays, a genius works ... [Thank you, Barbara Ann Kipfer]

[ ] A good business plan reads like a combination of the Wall Street Journal, a model of good business writing, and USA Today, a model of good storytelling ...

[ ] Choose the best word ...

[ ] Practice makes us better ...

[ ] Successful Innovators and entrepreneurs know how to reflect ... [Thank you, Patricia G Greene]

[ ] Technology: the application of scientific knowledge for practical purposes, especially in industry ...

[ ] Principles don't change with circumstances ... that's what makes them principles! ... [Thank you, George Colombo]

[ ] Understate rather than overstate ...

[ ] Estimate sales and revenue from several perspectives to see if they are in the same ballpark ...

[ ] Wonder is the beginning of wisdom ...

[ ] Lean Canvas: a version of the Business Model Canvas that focuses on addressing broad customer problems and low-development-cost solutions and delivering them to select customer segments to validate (or not) a particular value proposition ...

[ ] Conceit is the finest armor anyone can wear ... [Thank you, Jerome K Jerome]

[ ] A good business plan contains reasonable financial projections with key data explained and justified ... [Thank you, Mike Arnold]

[ ] How to attract new customers: offer a pleaser teaser to buy ...

[ ] Allow our colleagues to speak their minds and offer differing opinions ... [Thank you, Scott Isaksen]

[ ] See what new patents are being issued ...

[ ] Spoken words can't be recalled ... and emails are even worse because they will live in the cloud forever!

[ ] Conquer ignorance ... stupidity is forever, but ignorance can be fixed ...

[ ] Clearly assess our strengths and weaknesses ...

[ ] Create something ... something is better than nothing ...

[ ] Heroes take risks ... often without much thought ...

[ ] Send handwritten notes ... saying "thank you" is one of the nicest things you can do for someone ...

[ ] Cash flow: the total amount of money being transferred into and out of a business, especially as affecting liquidity ...

[ ] Build a loyal fan base by being better than everyone else ... customers, suppliers, employees, the community ...

[ ] Innovators often have good memories ... what worked before, and what didn't ...

[ ] Keep our team informed ... the bad news as well as the good ...

[ ] How can we answer this Question: What sets us apart from all our competition? ...

[ ] Promote our venture with mugs ...

[ ] Never run out of altitude, airspeed, and ideas at the same time ... [Thank you, Bob Willson]

[ ] Opportunity evaluation checklist: Is it timely, solvable, doable, important, potentially profitable? Does it have favorable regulatory and industry context? Does it have the potential to be positioned favorably relative to the competition? ...

[ ] How can we answer this Question: How was our company's intellectual property developed? ... who owns the rights? ...

[ ] Yada, yada, yada ... there are always more details than what we first may think ... [Thank you, Jerry Steinfeld]

[ ] We can't cut costs without making a better product ... [Thank you, W Edwards Deming]

[ ] Fame: being known because of notable achievement ...

[ ] Time: the indefinite continued progress of existence and events in the past, present, and future regarded as a whole ...

[ ] Intellectual Property: something that is the result of creativity, such as a manuscript or a design, to which one has rights and for which one may apply for a patent, copyright,or trademark ...

[ ] If we want to do something new, we gotta do something different!

[ ] There is a great difference between knowing and understanding ... we can know a lot about something but not really understand it ... [Thank you, Charles F Kettering]

[ ] Make a "preliminary" marketing brochure ... use it to "test market" a new product or service before it is actually launched for real ...

[ ] Jim Jindrick Rule of Thumb for Venture Success: Earn a Profit Solving Customer Problems with Something New and Better than the Competition! a critical success factor for every venture ...

[ ] Promote our venture with telephone pole signs ...

[ ] We may be blessed with brilliant brains, but they're not much good unless we use them ...

[ ] Don't look back ... something might be gaining on us! ... [Thank you, Satchel Paige]

[ ] We have to know the ropes in order to pull the strings ...

5280 TIPS for INNOVATORS and ENTREPRENEURS

[ ] It's hard to detect good luck ... it looks so much like something we've earned! ... [Thank you, Fred Clark]

[ ] Rule of Thumb: a commonly accepted truth-ism or way of doing something ... it may or may not be right, but it is probably a good place to start ...

[ ] Proofread, then proofread again ... [Thank you, Kenneth Roman]

[ ] It takes less time to do a thing right than to explain why we did it wrong ... [Thank you, Henry Wadsworth Longfellow]

[ ] Managers do things right ... leaders do the right things ... [Thank you, Daniel McCullum]

[ ] Put our money where our need is ... [Thank you, Madeline E Cohen]

[ ] It could be a good opportunity if the upside potential is significant and timely ...

[ ] Be willing to shift ... iterate, pivot, start all over again ...

[ ] Don't procrastinate ... (starting tomorrow, of course!) ...

[ ] Beware: tagalongs ... some folks are just there to bask in our glory without breaking a sweat to help get there ...

[ ] It is a capital mistake to theorize before one has data ... [Thank you, Sherlock Holmes]

[ ] We cannot undo anything that we did in the past ... all we can do is learn from it, and repeat the good and avoid the bad ...

[ ] One fantasy can transform one million realities ... [Thank you, Barbara Ann Kipfer]

[ ] The first rule of intelligent tinkering: "save all the pieces" ... [Thank you, Aldo Leopold]

17

[ ] ASP: abbreviation for Average Selling Price ...

[ ] Embrace change ... or brace for the consequences ...

[ ] End User: the ultimate consumer of our products and services ...

[ ] IPO: abbreviation for Initial Public Offering ...

[ ] Spend some time protecting the earth ... we've only got but one to go around ...

[ ] Make our writing active and personal ... [Thank you, Kenneth Roman]

[ ] When work is a pleasure, life is a joy ... when work is a duty, life is slavery! ... [Thank you, Maxim Gorky]

[ ] Experienced mentors can help innovators and entrepreneurs effectively and efficiently move their venture concept ahead ... that helps the team avoid many of the rabbit holes and booby traps that can hinder success ...

[ ] Insanity is doing the same thing over and over again and expecting different results ... [Thank you, Albert Einstein]

[ ] A wise man sometimes changes his mind, but a fool never will ...

[ ] Give ourselves an hour instead of the whole day ... get it done, now ...

[ ] A problem is an opportunity in disguise ... [Thank you, Pouria Valley]

[ ] Sometimes we gotta walk before we've even learned to crawl ...

[ ] Crucial Questions (the CQ's): Who? What? Where? When? Why? How? ... (Often called the six most powerful questions

in the world) ... [Thank you, Northwestern University, Journalism 101]

[ ] If they are selling dogs at a flea market, they are not reputable breeders ... [Thank you, Sarah Mister]

[ ] The person with a new idea is often considered a considered a crank until the idea succeeds ... [Thank you, John Goulding]

[ ] Haste makes waste ...

[ ] Praise competitors ... learn from them, too ... there are times when we can cooperate with them to their advantage and to ours! ... [Thank you, George Matthew Adams]

[ ] What one sees depends on where one sits ... [Thank you, James R Schlesinger]

[ ] People forget how fast we did a job, but they remember how well we did it ... good quality is benefit number one ... [Thank you, Howard Newton]

[ ] Don't get caught up in the latest and greatest fads ... they, too, shall pass. ... [Thank you, Sandy DeCesaro]

[ ] Key question for our venture: Do our marketing messages make sense? ... Check to see that all of our points are relevant and that everything is consistent with the tone and flow or our text ...

[ ] Ensure our message has important details and facts, but that nothing deters the focus of our message ...

[ ] Tardiness can rob us of opportunity ... [Thank you, Niccolo Machiavelli]

[ ] The easiest thing to achieve is a misunderstanding ...

[ ] Take responsibility, good or bad ... lavish credit on others when things go well, take it on the chin when they do not ...

[ ] Follow the advice we've been giving others ...

[ ] One person's leisure is another person's work ...

[ ] Skilled innovators and entrepreneurs have stamina ...

[ ] Branding mistake: lack of passion ... [Thank you, Jarad Hull]

[ ] The ultimate inspiration is a deadline ... [Thank you, Nolan Bushnell]

[ ] Get in low, get out high ...

[ ] Real or Imaginary ... what should we focus on today? ...

[ ] See everything as if it were for the first time ...

[ ] We need a buffer in the bank ... a little extra cash to hold us over on rainy days, weeks, months! margins are good safety features ...

[ ] Common cause of venture death: corruption ... someone on the team is taking something out the back door ...

[ ] Just do it ... [Thank you, Nike]

[ ] Beat them with service ... same product, customers will buy from whomever makes their buy and try experience easier.

[ ] Buy in bulk ... but only if we're really going to use it all ...

[ ] The traditional entrepreneurship process ... 1] Think of an idea ... 2] Do market research ... 3] Put together some financial projections ... 4] Put a team together ... 5] Write business plan ... 6] Find funding ... 7] Build a prototype and test it with prospective customers ... 8] Bring the product and/or service to market ... 9] Manage the business ... 10] Find an exit ...

[ ] How to kill creativity: "That's been done before ..." ...

[ ] Planning is what we do before we do something so when we do it, it's not all mixed up ... [Thank you, Winnie the Pooh]

[ ] If we can't win the game, kick over the table ... [Thank you, Nancy Hughes]

[ ] Key question for our venture: What have we learned from our competitors' mistakes? ...

[ ] Beware: scamming "consultants" ... are the advice givers giving good advice ...

[ ] Critical Success Factor: the elements necessary for an innovation or entrepreneurial venture to reach fruition ...

[ ] Successful entrepreneurs do not wait until "the Muse kisses them" and gives them a "bright idea" ... they go to work ... they do not look for the "biggie," the innovation that will "revolutionize the industry," create a "billion-dollar business" or "make one rich overnight." ... those entrepreneurs who start out with the idea that they'll make it big - and in a hurry - can be guaranteed failure ... [Thank you, Peter F Drucker]

[ ] An old dog can still learn new tricks ... it just might take a little patience in training ... [Thank you, John McCain]

[ ] Promote our venture with business networking ...

[ ] How to kill creativity: "Their ideas don't count ..."

[ ] The future changes everything and everyone ...

[ ] Ask many questions ... gather many answers before making a final decision ...

[ ] When we come to the end of our rope, tie a knot and hang on ...

[ ] Everybody is somebody we can learn from ...

[ ] Big oceans are full of big sharks ... little lakes and ponds, not so much ... occasionally, there might be a Loch Ness Monster-ish critter in there, but not so common ...

[ ] How to kill creativity: "That's crazy ..."

[ ] Banish the word "cannot" from our vocabulary ...

[ ] The worse the news, the more effort should go into communicating it ... [Thank you, Andy Grove]

[ ] Begin with the end in mind ... [Thank you, Stephen R Covey]

[ ] Key question for our venture: What is the critical mass for our venture? ... How much money, how many people, what resources, which customers do we absolutely need to make it a go? ...

[ ] The company of tomorrow will consist of a CEO with a cell phone ... [Thank you, Tom Peters]

[ ] Evolution of a Business Venture ... 1] Opportunity: there is a gap in market, there is new technology; maybe, just maybe, we can do something here ... 2] Idea: clear problems, viable solutions; hmmm, there is something here ... 3] Concept: viable strategies for earning a profit solving customer problems better than the competition ... 4] Venture: viable innovation concept (product, service, process, position, method); team (innovator, entrepreneur, money manager); resources (people, places, things, time, money) ... 5] Organization: team, roles, clear strategies ... 6] Company: legal formation, pre-sales, unstable financials (raising funds) ... 7] Business: low-hanging fruit, sales, customers, stable, positive EBITDA, viable business model ... 8] Enterprise: scale, scope, markets, growth, significant EBITDA, defined task and assignments, employees ... 9] Institution: significant market share, significant industry position, re-invention,

continual innovation ... 10] Tombstone: the cows have run out of milk ...

[ ] Successful teams respect each other ...

[ ] Refine roles, risks, and rewards ...

[ ] Don't make our employees come in on days they're normally not scheduled to work or call them while they're on vacation ... Give 'em a break ... they deserve it ... [Thank you, InsideCRM]

[ ] Needs, wants, desires ... the types of problems our customers have that we need to solve, ranging from painful needs to pleasurable desires ...

[ ] Courage is what it takes to stand up and speak ... courage is also what it takes to sit down and listen ... [Thank you, Winston Churchill]

[ ] Design for the world ... [Thank you, Sue Factor]

[ ] COGS: abbreviation for Cost of Good Sold, the cost of the components and labor required to produce a product ...

[ ] Most every problem has multiple solutions ...

[ ] Either or ... when we have a list of things that need to be prioritized, put the items in order by picking one or the other, then move down the list until all are sorted ...

[ ] The key to good research is to keep it simple ... focus on measuring one or two variables at a time to keep things manageable ... [Thank you, Jenn Kim]

[ ] Promote our venture with picket your establishment ...

[ ] Making a great presentation: Make pictures and diagrams easy to see ... [Thank you, Ian McKenzie]

[ ] Imagination is a good servant but a bad master ...

[ ] How can we answer this Question: Can we sell our products wholesale? ...

[ ] Make people feel good ...

[ ] There is a solution to every problem ... the difficulty is finding it ... [Thank you, Ewie Nef]

[ ] Look at the bright side of things ... even if we have to use a flashlight to find it ...

[ ] Write our own ending ...

[ ] One way to get high blood pressure is to go mountain climbing over molehills ... [Thank you, Earl Wilson]

[ ] Fear kills growth ... [Thank you, Gary Vee]

[ ] Successful innovators and entrepreneurs have tenacity ...

[ ] Google was not the first search engine ... they weren't first so they had to be better!

[ ] Imagination or Intuition ... what should we focus on today? ...

[ ] There's no crying in baseball ... there is a lot of crying in entrepreneurship ... it's how we keep going that will make us great ... [Thank you, Tom Hanks]

[ ] Offer direction instead of issuing orders ...

[ ] Without customers, we don't have a business ... we have but a hobby! ... [Thank you, Don Peppers]

[ ] There is no right way to do wrong ...

[ ] Don't act like a dumb idiot ... at least not in public. Do what we want in private ... [Thank you, J Browning]

[ ] Version 1.0 (one point oh) is the first out-the-door product that we're selling to any and all customers ...

[ ] Iterative, not linear ...

[ ] Anyone can say they are an investor ...

[ ] Potential business model: Transportation of people or products ...

[ ] Life is one experiment after another ... some work, some don't ...

[ ] First listen, then ask questions: repeat six times before talking ...

[ ] Key question for our venture: Is our name itself confusing? ...

[ ] There's always a reason to smile ... [Thank you, Bob Parsons]

[ ] Make sure everything is polished ... shiny, sparkling, looking like new, and ready to make a great impression on our customers!

[ ] Eighty percent of success is showing up ... [Thank you, Woody Allen]

[ ] Innovation is essential for achieving competitive advantage in today's high pressure business environment ... too few companies have successfully integrated systematic innovation into their operating methods and practices ... it is often too easy to become internally focused, losing site of key sources for inspiration and customer needs in changing marketplaces thus stifling creativity and long-term growth ... [Thank you, MIT]

[ ] We cannot become what we need to be by remaining what we are ... [Thank you, Max de Pree]

[ ] Job or Career ... what should we focus on today? ...

[ ] Common Mistake: underestimating the time to make a sale ...

[ ] The source is often more important than the story ...

[ ] Promote our venture with sponsorship of charitable events sponsorships ...

[ ] Champions are made from something they have deep inside them ... a desire, a dream, a vision ... [Thank you, Muhammad Ali]

[ ] Believing is seeing ... [Thank you, Naomi Klein]

[ ] Our attitude changes our reality ...

[ ] A new venture may be feasible if creating a solution is sustainable ...

[ ] Copy successful business models ...

[ ] Handle numbers consistently and coherently ... it's easier to understand $73 million than $73000000 or even $73,000,000 ...

[ ] Perhaps no one's lives depend on what we do ... but their livelihood might, so it's important that we do a good job ... [Thank you, Ian Lurie]

[ ] We can and should discover new things every day ...

[ ] Viral marketing is the ability to create entertaining or informative messages that are passed along in an exponential fashion, often electronically or by e-mail ... [Thank you, Andrew Corbett]

[ ] We cannot resist an idea whose time has come ... [Thank you, Victor Hugo]

[ ] Never was anything great achieved without danger ... [Thank you, Niccolo Machiavelli]

[ ] Move first, more fast ... if we're not first, we must be better. If we are first, we need to remember that it won't last ... we still need to be better ... move first, move fast ... move second, move faster ...

[ ] Research: the systematic investigation into and study of materials and sources in order to establish facts and reach new conclusions ...

[ ] Common bootstrapping strategy: don't give up the day job!

[ ] There is no time like the present ... [Thank you, Tyler Johanson]

[ ] How can we answer this Question: How will this venture grow, and over what time period? ...

[ ] We gotta polish it if we want it to shine! ... [Thank you, Len Goodman]

[ ] The number of members on the board of directors should be odd ... no tie votes ...

[ ] Buy low and sell high ... the basics of every good business model ... the value from the business lies in the "and" in between!

[ ] Don't assume it will get done ...

[ ] Summertime and the living is easy ... wintertime and we've got to keep the firing going ...

[ ] The biggest competition is the status-quo ...

[ ] Success is 99 percent failure ... [Thank you, Soichiro Honda]

[ ] Beware of the Ides of March ... it can be a killer day ... depending on our venture, some days are just naturally good for business, others not ... are we ready for either or both? ...

[ ] Act constructively ... [Thank you, Warren Donian]

[ ] The prime purpose of eloquence is to keep our customers listening to us instead of our competition ... [Thank you, Louis Vermeil]

[ ] Application: putting something into operation ...

[ ] Key question for our venture: What milestones will the financing get our venture to? ...

[ ] Bury "can't" and we'll find "can" ...

[ ] If it was easy to succeed, everyone would do it ...

[ ] In truth lies beauty ...

[ ] Always have a margin of safety, in case something goes wrong ... and it will! ... [Thank you, Warren Buffett]

[ ] The key to failure is trying to please everyone ...

[ ] Improvement requires change ...

[ ] The best judge of an argument is time ... [Thank you, Barbara Ann Kipfer]

[ ] Key question for our venture: Is our name pleasant to see?

[ ] People will forget what we said, people will forget what we did, but people will never forget how we made them feel ... [Thank you, Maya Angelou]

[ ] Learn from mistakes, ours and others ...

[ ] Light travels faster than sound ... this is why some people appear bright until we hear them speak!

[ ] Lose a small fish to catch a big one ...

[ ] Nothing is ever lost by courtesy ... it is the cheapest of pleasures, costs nothing, and conveys much ... [Thank you, Erastus Wiman]

[ ] Move our venture forward, from dream to concept to reality ...

[ ] Recognize the difference between the big and small ...

[ ] Sometimes apparent failures lead to great successes ... the glue didn't stick very well, but worked great on the back of the 3M Post-it Note ... [Thank you, Spencer Silver]

[ ] There are always obstacles and competitors ... there is never an open road, except the wide road that leads to failure ... every great success has always been achieved by fight ... every winner has scars ... those who succeed are the efficient few ... they are the few who have the ambition and willpower to develop themselves ... [Thank you, Herbert N Casson]

[ ] Be impeccable with our words ... if we can't say something good, don't say something at all ...

[ ] Strength comes from commitment ...

[ ] Skilled innovators and entrepreneurs are willing to question norms and assumptions ...

[ ] Key question for our venture: What traction has our venture generated? ... How can this traction be accelerated? What has been the principal reasons for this traction? ...

[ ] Use beta tests to gather primary research data ...

[ ] A leopard cannot change its spots ... at least not without a can of spray paint ...

[ ] The window of opportunity won't stay open forever ...

[ ] Promote our venture with seminars ...

[ ] Anything worth having is worth working for ...

[ ] Skill or Luck ... what should we focus on today? ...

[ ] Take one day at a time ... tomorrow is another day ...

[ ] Take hands out of pockets ...

[ ] If we're going through hell, keep going ... [Thank you, Winston Churchill]

[ ] Lean and mean, Jean! keep our profit-generating machine clean! ... [Thank you, Gene Tobey]

[ ] Treat our customers like guests ... [Thank you, Walt Disney]

[ ] Mental Error: "We'll capture 50% of the market in no time at all!" ... If our market size is two and one of them is mom, maybe. But if we're a normal venture, it's going to take some time. Further, a 50% market share is phenomenal ...

[ ] Common bootstrapping strategy: be frugal ...

[ ] Love to learn, learn to live, live to love, and so forth ... keep iterating ...

[ ] Learn every step of the way ... keep in step with learning ...

[ ] The most important single central fact about a free market is that no exchange takes place unless both parties benefit ... [Thank you, Milton Friedman]

[ ] Skilled innovators and entrepreneurs are aware of the world around them ...

[ ] Don't just be credible, be incredible ...

[ ] Create a PR campaign for our new product concept ... if after creating the campaign, the product concept still looks good, do it!

[ ] Key question for our venture: What are our unit economics? ...

[ ] Think things through, then follow through ... [Thank you, Eddie Rickenbacker]

[ ] Pursue opportunities with discipline, not emotion ... [Thank you, Cooper Kowalski]

[ ] Change is inevitable ... it will happen again. Always has, always will ...

[ ] Find problems, fix them ...

[ ] Opportunity knocks, but sometimes not very hard ...

[ ] Many hands make light work ...

[ ] If people listened to themselves more often, they'd talk less ...

[ ] Be brief ...

[ ] Each mind has its own method ... [Thank you, Oleh Fostiak]

[ ] Skilled innovators and entrepreneurs are able to use wide categories and images ...

[ ] Use social media to get the word out about our venture ...

[ ] How can we answer this Question: How will our venture earn a profit? ...

[ ] The C's of entrepreneurial motivation: challenge, creativity, control, cash, and celebrity ...

[ ] Thinking is the hardest work of all, and that's why so few of us do it ... [Thank you, Henry Ford]

[ ] How to kill creativity: "It's not your job ...".

[ ] A good business plan provides a clear explanation of what the investor will get for their investment ... [Thank you, Arizona State University Colleagues]

[ ] Mind our image online ... once it's on the internet, it's almost impossible to retract or retread ...

[ ] How to kill creativity: "It would cost too much ..." ...

[ ] There are no patent police ... we're on our own to go after suspected patent infringement ...

[ ] Our brand is our promise to our customers that they will have a consistent experience ... preferably a great experience with our venture ...

[ ] Failing to prepare is preparing to fail ... [Thank you, John Wooden]

[ ] Outsource when possible ... focus on our core competencies ...

[ ] The FUD Factor: Fear, Uncertainty, and Doubt ... careful we don't let FUD get in the way of our progress ...

[ ] Eighty percent of the work is done by twenty percent of the staff ...

[ ] Skilled innovators and entrepreneurs are have good communicative ability ...

[ ] Build products that are already in demand ...

[ ] Nothing is so contagious as an example ... [Thank you, François de la Rochefoucauld]

[ ] Innovation is art and science ... the art of seeing things that aren't there, the science of putting them there ...

[ ] Nothing succeeds like the appearance of success ... [Thank you, Christopher Lasch]

[ ] We are responsible for our own happiness ...

[ ] Brands require constant attention ... staying fresh and relevant in the marketplace takes work! ... [Thank you, Leslie Bromberg]

[ ] Seeking to please others is perilous ... but that is what we must do. Our customers are waiting ...

[ ] Develop multiple paths to success ...

[ ] Decide whether we're having a creative meeting to generate ideas, or an analytical meeting to make decisions ... don't try to do both in the same meeting ... we'll all go crazy!

[ ] TRIM: Team, Resources, Idea, Market ... a basic outline for a business venture ...

[ ] Excellence is our goal, understanding is our foundation ... [Thank you, Lew Sorensen]

[ ] When writing a business plan, avoid gimmicks ... serious investors want facts, not hype ... they may eat the chocolate rose that accompanies the business plan for our new florist shop, but it won't make them any more interested in investing in the venture ... [Thank you, Kaye Vivian]

[ ] We don't learn anything the second time we're kicked by a mule ...

[ ] Have an customer champion inside our venture ... that person looks at everything we do from a customer perspective so we can nip bad policies in the bud ...

[ ] Old habits die hard ... getting customers to try something new is not something easy to do ...

[ ] Skilled innovators and entrepreneurs are able to cope well with novelty ...

[ ] No reward, no risk ...

[ ] Low investment, low return ...

[ ] Me or Thee ... what should we focus on today? ...

[ ] Some 3 million new business ventures are launched each year in the US ... many more worldwide, of course!

[ ] Board of Directors: a group of persons chosen to govern the affairs of a corporation or other organization or institution.

[ ] If we think we're paying too little for our tattoos, there's probably a reason ...

[ ] Imagination trumps intelligence ...

[ ] With grace, ambidexterity, fitness, and poise ... how to stand in front of an audience ...

[ ] Encourage purposeful evolution ... [Thank you, S A Buckler]

[ ] When things go wrong, don't go with them ... [Thank you, Elvis Presley]

[ ] Key question for our venture: Can we list 100 potential customers for the products and services we offer in our venture ... If not, why not? ...

[ ] Different strokes for different folks ... tailor our marketing messages to market segment niches ...

[ ] The only thing we know for certain about the future is that it's going to be different ... [Thank you, Peter F Drucker]

[ ] Distance allows us to see things more clearly ...

[ ] We don't know until we try ...

[ ] It is difficult to believe that someone can differ from us and be right ... [Thank you, Bob Swelgin]

[ ] The most important person in the room is the one who knows what to do next ... [Thank you, James Webb]

[ ] Be guided by our vision and mission ...

[ ] People act differently in a crowd than when they are alone ... groupthink usually rules ...

[ ] Appeal to their emotions ... subjective benefits are often ranked higher than objective benefits ...

[ ] Price is a strategy ...

[ ] An expert is a person who has made all the mistakes that can be made in a very narrow field ... [Thank you, Niels Bohr]

[ ] Everyone is a fool for at least five minutes every day ... wisdom comes from not exceeding the limit! ... [Thank you, Elbert Hubbard]

[ ] If it weren't for the last minute, a lot of things wouldn't get done ... [Thank you, Michael Traylor]

[ ] Deploy: bring into effective action ...

[ ] Acquisition: an asset or object bought or obtained ... Sometimes big companies buy little companies because they want what they got! But big companies also buy little companies because they want what the little company's got gone!

[ ] Stage: a particular point in a process ...

[ ] Probability: the likelihood of something happening ... rarely is something 100% certain to happen or 0% certain not to happen ... what are the real odds we're dealing with? ...

[ ] Get the details right ... the devil is in there! ...

[ ] Chance favors the prepared ... [Thank you, Louis Pasteur]

[ ] Home Run or Touchdown ... what game are we playing today? ...

[ ] Promote our venture with grocery store cart signs ...

[ ] Passion: an intense desire or enthusiasm for something ...

[ ] Under-promise, over-deliver ...

[ ] Keep away from people who try to belittle our ambitions ... small people always do that, but the really great make us feel that we can become great, too ... [Thank you, Samuel Clemens]

[ ] Imagination rules the world ...

[ ] In God we trust, all others bring data!

[ ] Software: the programs and other operating information used by a computer ... sometimes, software is used to describe the variable content of something. For example, a music player needs "software" (the music) to be of any value to the user ...

[ ] All creative endeavor begins with just fooling around, not doing much of anything, just noodling and letting the different parts of our mind talk to each other ... science and art and invention spring forth when we do the unexpected and so coax our brains into letting some imaginative combinations of ideas and concepts jangle together ... [Thank you, Cory Doctorow]

[ ] Be stubborn about our vision but flexible with our plan ... [Thank you, John C Maxwell]

[ ] When in over our heads, grab a life preserver ...

[ ] I didn't fail, I just found 1,000 ways that don't work ... [Thank you, Thomas A Edison]

[ ] Programming today is a race between software engineers striving to build bigger and better idiot-proof programs, and the Universe trying to produce bigger and better idiots ... so far, the Universe is winning ... [Thank you, Rick Cook]

[ ] Obstacles are what we see when we take our eyes off our goals ...

[ ] Skilled innovators and entrepreneurs are alert to gaps in their knowledge ...

[ ] The person who says they are willing to meet us halfway is usually a poor judge of distance ... [Thank you, Laurence J Peter]

[ ] Possible but not probable, possible but not plausible ...

[ ] Skilled innovators and entrepreneurs are able to think metaphorically ...

[ ] Dare to take calculated risks in order to bring innovative ideas to fruition ... [Thank you, Walt Disney]

[ ] Innovators and entrepreneurs are agents of change ... can't have one without the other!

[ ] Relax ... don't let our emotions get in the way of progress ...

[ ] Every millisecond counts ... [Thank you, Sue Factor]

[ ] To create a new product, apply SCAMPER to an old one ... Substitute; Combine; Adapt; Modify, minimize, magnify; Put to another use; Eliminate, elaborate; Rearrange, reverse ... [Thank you, Bob Eberle]

[ ] Do our best ... why would we do any less? ...

[ ] Making a great presentation: Use color carefully ... [Thank you, Ian McKenzie]

[ ] Any jackass can kick a barn door down ... but it takes a skilled carpenter to build one ...

[ ] Push in just one direction, not in two ... [Thank you, Rita Levi-Montalcini]

[ ] A good business plan is plausible throughout ... [Thank you, BottleKnows]

[ ] People always pay too much attention to things that are easy to quantify ... money vs happiness, blood pressure vs fitness, grades vs competency ...

[ ] Courage is not the absence of fear but the ability to carry on with dignity in spite of it ... [Thank you, Scott Turow]

[ ] Buy quality ... sell value ...

[ ] It is the supreme art of the teacher to awaken the joy of creative expression and knowledge in the student ... [Thank you, Albert Einstein]

[ ] Keep an eye on what we want to happen ...

[ ] Promote our venture with telemarketing ...

[ ] Key question for our venture: Is our name limiting? ...

[ ] Types of customer segments ... mass market, niche market, segmented market, diversified market, multi-sided market ...

[ ] Insight and knowledge produce enlightenment ... [Thank you, Barbara Ann Kipfer]

[ ] Capitalization Table: a capitalization table (Cap Table) lists who owns what in a startup ... it calculates how the option pool shuffle and the seed debt lower the Series A share price ...

[ ] Never throw away an idea ... [Thank you, 3M]

[ ] She has half the deed done, who has made a beginning ... [Thank you, Horace]

[ ] Successful teams are doers ...

[ ] Improve current products ...

[ ] Necessity is the mother of innovation ...

[ ] Skilled innovators and entrepreneurs are intelligent ...

[ ] Half of the prospects that contact us are going to buy, if not from us from someone else ... if we can sell half the contacts we get, we're doing great ... if we only sell one in ten, ninety percent of our potential customers went somewhere else! ... [Thank you, Mike Rymsza]

[ ] Time waits for no one ... any time wasted cannot be recovered ...

[ ] Invest in solid technology ... leave the flim-flam to our competition ...

[ ] Entrepreneurs have a knack for turning the commonplace into the unique and unexpected ... [Thank you, D G Mitton]

[ ] An innovation is [simply] something new and better ... while "innovation" may have a revolutionary reputation, it has an evolutionary reality ... get there step by step, inch by inch ...

[ ] Appreciate the questions as much as the answers ... [Thank you, University of Wisconsin - Parkside teachers] ...

[ ] The number one factor that contributed to our success at Google is luck ... we followed our hearts, and worked on search because it was useful and an interesting problem ... [Thank you, Sergey Brin]

[ ] Carefully craft our story ... make sure our customers "get it" ...

[ ] Common cause of venture death: poor products and/or services ...

[ ] Public Relations: the professional maintenance of a favorable public image by a company or other organization or a famous person ...

[ ] Promote our venture with news releases ...

[ ] Support, empower, and reward employees ... [Thank you, Walt Disney]

[ ] Acknowledge a gift, no matter how small ... [Thank you, Barbara Ann Kipfer]

[ ] Borrowing money often costs too much ... do we really need it? ... will we use it wisely? ...

[ ] Don't hope, pray, or wish for success ... we've got to get out there and make it happen ...

[ ] Nothing is so amusingly arrogant as someone who has just discovered an old idea and thinks it is their own ... [Thank you, Sidney J Harris]

[ ] Less than one-tenth of one percent of all start-ups receive VC money, accounting for less than 2 percent of all small business financing ...

[ ] The harder it is to do something, the better we'll feel after doing it ... [Thank you, Marguerite de Angeli]

[ ] Replace an empty mind with an open one ...

[ ] Our time will come ... we need to be ready when it does ...

[ ] Resources: a stock or supply of money, materials, facilities, staff, time, and other assets that can be drawn on by an organization in order to function effectively ...

[ ] Key question for our venture: Do we know what to put in our business plan, and why? ...

[ ] Oh, the creatures of habit ... not all habits are bad ... consciously build good habits so we continue to do them without a second thought ...

[ ] B2B: abbreviation for a Business-to-Business relationship ...

[ ] Every industry has a rock star or two ... how can that be us? ...

[ ] Potential business model: Provide labor resources ...

[ ] Entertain our fears, get them totally blitzed, then cut off their heads with a sharp knife and get on with life ...

[ ] Skilled innovators and entrepreneurs have wide and varied interests ...

[ ] We are prisoners of our own experience ...

[ ] Product Development Triangle: the relationship between the Customer Needs, Wants, Desires Profile; the Fit, Form, Functions, Features Product Profile; and the Product Benefit Goals when developing a new product, service, process, or method ...

[ ] Customers rely on our dependability, and depend on our reliability ...

[ ] Creativity is a critical skill for innovators and entrepreneurs ... [Thank you, P G Greene]

[ ] How to improve our financial bottom line: change our pricing ...

[ ] Give or Grovel ... what should we focus on today? ...

[ ] Entrepreneurship is putting innovation to work ...

[ ] Give credit when it's due ...

[ ] Successful entrepreneurs have an ability to manage ongoing business operations ... [Thank you, Lynda Applegate]

[ ] Whatever is worth doing at all is worth doing well ... [Thank you, Philip Dormer Stanhope]

[ ] We're no good dead ... we need to be healthy if we're going to continue to serve our customers in new and better ways! ... [Thank you, Tom Brown]

[ ] The entrepreneurial process is not linear ... [Thank you, Kathleen Allen]

[ ] Be personal, direct, and natural ...

[ ] I believe there are numerous potential trim-tabbers in every organization who can lead and spread their influence no matter what position they hold ... they can move themselves and their team or department in such a way that it positively affects the entire organization. ... [Thank you, Stephen R Covey]

[ ] When there is less to see, our customer looks more carefully ... [Thank you, Anne Marie Russell]

[ ] There is a price for rewards ... no such thing as a freebie!

[ ] Types of barriers to competition: investment requirements of a venture; well-established brand; market saturation; economies of scale; customer loyalty; low-ball pricing; intellectual property; government regulation ...

[ ] The less we speak, the more we will hear ... [Thank you, Alexander Solzhenitsyn]

[ ] Much of what ultimately becomes an innovative product, service, or process is due to the hard work that goes into working out glitches and false starts along the way ... innovation takes discipline, a fact many folks overlook when they consider innovation as representing only the next "big idea" ... [Thank you, Dee McCrorey]

[ ] Don't wait for others to do it ... it's up to us ...

[ ] Show, don't tell ... demonstrate how our products work, not just talk about it!

[ ] Rise above the little things ... that'll keep us busy all day ...

[ ] We will be taxed ... and then taxed some more!

[ ] Business Plan: a formal statement of a set of business goals, the reasons they are believed attainable, the proposal for reaching those goals, and information about the organization or team attempting to reach those goals ...

[ ] Empower our team ...

[ ] When memories exceed dreams, the end is near ... the hallmark of a truly successful organization is the willingness to abandon what made it successful and start fresh. ... [Thank you, Michael Hammer]

[ ] Get out of the office every day ... talk to customers, feel what they feel ...

[ ] Tip for creating a good venture plan: Fairly and logically size up the competition ...

[ ] Corporate entrepreneur credo: Do any job needed to make the project work, regardless of job description ... [Thank you, Gifford Pinchot III]

[ ] Us or Them ... what should we focus on today? ...

[ ] We have two ears and one mouth ... use them in the same proportion!

[ ] Successful teams are honest and direct ...

[ ] We manage things, we lead people ... [Thank you, Grace Hopper]

[ ] Risk and Reward ... no risk, no reward ...

[ ] The more people that participate, the more accurate the survey ...

[ ] Learn faster than our competition ...

[ ] Assume the competition is smarter than us ... learn from them ... see what they do that is so smart ... then we can do it smarter and better than them ...

[ ] Resolve interpersonal conflicts as quickly as possible or they may escalate to the point where they are destructive ... [Thank you, Andrew Corbett]

[ ] She has the attention span of a gnat ... his is less. So how are we going to sell our story to them in the time we have? ...

[ ] Subjective benefits ...

[ ] How to kill creativity: "Well, maybe next week ..."

[ ] Look the part ... if we want to be successful, look the part to start ...

[ ] Dip our toes in the water before jumping in the ocean ... [Thank you, Nelson Wang]

[ ] Slow down ... that person looks at everything we do from a customer perspective so we can nip bad policies in the bud ...

[ ] Find a better solution for the problem ...

[ ] Pitch: clearly describing a product or service to others ...

[ ] Common cause of venture death: an inferior business model ...

[ ] Take a walk, and talk ... beats sitting behind a desk all day! A little change of scenery, a little exercise can stimulate some new thinking ... [Thank you, Nelson Wang]

[ ] Marketing is not a battle of products, it's a battle of perceptions ...

[ ] Common cause of venture death: disharmony with investors ...

[ ] Skilled innovators and entrepreneurs are able to organize ...

[ ] Breakfast or Lunch or Dinner ... which one do we want to serve to our customers, and why? ...

[ ] Pay close attention to details ... [Thank you, Walt Disney]

[ ] Be patient with all ...

[ ] Be positively unique as a manager ... positively, not negatively!

[ ] The more choices the more difficult the choice ...

[ ] Actively solicit ideas from the outside ...

[ ] Many successful business ventures started over lunch and a sketch on the back of a napkin ...

[ ] There is no such thing as an unimportant day ... [Thank you, Alexander Woolcott]

[ ] Successful teams are open to new ideas ...

[ ] The innovation process may be divided into three areas: the fuzzy front end, new product development, and commercialization ... [Thank you, P A Koen]

[ ] Celebrate ... big things, little things ... keep our positive attitude

[ ] One is not enough ... build a range of products, services, customers, suppliers, partners ...

[ ] Learn from children ... the teacher, looking over a little child's shoulder, asks, "What are you drawing?" ... Child: "I'm drawing a picture of God." ... Teacher: "But nobody knows

what God looks like." ... Child: "They will in a minute." ... [Thank you, Ken Robinson]

[ ] Making a great presentation: Avoid miscellaneous visuals ... [Thank you, Ian McKenzie]

[ ] Be a lifter, not a leaner ...

[ ] The value is in the hard ... easy anyone can do ...

[ ] Stop, think, thank ...

[ ] Exit Plan: a means of leaving a current situation after a predetermined objective has been achieved ...

[ ] A good business plan identifies all the alternatives available to prospective customers ... [Thank you, SHAW Wearables]

[ ] Identify clearly who in our venture is responsible for meeting our sales objectives ...

[ ] Facts may be colored by the personalities of the people who present them ... [Thank you, Reginald Rose]

[ ] Successful teams share learning ...

[ ] Push - pull marketing ... push to our distribution and sales channels, pull from our users and customers ...

[ ] When opportunity knocks, open the door ... sometimes the knock is not very loud ...

[ ] Successful teams reach most decisions reached by consensus ...

[ ] If we would have new knowledge, we must get us a whole world of new questions ... [Thank you, Susanne Langer]

[ ] Common bootstrapping strategy: don't hire anyone ...

[ ] Tag along on their coattails ...

[ ] Business is like a dog-sled team ... if we ain't the lead dog, the scenery never changes ... [Thank you, Lewis Grizzard]

[ ] Call people by name ... people love to hear their name spoken aloud, in reverence and honor, because someone else thinks they are worthwhile ... do not tread on their body and soul ...

[ ] Stay in the loop ... keep in the know ... [Thank you, LOOP Venture Team]

[ ] Hire the best, fire the worst!

[ ] Successful teams are calculated risk-takers ...

[ ] As long as people will accept crap, it will be financially profitable to dispense it ... [Thank you, Dick Cavett]

[ ] Allocate resources where they will do the most good ...

[ ] Inspiration: ...

[ ] Red ocean, blue bay ... let's try to stay away from the blood-thirsty shark frenzy fighting for customers ...

[ ] Algorithm: a process or set of rules to be followed in calculations or other problem-solving operations ...

[ ] Hitch our wagon to a star ... how can we benefit from the trends and flow that's already out there? ... [Thank you, Ralph Waldo Emerson]

[ ] The most important aspect of writing the business plan is the learning that goes on as we identify and research the concept, the industry, the competitors, and customers ... [Thank you, William Bygrave,]

[ ] We'll always have a boss: our customers ...

[ ] Some solutions are better than others ...

[ ] Venture Development Phases: Discover, Define, Design, Develop, Deploy ...

[ ] Don't let a winning business turn into a losing one ...

[ ] Skilled innovators and entrepreneurs are able to use existing knowledge as base for new ideas ...

[ ] Ignorance can be fixed ... stupid is forever! ... [Thank you, Don Wood]

[ ] A new venture may be feasible if there are both short-term and long-term market potentials ...

[ ] Key question for our venture: Do our customers know what we want them to do? ... Do we show them how to do it? ... (Sometimes in some companies it's not so easy to place an order!) ...

[ ] Key question for our venture: What kind of culture do we want in our venture? ... What do we need to do to make that happen? ...

[ ] Do not be afraid of making mistakes ...

[ ] The truth is more important than the facts ... [Thank you, Frank Lloyd Wright]

[ ] Watch out for gaps and holes and speed bumps and roadblocks ...

[ ] A venture operations manual can help identify problems before they arise, minimizing "crisis management" ...

[ ] A nap a day keeps the doctor away (especially if we snore really loud) ... a little snooze every now and then can be a good thing (but usually not in the middle of a company meeting!) ...

[ ] Key question for our venture: are we putting up artificial roadblocks? ... let's make life as easy as possible for our customers ...

[ ] The brightest sunshine produces the darkest shadows ...

[ ] Divide and conquer ... [Thank you, Julius Caesar]

[ ] Serendipity and fortuitous circumstances are bonuses in life ...

[ ] Like life, our venture is what we make it to be ...

[ ] Use the most conservative figures ...

[ ] Jump around!

[ ] Impossible or Improbable ... what should we focus on today? ...

[ ] Skilled innovators and entrepreneurs listen ...

[ ] Common bootstrapping strategy: reimburse advisors and consultants with equity and good will ...

[ ] Sharpen our skills and strengths ...

[ ] Experimentation is key to innovation because they seldom turn out as expected but we can learn so much in the process ... [Thank you, Jeff Bezos]

[ ] Iteration: a new version with carefully implemented improvements from a previous version ...

[ ] Describe the major suppliers to ventures in our industry ... how strong is supplier power? ...

[ ] A good business plan addresses how the venture will develop and sustain a proprietary position ... [Thank you, Leonard Brown]

[ ] Dreams are the sparks of passion ... [Thank you, Daniel Chabot]

[ ] Give it some time ... something great is never created quickly ...

[ ] Just because everything's different doesn't mean anything has changed ... [Thank you, Irene Peter]

[ ] The future comes one day at a time ... [Thank you, Dean Acheson]

[ ] A disease known is half cured ... if we understand our customer's problems, we're on our way to solving them ...

[ ] Gross Margin: a ratio, usually expressed as a percentage, equal to the selling price minus the cost of goods sold (COGS) ...

[ ] Promote our venture with signs on our building ...

[ ] A committee should consist of no more than three people, two of whom are absent ... [Thank you, Robert Copeland]

[ ] Be persistent in our mission ... don't give up when the going gets tough, and it will ...

[ ] Enclose our business card or mini-brochure with every letter and note and bill we send ...

[ ] Knowledge will give us power, but character respect ... [Thank you, Bruce Lee]

[ ] Quality is not an act, it's a habit ... [Thank you, Aristotle]

[ ] Survive or thrive ... what should we focus on today? The one we pick will point us in the direction we'll need to go with our venture ...

[ ] Business Model Canvas: a popular visual tool for developing new business models or documenting existing ones ... used in companies of all sizes, we can use the canvas to describe, design, challenge, iterate, and pivot our business model ... [Thank you, Yves Pigneur]

[ ] Success is 1 percent inspiration and 99 percent perspiration ... [Thank you, Thomas A Edison]

[ ] Promote our venture with television spots ...

[ ] Make new friends and keep the old ones ...

[ ] Keep our ears wide open ...

[ ] Key question for our venture: What are our key strengths? ...

[ ] Know how to use the "cloud" to store and share information among team members ...

[ ] Show our work, our logic, our assumptions ... numbers alone mean nothing!

[ ] Exercise: List 10 new revenue sources for our venture ...

[ ] Turn a little knowledge of this and a little knowledge of that and make it into something new and better ...

[ ] Key question for our venture: Got a grumpy team? ... A: Let's call it a day and go get a beer!

[ ] Use history as a guide, not a jailer ...

[ ] Buy comfortable furniture ...

[ ] Recognize opportunities ... practice the recognition skill!

[ ] Making a great presentation: Graph data whenever possible ... [Thank you, Ian McKenzie]

[ ] Skilled innovators and entrepreneurs are willing to work hard ... and smart ...

[ ] Build, measure, learn, and make mistakes as we go ... we'll know more about what we're doing as we're doing it, instead of before we do it ... [Thank you, Jason Fried]

[ ] An imitation is never as good as the original ... sometimes it's better!

[ ] Exploit untapped opportunities ...

[ ] Entrepreneurial Myth: Most entrepreneurs are successful financially ... yes, some entrepreneurs do become rich ... most, however, do not ... [Thank you, Scott Shane]

[ ] 72 divided by the annual interest rate as a percentage is approximately equal to the number years until an investment doubles in value ... example: At 8% interest, our money will double in approximately 9 years (72/8 = 9) ...

[ ] In an information economy, the most valuable company assets drive themselves home every night ... if they are not treated well, they do not return the next morning ... [Thank you, Peter Chang]

[ ] Why join the navy if you can be a pirate! ... [Thank you, Steve Jobs]

[ ] Allocate money and resources for new ideas ... [Thank you, Don Treffinger]

[ ] Get rich in a niche ... but sometimes finding a rich niche is a bitch!

[ ] Great things will never happen with VCs or professional managers ... they have high drive, but they don't have creativity or insight ... [Thank you, Elon Musk]

[ ] Keep our promises ...

[ ] Every problem is an opportunity ... maybe for us, maybe not ... pragmatically pick our problems ...

[ ] There is a time for every purpose ... A time to be born, a time to die; A time to plant, a time to reap; A time to kill, a time to heal; A time to laugh, a time to weep ... (Thank you, Byrds)

[ ] The world likes happy ... don't disappoint ...

[ ] Skilled innovators and entrepreneurs are able to creates internal visualizations ...

[ ] We only see the rainbow when we turn our backs to the sun ... [Thank you, Aage Gribskov]

[ ] Only by trying to go too far can we find out how far we really can go ...

[ ] Do our job better than anyone else ...

[ ] Allow for human nature ... it is the humans that make the decisions that most directly impact our venture ...

[ ] There is no substitute for hard work ... [Thank you, Thomas Alva Edison]

[ ] Objective benefits ... list the measurable values we can deliver to our customers ... the more the merrier!

[ ] Promote our venture with sales incentives ...

[ ] Key question for our venture: Do our promotions and advertising develop a desire in our prospective customers to do something? ...

[ ] Four types of intellectual property: copyrights, trade secrets, trademarks (and service marks), and patents ...

[ ] Pacesetting leadership style ... the leader sets high standards for performance ... [Thank you, Daniel Goleman]

[ ] How to attract new customers: have an introductory offer ...

[ ] Discover, Define, Design, Develop, Deploy: the typical development stages for a new product, service, process, method, venture, organization, et al ...

[ ] We won't always have all the facts ... so we'll need to have our best judgment ready to go!

[ ] Repeat back what we hear ... did the speaker really say what we think they said? ...

[ ] Entrepreneurial Myth: Most entrepreneurs start businesses in attractive industries ... unfortunately, the opposite is true ... [Thank you, Scott Shane]

[ ] Back or Forth ... which way are we going, which way do we really need to go? ...

[ ] Reinforce the factors that have contributed to our past success ...

[ ] Many new discoveries are suddenly seeing things that were always there ... [Thank you, Susanne K Langer]

[ ] Key question for our venture: What are their weaknesses? ... our venture, our competitors, our customers ... what are we going to do about that? ...

[ ] Direct price: how much it costs our customers to buy our products and services ...

[ ] Business plan competitions: the best plan does not always win ...

[ ] Key question for our venture: Is our venture and product mix aligned with the current industry trends? ...

[ ] Identify our customer's buying frequency and their willingness to pay ... [Thank you, Andrew Zacharakis]

[ ] Be as useful as we can to our customers ...

[ ] The customer is king/queen ... treat them as royalty (if we want to earn royalties!)

[ ] What we do speaks louder than what we say ... [Thank you, Ralph Waldo Emerson]

[ ] Invention: something created that is new and useful and not obvious ... an important note here: an invention is NOT

necessarily better than what already exists ... an invention is NOT necessarily an innovation (something new AND better!) ... most inventions are not innovations ... they are simply different ways of doing something ... [Thank you, IEEE]

[ ] Persevere ... last longer than the other guy/gal ... that'll show 'em ...

[ ] Don't play favorites ... be upfront and fair all around ...

[ ] Imagine that ... we can imagine whatever we want; whenever we want; wherever we want ...

[ ] Phase: a distinct period or stage in a process of change or forming part of something's development ...

[ ] Make it better and cheaper before our competitors do ... once we do that, do it again!

[ ] Risk is a necessary evil ...

[ ] Try not to keep going back to the well for more water ... stakeholders get irritated if we can't manage what we already have ...

[ ] Trust: firm belief in the reliability, truth, and strength of someone or something ...

[ ] Just suppose ... we can "just suppose" anything we want ... just suppose there are no restraints, no limitations, no roadblocks to our thinking, to what we want to accomplish ... just suppose we can think whatever we want, wherever we want, whenever we want, and no one can stop us ... just suppose anything we want!

[ ] Potential business model: Provide infrastructure support to other business ventures ...

[ ] The best questions have more than one answer ... but that doesn't mean all the answers are all right ...

[ ] Common bootstrapping strategy: live with relatives ...

[ ] Do our own thing ...

[ ] Promote our venture with trade and technical magazines and newspapers ...

[ ] Key question for our venture: Have we defined our target customer profile accurately? ...

[ ] Objective and subjective specifications ...

[ ] Learning has no limit ... it goes on forever, and that's not a bad thing ...

[ ] Key question for our venture: What are our competitive positions? ...

[ ] Forecast: a prediction or estimate of future events ...

[ ] Don't lose our sense of humor ... life is short, might as well enjoy it while we can ...

[ ] Successful companies can indeed "make money" ... called "stock certificates", they are redeemable for real dollars ...

[ ] Technology will literally transform every aspect of business, every aspect of life, and every aspect of society ... [Thank you, Carly Fiorina]

[ ] Objective: a thing aimed at or sought ...

[ ] Put all our eggs in one basket ... don't spread ourselves thin ... but we better be really, really careful about what we do with that basket!

[ ] Key question for our venture: What is the lifetime value of a customer? ...

[ ] Tomorrow is a new day ... and a new day is neither better nor worse until we make it so ...

[ ] Great things are not accomplished without passion ... when the skills are light and the luck is low, fill in the void with passion ...

[ ] Grasp a little and we may get it ... grasp too much and we may not ...

[ ] Humor is the most significant activity of the human brain ... [Thank you, Edward De Bono]

[ ] It takes years to build trust ... but only seconds to destroy it ...

[ ] There is no harm in asking ... what's the worse they could answer? ...

[ ] SWOTT: an abbreviation / acronym for Strengths, Weaknesses, Opportunities, Threats, and Trends ... use for analyzing an industry, the competition, customers, our own venture ...

[ ] Promote our venture with bus and streetcar and taxi ads ...

[ ] Create our own special ocean where we're the big fish and the sharks are somewhere else ...

[ ] Adversity: difficulties, misfortune ... facts of life ... what are we going to do about them? ...

[ ] People resist change ... even little ones ...

[ ] Don't do what they don't want ... do do what they do ...

[ ] Build and maintain an environment that is conducive to high motivation ... [Thank you, K A Zein]

[ ] Entrepreneurial Myth: Venture capitalists are a good place to go for start-up money ... it depends on the type of venture ... some high-tech ventures do start with VC money, particularly when the investors are an integral part of the

planning team ... however, most new and early-stage ventures do not receive VC fundings and never will ... [Thank you, Scott Shane]

[ ] Give 'em some room to breathe ... some days, we all need a little extra space ...

[ ] Break the problem into pieces ... solve for the pieces, then put them back together again ...

[ ] Work with the people you like ... like the people you work with ...

[ ] Don't "wing it" ... unless we really, really have to or else we'll get hit by a train. A big train. Not an ordinary train, but a 200-car fully-loaded freight train. That would hurt ... So then, maybe we wing it and fly in the sky?

[ ] Never say never ... if we should, we can and would!

[ ] Key question for our venture: What do we need to know about our industry that we don't already know? ...

[ ] What we don't know would make a good book ... [Thank you, Sydney Smith]

[ ] Skilled innovators and entrepreneurs have a sense of humor ...

[ ] Try to avoid the speed bumps and potholes ...

[ ] Entrepreneurs are usually good at forming strategies ...

[ ] Rotate jobs ... see how the other shoes fit and feel!

[ ] It's not all about us ... it is all about our customers!

[ ] Time is far more valuable than money ... money can be replaced, time can not ... [Thank you, Curt Van Lydegraf]

[ ] Dream a big dream ... what do we have to lose? ...

[ ] One home run does not win a ball game, unless we keep the opposing team from scoring two ... [Thank you, Kenny Lofton]

[ ] A happy venture is a productive venture ...

[ ] A good venture operations manual offers examples of standard forms, reducing the number and variety of forms used ...

[ ] Wake up! stop what you're doing right now! (OK, so you're reading this book ... it'll still be here when you come back!) ... but right now, Wake Up! open your eyes and look around ... keep looking until you see something new ... capture the moment ... a picture, a note, a memory ...

[ ] Give more ... take less ... keep improving our value proposition!

[ ] Technology happens ... it's not good, it's not bad, it just happens ... [Thank you, Andy Grove]

[ ] As a cure for worrying, work is better than whiskey ... [Thank you, Thomas A Edison]

[ ] Test it first at home ... if we don't like it, why do we think our customers would ...

[ ] Get a good accountant ...

[ ] A new venture should have a very clear, crisp, descriptive tagline ... nobody knows what a new business even does in the early days, so use a tag line to tell 'em ... in the early days, McDonald's tag line was simply "Hamburgers" because back then, nobody knew what a McDonald's did ...

[ ] The unfinished is nothing ... [Thank you, Henri Frederic Amiel]

[ ] Nothing is so contagious as enthusiasm ... [Thank you, Samuel Taylor Coleridge]

[ ] How can we answer this Question: Can we sell our products directly to other business ventures? ...

[ ] Success requires some order ...

[ ] Better is better than best! As we think, so shall we be ...

[ ] Skilled innovators and entrepreneurs are knowledgeable ...

[ ] Forming, storming, norming, performing ... a model of group development wherein these phases are all necessary and inevitable in order for the team to grow, to face up to challenges, to tackle problems, to find solutions, to plan work, and to deliver results ... [Thank you, Bruce Tuckman]

[ ] When seldom is heard an encouraging word, the sky is just cloudy all day ... sock that one away, boss people ...

[ ] Good people, good business ...

[ ] Get what we can, and what we get, hold ...

[ ] More heroes, not zeros ... [Thank you, Michael Bassey Johnson]

[ ] Successful launches are iterative ...

[ ] Don't be boring ... if we are, let's at least be short ...

[ ] Don't rely on just one big customer or client ...

[ ] How long does it take for a new idea to take hold? ... a day, a week, a month, a year, a lifetime? ...

[ ] A successful relationship needs both sides believing in each other ... our customers have to believe that we will deliver the best value to them, and we have to believe they will find that value worthy enough to pay our price ...

[ ] Passion pays, sex sells, weird works ... what do we put in our advertising campaign? ...

[ ] What we like, or what our customers like ... what should we focus on today? ...

[ ] Save the whales, the elephants, and the Oxford Comma ... [Thank you, James Arnold]

[ ] It could be a good opportunity if our solution can generate a sustainable profit ...

[ ] Build a personal brand ... [Thank you, Nelson Wang]

[ ] 0 to 100 ... how long is it going to take our venture to get up to speed? ... [Thank you, Michael DeCesaro]

[ ] Potential business model: Design products ...

[ ] If we stay in the middle of the road, we'll get run over ...

[ ] Vegetables or Minerals ... what should we focus on today? ...

[ ] Do not let what we cannot do interfere with what we can ... [Thank you, John Wooden]

[ ] Numbers can be bent to the will of whoever happens to be wielding them ... [Thank you, Darrell Huff]

[ ] Business plan outline: Executive summary; Company description; Industry analysis and trends; Target market; Competition; Strategic position and risk assessment; Marketing plan and sales strategy; Operations; Technology plan; Management and organization; Community involvement and social responsibility; Development, milestones, and exit plan; The financials ... [Thank you, Rhonda Abrams]

[ ] Elvis has left the building ...

[ ] Cutting costs without improving quality is futile ... [Thank you, W Edwards Deming]

[ ] Common cause of venture death: lack of resources ...

[ ] Giving advice is easy ... taking it is hard!

[ ] When writing our business plan, avoid overestimating on our financial projections ... sure we want to look good, but resist optimism here ... use half of what we think is reasonable ... better to underestimate than set expectations that aren't fulfilled ... [Thank you, Kaye Vivian]

[ ] When the cat's out of the bag ... it's fair game for us to chase it! ... [Thank you, Paul Biegler]

[ ] Skilled innovators and entrepreneurs are expressive ...

[ ] The right to do something does not mean that doing it is right ... [Thank you, William Safire]

[ ] Innovation barely exists until it is communicated and brought to life in the minds of others ...

[ ] Ideas build upon each other ...

[ ] Use customer interviews to gather primary research data ...

[ ] Leaders are innovative and entrepreneurial ...

[ ] Customers are easily satisfied with the best ...

[ ] Key question for our venture: Does our name fit customers' expectations? ...

[ ] Keep our fingers crossed ... and our toes on the road ...

[ ] Some people never miss an opportunity to miss an opportunity ... [Thank you, Algernon West]

[ ] One experiment after another ... so goes life!

[ ] SCAMPER: Substitute; Combine; Adapt; Modify, Minimize, Magnify; Put to Another Use; Eliminate, Elaborate; Rearrange, Reverse ... a great tool to use when creating a new product, service, process, or business methodology ... [Thank you, Robert Eberle and Alex Osborn]

[ ] Operations: the harvesting of value from assets owned by a business venture; manufacturing, production, and delivery of goods and services ... deliver the right product at the right price to the right customers at the right time and right place ...

[ ] Successful entrepreneurs collaborate more than they compete ... rarely can one person do it alone and succeed ... [Thank you, Heidi M Neck]

[ ] Whatever we believe, we become ...

[ ] Innovating is competitive creativity ...

[ ] Use our best judgment at all times ...

[ ] Entrepreneurs act more than they plan to act ... they just don't like to sit around and talk ...

[ ] Make sure we have our raw material suppliers lined up and ready to go when we launch a new product ...

[ ] Web site for government statistics: www.fedstats.gov ...

[ ] Furious activity is no substitute for understanding ... [Thank you, H H Williams]

[ ] The most terrifying words in the English language are: I'm from the government and I'm here to help ... [Thank you, Ronald Reagan]

[ ] The less time and money it takes to start and manage a business, the more likely it is to succeed ... [Thank you, Robert Kessler]

[ ] Genius is initiative on fire ... [Thank you, Holbrook Jackson]

[ ] Be original ...

[ ] A closed mind is like a closed book: just a block of wood ...

[ ] Key question for our venture: Who do we need in our venture? ... Who don't we need? ...

[ ] The window of opportunity is only open so long ... and tends to close with a bang! ... [Thank you, Bill Gates]

[ ] Doing something we love is never a waste of time ...

[ ] Angel Advocate: someone who builds on new ideas ...

[ ] Entrepreneurship is a methodology ... a set of practices, continuous learning, iteration and improvements, a focus on action, and collaboration ... [Thank you, Candida G Brush]

[ ] Nothing is forever except change ...

[ ] Nobody ever said we had to start at ground zero ...

[ ] Make the time to listen and be available to our customer for their questions and comments ...

[ ] The world has always been and will always be full of new opportunities ...

[ ] Key question for our venture: Is our name instantly recognized? ...

[ ] We'll never run out of great ideas! Paul Efron ...

[ ] Lightning doesn't strike twice in the same place ... the same place isn't there the second time!

[ ] Most innovations are just incremental improvements of things that already exist ...

[ ] There are three ways to get to the top of a tree: sit on an acorn; make friends with a bird; climb to the top ... [Thank you, Ray Rolland]

[ ] Time is not money ... money cannot buy us more time, but with time we can make more money!

[ ] Entrepreneurs are usually logical thinkers ...

[ ] LLC: abbreviation for Limited Liability Company ...

[ ] A little impatience spoils great plans ...

[ ] Know how to find the right moment ...

[ ] If we really want to learn about something, we've got to experience it ourselves ...

[ ] Key question for our venture: Are there any negative connotations with our name ...

[ ] Karma exists: treat customers with respect and they'll reciprocate ... spam them, annoy them, and lie to them, and they'll retaliate ... [Thank you, Ian Lurie]

[ ] Branding mistake: inconsistencies ... such as different logos, different colors, et al ... our brand needs to be consistent everywhere in order to reinforce and remind our customers of what we are all about ... [Thank you, Jarad Hull]

[ ] I'm going to make them an offer they can't refuse ... What offer can we make to our customers that they just can't refuse? ... [Thank you, Marlon Brando]

[ ] There are no rules ... [Thank you, Nike]

[ ] Once the term sheet is signed, the power shifts away from the startup to the purchaser ... the typical term sheet will give the purchaser the discretion to step away from the deal if due diligence is unsatisfactory, or if the necessary internal approvals are not obtained ... [Thank you, Suzanne Williams]

[ ] New technology is common, new thinking is not ... [Thank you, Peter Blake]

[ ] What would you do for free? ...

[ ] Key question for our venture: What is our vision for our venture five to 10 years from now? ...

[ ] Enjoy what we have instead of feeling sorry for what we do not ...

[ ] We do not need an invitation to help others ...

[ ] Maslow's Hierarchy of Needs (basic, psychological, self-fulfillment) ... 1] Physiological needs (food, water, warmth, rest); 2] Safety needs (security, safety); 3] Belongingness (intimate relationships, friends); 4] Esteem needs (prestige and feelings of accomplishment); 5] Self-actualization (achieving one's full potential, including creative activities) ... [Thank you, Abraham Maslow]

[ ] Replace wishing and wanting with acting and doing ...

[ ] Our messages should be brief and to the point ... why communicate our message in six sentences when we can do it in three? ...

[ ] Be on a mission ...

[ ] An ellipsis... three periods (stops) followed by a space ... a pauseandthink ... a space followed by three dots and another space ... it is a suggestion to the reader to "pause and think" about what they've just read ...

[ ] There are some 28 million registered business in the US ... many more worldwide, of course!

[ ] One of the tests of leadership is the ability to recognize a problem before it becomes an emergency ... [Thank you, Arnold H Glasow]

[ ] Margin: an amount of something included so as to be sure of success or safety ... [Thank you, Google Dictionary]

[ ] Key question for our venture: When do we need who in our venture? ...

[ ] Work: activity involving mental or physical effort done in order to achieve a purpose or result ...

[ ] Express ourselves ...

[ ] Scope it out ... scoop it up!

[ ] Buy low, sell high ...

[ ] Be sincere about our desire to help the prospect ... Making the sale should be our secondary objective. This attitude will come through in every encounter and will help us build long-term relationships ...

[ ] Accentuate the positive ... eliminate the negative, latch on to the affirmative, don't mess with Mister In-Between! ... [Thank you, Johnny Mercer]

[ ] Make it more accessible ... [Thank you, Bikram Choudhury]

[ ] Be careful of commitments ... we need to make sure we can meet them!

[ ] Sight ...

[ ] Relationships can wear out ... it takes some work to keep them fresh ...

[ ] Tip for creating a good venture plan: Planning is like steering, and steering means constantly correcting errors ... [Thank you, Tim Berry]

[ ] Creative people tolerate acceptable losses ... two steps ahead, one step back ... if the road ahead was like a freeway, it

means someone else has already been there and back ...
[Thank you, Christopher P Neck]

[ ] Making something complicated is easy, making something
simple is not ...

[ ] Say thanks ... and mean it ...

[ ] How deep is the ocean? ... depends where we jump in ...
it's only a few inches at the beach, but thousands of feet in the
middle ...

[ ] Keep breathing ... deep, long, and slow ...

[ ] Aim high ...

[ ] Common cause of venture death: out-competed ...

[ ] Intuitive or Inductive ... what should we focus on today? ...

[ ] A good business plan succinctly explains customer
benefits in qualitative and quantitative terms ... [Thank you,
Carol Shaughnessy]

[ ] The truth must be pursued ... [Thank you, New York
Times]

[ ] Some business plans are simple sketches ...

[ ] Don't argue with someone who is right ... cut your losses,
take your bat and ball and go home ...

[ ] Knowledge is a precious treasure that cannot be given
away nor stolen ...

[ ] Maintain an environment that allows risk taking ...
[Thank you, Scott Isaksen]

[ ] How to kill creativity: "That's a stupid idea ..."

[ ] KISS: acronym for Keep It Simple, Stupid; a guiding
philosophy widely used in organizations that aims to focus

management attention on the core attributes of a product, service, process, methodology, or task ...

[ ] There is always money ... to support a great idea. The problem is finding it ...

[ ] How to kill creativity: "Why don't you write a report ..."

[ ] Critical Path: the sequence of stages determining the optimal route to success ...

[ ] Imagine great things ... now imagine making them happen ...

[ ] Since everything is a reflection of our minds, everything can be changed by our minds ... [Thank you, Buddha]

[ ] Attitudes are more important than facts ...

[ ] First Base or Home Run ... what should we focus on today? ...

[ ] Same old, same old ... some things never change, so it seems, until someone somewhere makes them change ...

[ ] Diversify our investments ...

[ ] Neat and clean ...

[ ] Promote our venture with offer a reward for referrals ...

[ ] A good business plan presents a quality, sophisticated, experienced management team, advisors, and board of directors with complementary and encompassing business skills ... [Thank you, CloisterVR]

[ ] Directly collect information about our markets and customers ... go talk to real prospective customers ...

[ ] Fear is a great inventor ... it's fearless that gets into trouble ...

[ ] Key question for our venture: What are the major weaknesses of our industry? ...

[ ] Use the passive voice sparingly ... [Thank you, Randy Accetta]

[ ] Copy from the greats ...

[ ] Describe the substitutes available to buyers ...

[ ] To build a good relationship with our customers, spend half as much money but twice as much time ...

[ ] Promote our venture with employee events ...

[ ] Innovation is the primary instrument of entrepreneurship ... the act that endows resources with a new capacity to create wealth ... [Thank you, Peter F Drucker]

[ ] Focus on measuring one or two variables at a time ... [Thank you, Jenn Kim]

[ ] A brand is a promise ... [Thank you, Alaina Levine]

[ ] Investability: a venture that is able to attract funding from investors that have the expectation of achieving a profit or material result by putting it into financial schemes, shares, or property ...

[ ] A goal is a dream with a deadline ... [Thank you, Leo Helzel]

[ ] Don't ask for a Porsche in the first round of funding ...

[ ] Quality is remembered long after the price is forgotten ... [Thank you, Gucci]

[ ] Successful innovators and entrepreneurs have a commitment to test knowledge through experience, persistence, and a willingness to learn from mistakes ... [Thank you, Michael J Gelb]

[ ] Pre-Money Valuation: the financial value or worth established for a company immediately prior to a financing round ...

[ ] Explore, incubate, stimulate, illuminate, select, plan, implement, evaluate ...

[ ] Not everything that can be counted counts, and not everything that counts can be counted ... [Thank you, Albert Einstein]

[ ] Leaders are facilitators, not order givers ...

[ ] Common bootstrapping strategy: give discounts to early customers ...

[ ] Create and nourish a customer community ...

[ ] Vision is the art of seeing things invisible ... [Thank you, Jonathan Swift]

[ ] Luck affects everything ...

[ ] Make sure the cost of producing our product is significantly lower than the future sales price ...

[ ] Know how to use at least one good word processing program ... Microsoft Word is most popular, Google Docs is good, too, as are others ...

[ ] Keep our plan as close to the "general format" as possible ... if a venture capitalist becomes frustrated with an unfamiliar format, it is more likely that she will reject it rather than try to pull out the pertinent information ... [Thank you, Andrew Zacharakis]

[ ] Our knowledge is finite, our ignorance infinite ...

[ ] Wonders will never cease ... never ...

[ ] Even a blind squirrel will find an acorn once in awhile ... [Thank you, Mike Novy]

[ ] Key question for our venture: What is happening in our industry around the world, not just in our world? ...

[ ] Cutting prices or putting things on sale is not a sustainable business model ... [Thank you, Howard Schultz]

[ ] Exercise: List 100 potential new customers for our new product or service ...

[ ] Think fast ...

[ ] Make ourselves necessary to someone ... [Thank you, Ralph Waldo Emerson]

[ ] Scratch where it itches ... but maybe not in public ...

[ ] Ideas are funny things ... they don't work unless we do ...

[ ] We've solved the crime, now all that's left is to make the evidence fit ...

[ ] Speaking softly will often gain more attention than shouting ...

[ ] Whatever can go wrong, will ... and at the most inopportune time ... [Thank you, Murphy]

[ ] Skilled innovators and entrepreneurs are willing to ask "why?" and "why not?" ...

[ ] Key question for our venture: What are the barriers to entry, for us and for our competitors? ...

[ ] To get something we never had, we have to do something we never did ... [Thank you, Albert Einstein]

[ ] Common cause of venture death: lack of money ...

[ ] Potential opportunities have potential economic value ... [Thank you, IDEO]

[ ] A good read: Integrity is All You've Got (Karl Eller) ...

[ ] Key question for our venture: Does the name work in all target markets? ...

[ ] Debt Funding: ...

[ ] We are continually faced with a series of great opportunities brilliantly disguised as insoluble problems ... [Thank you, John W Gardner]

[ ] Core Competency: the defining capabilities or advantages that distinguishes a venture from its competitors ...

[ ] Success begets success ...

[ ] Do an intensely good job ... even in our sleep! ... [Thank you, Frank DeCesaro]

[ ] Don't fall in love ...

[ ] Do not do what is already done ... take what is already done and do it better ...

[ ] Key question for our venture: What relevant domain experience does our venture team have? ... What do we need? ...

[ ] Profit is our best source of funding ...

[ ] Common Mistake: underestimating the time it takes to become a stable venture ...

[ ] Skilled innovators and entrepreneurs are able to resist jumping to premature conclusions ...

[ ] Getting to know anything takes time ...

[ ] Comprehension: classify, describe, discuss, explain, express, identify, indicate, locate, recognize, report, restate, review, select, translate, ...

[ ] In unity comes strength ...

[ ] A picture is worth a thousand words ... a prototype is worth a thousand pictures ... [Thank you, Ray Knutson]

[ ] Exploration: traveling in or through an unfamiliar area in order to learn about it and uncover new opportunities ...

[ ] There are seven sins in the world ... wealth without work, pleasure without conscience, knowledge without character, commerce without morality, science without humanity, worship without sacrifice, and politics without principle ... [Thank you, Mohandas Gandhi]

[ ] Sales revenues are important, yes ... but sustainable earnings are quite often more critical for venture success ... [Thank you, Ted Turner]

[ ] Tell them what they get, not what we do ... [Thank you, Rhonda Abrams]

[ ] We can never get the past back ... but we can make the most of now ...

[ ] Always look for what we can throw away in our writing ... make it simple ... [Thank you, Randy Accetta]

[ ] Differentiation: ...

[ ] Do what we can, with what we have, where we are ... [Thank you, Teddy Roosevelt]

[ ] We are not our customer ... the customer is the customer and we need to know what they think ...

[ ] Faced with the choice between changing one's mind and proving there is no need to do so, almost everyone gets busy on the proof ... [Thank you, John Kenneth Galbraith]

[ ] Key question for our venture: How can we define our marketing strategy? ...

[ ] Service: the action of helping or doing work for someone ...

[ ] How can we answer this Question: Is our venture an incremental innovation or something completely new? ... if it is completely new, we may have more issues in going to market than if we had something similar but better than what already exists ...

[ ] If we pay peanuts ... we get monkeys!

[ ] How can we answer this Question: Is our venture compelling? ...

[ ] There is only the future: the present just became the past, the past is now ancient history ...

[ ] A good cookbook never gets outdated, it just gets better with practice ... [Thank you, Carol Willson]

[ ] Something posted on-line spreads, like it or not ...

[ ] A good business plan explains how and when the venture will generate sustainable positive cash flow streams ... [Thank you, October Sports]

[ ] Don't say one thing and mean another ... don't beat around the bush ...

[ ] Expect chaos ...

[ ] By the work one knows the workman ... [Thank you, Jean de la Fontaine]

[ ] Choose markets that are in harmony with our values ...

[ ] Stay in touch with our customers; their needs are the basis of our business ... [Thank you, Mike Dell]

[ ] An expanded business plan executive summary is typically 4 to 6 pages in length ...

[ ] The most exciting phrase in science, the one that heralds new discoveries, is not "Eureka, I've found it!", it is "That's funny ..." ... [Thank you, Isaac Asimov]

[ ] Valuation: the monetary worth of something, especially as estimated by an appraiser and industry experts ...

[ ] Writing about music is like dancing about architecture ... what's the best way to communicate with our customers? Maybe give them a little sample of the goods? ... [Thank you, Elvis Costello]

[ ] The real question is not whether machines think but whether people do ... [Thank you, Vinay Nenwani]

[ ] The secret of genius is to carry the spirit of the child into old age ... which means never losing our enthusiasm ... [Thank you, Aldous Huxley]

[ ] The truth is hard ...

[ ] Stress less, mess more, more or less ...

[ ] Do not fight a battle if there is nothing to win ...

[ ] Use the right language ... talk the talk, walk the walk, write the right way to fit your target audience ... if it's a techie audience, talk techie; if it's a financial audience, talk money; if it's a customer audience, talk benefits and features ...

[ ] Real integrity is doing the right thing, knowing nobody is going to know whether we did it or not ... [Thank you, Oprah Winfrey]

[ ] Nobody likes change ... even change for the better has its detractors!

[ ] Keep good company ...

[ ] Customers don't always know what they really need, want, desire until we show it to them ...

[ ] Finance is the art of passing money from hand to hand until it finally disappears ... [Thank you, Robert W Sarnoff]

[ ] Surround ourselves with people who are more intelligent than us ...

[ ] Promote our venture with vehicle signs ...

[ ] Seeing opportunity and seizing it are two different things ... [Thank you, Grover Cleveland]

[ ] If an idea is worth having once, it's worth having twice ... [Thank you, Tom Stoppard]

[ ] Neat or messy ... what should we focus on today? ...

[ ] Don't mumble ...

[ ] Have a nice day ... we might not get another chance ...

[ ] minimal viable product (mvp) or Maximum Value Product (MVP) ... creating an mvp first can be the right strategy for some products, but a major setback for others ... hard to have an mvp airplane!

[ ] Skilled innovators and entrepreneurs are articulate ...

[ ] Il n'y a au monde que deux manières de s'élever, ou par sa propre industrie, ou par l'imbécilitè des autres ... There are but two ways of rising in the world, either by one's own industry or profiting by the foolishness of others ... [Thank you, Jean de La Bruyère]

[ ] Be the change we want to see in the world ... [Thank you, Fernando Garcia for reminding me of this quote (often attributed to Mahatma Gandhi, but no solid evidence he actually said that)]

[ ] Promote our venture with charitable contributions ...

[ ] Don't waste time on market research ... instead, launch test versions as early as possible, then keep improving the product in the open ... [Thank you, Loic Le Meur]

[ ] Intersperse market and business needs with technological advances ... [Thank you, S Fountoulakis]

[ ] Through many dangers, toils, and snares we have already come ... [Thank you, Amazing Grace]

[ ] Attention: notice taken of someone or something ... if our prospects don't pay attention to us, how will they possibly become customers? ...

[ ] Making a great presentation: Make visuals attractive ... avoid clutter and work for simplicity and clarity ... [Thank you, Ian McKenzie]

[ ] To maximize miles-per-gallon, aim for the lowest rpm in the highest gear ... how does that apply to our venture? ... [Thank you, Rick Newman]

[ ] If we can't say anything nice, don't say anything at all ...

[ ] An investment in knowledge pays the best interest ...

[ ] Skilled innovators and entrepreneurs are adaptable ...

[ ] Any change generates wasted heat ...

[ ] She who laughs last remembers our commercial ... she who laughs last, laughs best ...

[ ] Be careful about mixing friendships inside and outside of work ...

[ ] Play is a critical skill for innovators and entrepreneurs ... [Thank you, P G Greene]

[ ] Promote our venture with shopper classified newspapers ...

[ ] Promote our venture with contests ...

[ ] Advertising: describe or draw attention to a product, service, or event in a public medium in order to promote sales or attendance ... [Thank you, Google Dictionary]

[ ] Constantly look at things in a different way ... [Thank you, John Keating]

[ ] Talent hits a target no one else can hit ... genius hits a target no one else can see ... [Thank you, Arthur Schopenhauer]

[ ] Courtesy costs nothing ...

[ ] Knowledge is knowing a fact, wisdom is knowing what to do with that fact ...

[ ] Answer all the questions ... if we don't know the answers, we need to find out ...

[ ] Skilled innovators and entrepreneurs are exciting ...

[ ] Skilled innovators and entrepreneurs are able to focus ...

[ ] Make the bed right in the morning ... Learn to do the little things well, learn to make the bed right and that transcends into a lot of other things we do ... [Thank you, William McRaven]

[ ] The gentle calf sucks all the cows ... [Thank you, Mike Novy]

[ ] If we don't do it, how will we feel when someone else does? ...

[ ] Set sales objectives, not sales projections ... Objectives are personal, projections are not ...

[ ] Never insult an alligator until after we've crossed the river ... [Thank you, Cordell Hunt]

[ ] I'm sorry, Moe, it was an accident ... accidents happen, it's how we handle them that counts ... [Thank you, Curly Howard]

[ ] Promote our venture with special sales ...

[ ] Duplicate what works here over there ...

[ ] Promote our venture with email ...

[ ] Always make it easier for our customers ...

[ ] Most successful innovators and entrepreneurs want to do something good for the environment and humanity ...

[ ] We have a right, an obligation to our customers, to earn a fair and reasonable profit ...

[ ] Relish the details ...

[ ] We cannot change the cards we are dealt, just how we play the hand ... [Thank you, Randy Pausch]

[ ] If it's not growing, it's going to die ... [Thank you, Michael Eisner]

[ ] The most important attribute for any entrepreneur: Passion ... [Thank you, Paul Allen]

[ ] Nobody made a greater mistake than she who did nothing because she could do only a little ... [Thank you, Edmund Burke]

[ ] Actively engage trade booth visitors ... [Thank you, Susan Ward]

[ ] Promote our venture with direct mail with co-op advertising ...

[ ] Make life easier for our customers ... that will keep them coming back ...

[ ] Love ...

[ ] Make a big splash ... don't just wade in the water, do a cannonball ... [Thank you, Jonah]

[ ] PR: abbreviation for Public Relations ...

[ ] Mistakes are there waiting to be made ... and made they will be. Then what? ...

[ ] HALT stress: make sure we're not Hungry, Angry, Lonely, or Tired ... take care of those four things and less likely to be stressed ... [Thank you, Keith King]

[ ] The difficult we can do right now ... the impossible will take a little while! ... [Thank you, Billie Holliday]

[ ] Capital effectiveness ...

[ ] With the internet, we can always find data to support our opinion ... no matter how wrong that data may be!

[ ] Do not look where we fell, but where we slipped ...

[ ] Just stick with it ... [Thank you, Harry Coover]

[ ] The only way I can get them to do anything is by giving them what they want ... [Thank you, Dale Carnegie]

[ ] To start a trend, we have to first give our product away for free ... [Thank you, Mark Hughes]

[ ] To make enemies, talk ... to make friends, listen ...

[ ] We are not the customer ... dangerous to think we are!

[ ] The right brain creates energy, the left brain consumes it!

[ ] Debt: borrowed funds; money, goods or services owed by one person or organization to another ...

[ ] Difficult and painful times should make you better, not bitter ... [Thank you, Barbara Ann Kipfer]

[ ] Match form to function ...

[ ] Ability is what we're capable of doing ... motivation determines what we do, attitude determines how well we do it ... [Thank you, Lou Holtz]

[ ] Keep the daily to-do list small ...

[ ] Entrepreneurship is a team sport ...

[ ] Garbage in, garbage out ...

[ ] It is better to know than to be ignorant ... [Thank you, H L Mencken]

[ ] Show our brochure to as many prospective customers as possible ... can we capture some advanced orders by doing so? ...

[ ] We can be excellent without being perfect ...

[ ] Do the right thing ... no matter what others may think ...

[ ] Here's your desk, here's your phone, lots of luck, you're on your own ... (how not to train new salespeople!) ... [Thank you, Brad Thompson]

[ ] Key question for our venture: How can we research our target market? ... what do we really, really need to know about them? ...

[ ] Our venture is only as strong as our weakest link ... be it skills, passion, luck, or ethics ...

[ ] Give people more than they normally expect ...

[ ] Key question for our venture: Who are our future competitors? ...

[ ] Make feedback to us as painless as possible for our customers ... if they aren't happy with what we're doing, we need to know and need to know quickly!

[ ] The truth makes us free ... lies make us cheap ...

[ ] Promote our venture with public relations and publicity ...

[ ] Resource or Pre-source ... what should we focus on today? ...

[ ] Innovators and entrepreneurs should be out there innovating and entrepreneuring, not sitting around reading about innovating and entrepreneuring ... they are doers, not stewers ... but they also need to take a break every now and then or their brains will overheat ...

[ ] Use carefully-crafted surveys to gather primary research data ...

[ ] Focus on the key success factors that lead customers to buy our products and services ...

[ ] There is a limit to everything ... but don't stop pushing until we reach it ...

[ ] Skilled innovators and entrepreneurs are able to concentrate ...

[ ] We may not hear everything that's true ...

[ ] Promote our venture with proposals ... propose to our customers and tell them how a marriage to our venture will

make their lives so very much better ... (mean it, and deliver!) ...

[ ] Innovators are creative ... it's basic to being innovative ...

[ ] Ask our hearts what action to take ... in our hearts, we usually right ...

[ ] Use the storyboarding technique to solve planning and communication problems ... [Thank you, Walt Disney]

[ ] Be ready to pivot if needed ... but don't react too quickly to set backs or our venture may wind up going around in pivot circles ...

[ ] Network ... get around and make connections ...

[ ] If they're laughing, they're listening ... if they're listening, they're learning!

[ ] Give encouragement ... not grief ...

[ ] Pro Forma: forward-looking or predicting future financial performance ...

[ ] If we can't be interesting, at least be brief ... say it, then sit ...

[ ] Things are not always what they seem ... sometimes they're better, sometimes they're worse ...

[ ] 'Tis better to have loved and lost, than never to have loved at all ... better to have "ventured" and failed, than never to "ventured" at all ... [Thank you, Alfred Lord Tennyson]

[ ] Promote our venture with greeting cards ...

[ ] Have a picnic ... get the team together off-site for a day of fun and games ...

[ ] Courtesy is contagious ... we be nice to them and they be nice to us ...

[ ] They are what they are ... if we can't change them, think hard about whether we should join them ...

[ ] Process: a series of actions or steps taken in order to achieve a particular end ...

[ ] Quantitative or Qualitative ... what should we focus on today? ...

[ ] Promote our venture with walking signs ...

[ ] Years don't always add wisdom, but they do add perspective and grey hair ... why we need both "grey hairs" and "young pups" on our team ... grey hairs with experience, young pups with energy ... [Thank you, Paul Harvey]

[ ] Add our new (and hopefully big) twist and quickly blend with tested bits borrowed from anyone and everyone ... [Thank you, Tom Peters]

[ ] The fear of the change is usually worse than the change itself ...

[ ] Entrepreneurs do not have a special set of personality traits ... rather they combine their personal strengths together in ways that yield new results ... [Thank you, Heidi M Neck]

[ ] The best value wins the business ...

[ ] We can always ask questions ... and we should ...

[ ] Get a good attorney ... on second thought, make that a "great attorney"! ... [Thank you, Larry Hecker]

[ ] Dream, explore, ideate, vision, mission, goals, objectives, strategies, tactics, tasks, assignments ... common stages in new venture development ...

[ ] Fit, form, function, features ... a quick little 4-point checklist for new product or service design and development ... where does it fit, what form is it in, what functions does it

perform, what features does it have that make it different from everything else like it? ...

[ ] Creativity is like driving a car at night ... we never see further than our headlights, but we can make the whole trip that way ...

[ ] Good people can fix a lot of flaws in poor planning, but it's never the other way around ... [Thank you, Roland Schmitt]

[ ] Delight our customers ... that'll get 'em talkin'!

[ ] Our brand conveys our set of venture values to our customers ...

[ ] We may call it madness, but I call it love ... [Thank you, Don Byas]

[ ] Skilled innovators and entrepreneurs are considerate ...

[ ] Some problems are not really understood until a they are solved ...

[ ] Hit a brick wall ...

[ ] Ideas die quickly in some minds because they can't stand solitary confinement ...

[ ] If I had nine hours to cut down a tree, I'd spend the first six sharpening my axe ... [Thank you, Abraham Lincoln]

[ ] Creative mess is preferable to idle neatness ...

[ ] Interest: 1] money paid regularly at a particular rate for the use of money lent, or for delaying the repayment of a debt; 2] the state of wanting to know or learn about something or someone ...

[ ] When in doubt, don't ...

[ ] Promote our venture with Youtube ...

[ ] Monotony may be the best condition for creativity ... [Thank you, Margaret Sackville]

[ ] Market: a demand for a particular commodity or service, and the customers that create that demand ...

[ ] Line up funding commitments in advance ... ideally, we will have enough funding commitments to carry us over until we can reach self-funding stability ...

[ ] When we compete against another company, we just have to be better to win ... if we compete with ourselves, there is no limitation on how good we can become ... [Thank you, Chu Chin-ning]

[ ] Where there is money there is mischief ...

[ ] Lean: efficient and with no waste, offering little reward or substance, having no superfluous fat ...

[ ] The most powerful word in the English language is "free" ... "sale" is second ...

[ ] EXP: common abbreviation for Experimental ... "X" often is used the same way, too ...

[ ] Nothing is more valuable than a workable idea ... [Thank you, Ed Veverka]

[ ] Hire for attitude, train for skills ... [Thank you, Herb Kelleher]

[ ] Make it easy for us <or> Make it easy for them ... which one describes what we should be doing today? ...

[ ] Discovery consists of looking at the same thing as everyone else and thinking something different ... [Thank you, Albert Szent-Gyorgyi]

[ ] Experimental: a new invention or product based on untested ideas or techniques and not yet established or finalized ...

[ ] It's not just who we want to reach, it's how they can reach us, too! ... [Thank you, Jack Hardy]

[ ] Skilled innovators and entrepreneurs are alert to novelty ...

[ ] Focus on an industry that is new, growing, and/or expanding significantly ...

[ ] When we have eliminated the impossible, whatever remains, however improbable, must be the truth ... [Thank you, Arthur Conan Doyle]

[ ] Take time in turning a corner ... less we take a tumble in time ...

[ ] Take a hike ...

[ ] Identify the key questions and actions ...

[ ] Nothing endures but change ... [Thank you, Heraclitus of Ephesus]

[ ] Time makes more converts than reason ... [Thank you, Thomas Paine]

[ ] Turn fixed costs into variable costs whenever we can ...

[ ] Cultivate a pool of potential investors ... if one drops out, we have some backup ... [Thank you, Pamela Morrone]

[ ] Develop the habit of creativity ... reinvent everything we see, at least in our heads ...

[ ] Every venture has a unique past, present, and future ...

[ ] The trick to getting things done is knowing what to leave undone ... [Thank you, Stella Reading]

[ ] Finish before it's due ...

[ ] Fuzzy Front-End: the period between when an opportunity is first considered and when it is judged ready to enter formal development ... [Thank you, A Clamen]

[ ] Passion leads to success ... success feeds passion!

[ ] Promote our venture with sidewalk signs ...

[ ] Just the facts, Jack or Jill, just the facts ...

[ ] Sometimes we need a little push to get us back on track ...

[ ] Read every day ...

[ ] A day lost is gone forever ...

[ ] The door to success is closed until we open it ...

[ ] A good read: Thinking, Fast and Slow (Daniel Kahneman) ...

[ ] Money makes money ...

[ ] Some people who enter our lives change it forever ... for better or for worse ...

[ ] Sometimes we just need to shut up ...

[ ] What do you find easy? ...

[ ] It's the hard that will make us great ...

[ ] Innovate: make something new and better or improvements in something by introducing new methods, ideas, products, services, processes, market positions, paradigms, or combinations thereof ...

[ ] Ready! Fire! Aim! ... [Thank you, Dick Cheney]

[ ] In horse racing, the favorites win about 30% of the time ... [Thank you, Bill Finley]

[ ] Plan for today's and tomorrow's business ... [Thank you, Google]

[ ] Cost of Goods Sold: the cost of the components and labor required to produce a product (the Goods) ...

[ ] Know when to hold 'em, know when to fold 'em, know when to walk away, know when to run ... [Thank you, Kenny Rogers]

[ ] Common cause of venture death: inadequate time to become a stable organization ... time and money, can't live with them, can't live without them ...

[ ] Goal: a long-term aim or desired result ...

[ ] A roving eye misses opportunities close by ... [Thank you, Barbara Ann Kipfer]

[ ] Give each customer individualized attention ...

[ ] Fools rush in where angels fear to tread ...

[ ] Constant kindness can accomplish much ... as the sun makes ice melt, kindness causes misunderstanding, mistrust, and hostility to evaporate ... [Thank you, Albert Schweitzer]

[ ] Be different, be better ...

[ ] Follow our passions ...

[ ] Front or Back ... what should we focus on today? ...

[ ] Eat food, not too much, mostly plants ... [Thank you, Michael Pollan]

[ ] Some people who seem smart aren't ...

[ ] Skilled innovators and entrepreneurs are high achievers ...

[ ] MVP: abbreviation for Maximum Value Product ... MVP is often capitalized to differentiate it from mvp (minimal viable product) ...

[ ] Key question for our venture: What are the three-year projections for our venture? ...

[ ] If we want people to pay attention, make it quantifiable ... [Thank you, Jim Ehrlich]

[ ] Exactitude is not truth ... [Thank you, Henri Matisse]

[ ] Motion is not necessarily action ...

[ ] What are we waiting for? ... are we sure waiting is worth it? ...

[ ] People make decisions emotionally ... they make decisions based on a feeling, need, or emotion, not necessarily though a logical thought process ... [Thank you, Dean Rieck]

[ ] Where is our venture going to be located? ...

[ ] Write down our thoughts as we have them ... capture our ideas, never know when that great one is going to hit!

[ ] Are they really a competitor or a potential collaborator? ... maybe we can work with them instead of against them ...

[ ] Without innovation, don't bother!

[ ] Do not try to fix our venture all at once ... piece by piece, inch by inch ...

[ ] Successful innovators and entrepreneurs have unbounded determination to succeed ...

[ ] Capital: money, in particular, funds contributed by investors or lenders to a company for the purpose of funding

...

[ ] Someone who may be nice to us but is rude to the waiter is not a nice person ...

[ ] Niche versus broad markets ...

[ ] Key question for our venture: Is our name pleasant to say? ...

[ ] Reach is the percentage of a company's target market that is exposed to an ad campaign within a specific period of time ... [Thank you, Andrew Corbett]

[ ] Business Development: business function focused on creating strategy, strategic partnerships, and long-term relationships with suppliers and customers ...

[ ] Change costs ... nothing is ever free, is it? ...

[ ] Do a SWOTT Analysis ... Strengths (internal factors): What are the attributes of the organization that are helpful to achieving the objective? How can we use each strength? ... Weaknesses (internal factors): What are the attributes of the organization that are harmful to achieving the objective? How can we eliminate each weakness? ... Opportunities (external factors): What are the external conditions that are helpful to achieving the objective? How can we exploit each opportunity? ... Threats (external factors): What are the external conditions which could do damage to the business's performance? How can we defend against each threat? ... Trends (internal and external factors): What are the current trends that will affect the strengths, weaknesses, opportunities, and threats in the near and long term? What should the organization do to take advantage of the positive trends and avoid the negative? ...

[ ] Sometimes start-up ventures have too much money ... it's a nice problem, yes, but still a problem if we don't know how to use it right ...

[ ] Turn dreams into reality ...

[ ] Customers pay our salaries ... they are the most important visitors on our premises ... they are not dependent on us, we are dependent on them ... they are not an interruption in our work, they are the purpose of it ... we are not doing them a favor by serving them, they are doing us a favor by giving us the opportunity to serve them ... [Thank you, Mohandas Gandhi]

[ ] Many new discoveries are just seeing things that were already there ... but seeing them in a different way ...

[ ] If we can sell it to us, we can sell it to anyone ...

[ ] History is only as accurate as the historian ...

[ ] Encourage active participation from our customers ...

[ ] It's easy to sit up and take notice ... what's difficult is getting up and taking action! ... [Thank you, Al Batt]

[ ] Mistakes are lessons of wisdom ... [Thank you, Hugh White]

[ ] Focus on a particular demographic niche ...

[ ] Feature: a distinctive attribute or aspect of something ...

[ ] Take responsibility ... good, bad, or ugly ...

[ ] We'll know we've really made it when our brand becomes a verb ... like Google or Xerox!

[ ] Good products are desirable, feasible, and viable ... [Thank you, IDEO]

[ ] Do what we can't ... [Thank you, Casey Neistat]

[ ] Balance sheet formula: Assets - Liabilities - Shareholder Equity = 0 ... [Thank you, Chip Ruscher]

[ ] Early Adopter: individuals or organizations that enthusiastically embrace (try and buy) new technologies or tech-based products before the vast majority of potential buyers consider it ...

[ ] The results of a recipe depend on the quality of the ingredients and the skills of the cook ...

[ ] We can make more friends in two months by becoming really interested in other people than we can in two years by trying to get other people interested in us ... which is just another way of saying that the way to make a friend is to be one. ... [Thank you, Dale Carnegie]

[ ] An early-stage company should have 5 board members: CEO, CFO, two members from the lead investors, and an independent outsider ... [Thank you, Andrew Zacharakis]

[ ] Progress: moving forward toward a goal ...

[ ] The past cannot be changed ...

[ ] Think about how we can help others ...

[ ] Fortune: luck, especially good luck; a large amount of money ... yes, luck and money go together ...

[ ] Fresh eggs sink in cool saltwater, old eggs don't ... new ventures often may sink, old ones usually don't ...

[ ] The more we know, the more we know we ought to know ...

[ ] Hang loose ... keep easy ...

[ ] Promote our venture with local newspapers ...

[ ] Opportunity: A business or technology gap, that a venture or individual realizes, that exists between the current situation and an envisioned future in order to capture

competitive advantage, respond to a threat, solve a problem, or ameliorate a difficulty ... [Thank you, P Puri]

[ ] Key question for our venture: What are the factors that limit our growth? ...

[ ] A good business plan is the "right length" ... not too long, not too short ... to convey all the pertinent information ... [Thank you, Patty Sias]

[ ] Stand out ...

[ ] In programming, the first 90% of the code accounts for the first 90% of the development time ... the remaining 10% of the code accounts for the other 90% of the development time!

[ ] We simply hate, detest, loathe, despise, and abhor redundancy and duplication and repetition ... [Thank you, Department of Redundancy Department]

[ ] Don't gossip ... it's a waste of time and energy and ethics ...

[ ] Customer discovery, customer validation, iteration/pivot, customer creation, company building ... the stages in building a new venture, product, service, or process ...

[ ] Let's be a class act ... not a class acting classy ...

[ ] Skilled innovators and entrepreneurs are emotionally expressive ...

[ ] We need to take responsibility for our goals and objectives ... they don't happen by magic ...

[ ] A good business plan supports credible growth projections ... [Thank you, Charlie HIggins]

[ ] Go whole hog ...

[ ] Instruct rather than order ...

[ ] Put words together that don't usually go together ... way back when, someone put "personal" and "computer" together ... a very avant-garde thought at the time ...

[ ] The competition is a very good teacher ...

[ ] Successful entrepreneurs are comfortable with uncertainty ... [Thank you, Timothy Butler]

[ ] Without action, we aren't going anywhere ... [Thank you, Mahatma Ghandi]

[ ] TV networks are built on the assumption that audience size is what matters most ... content is secondary; it exists to attract passive viewers who will sit still for advertisements ... traditional market-driven media always attempts to treat devices, audiences, and content as bulk commodities ... as users acquire the means to produce and distribute content, the authority and profit potential of large traditional networks are directly challenged. ... [Thank you, John Hockenberry]

[ ] Entrepreneurs understand there is little difference between obstacles and opportunities ... they turn both into their advantage ...

[ ] Seize good luck ... it doesn't happen often enough ...

[ ] A watched pot never boils ...

[ ] The more things change, the more they are the same ... [Thank you, Alphonse Karr]

[ ] All investors are not the same ...

[ ] It could be a good opportunity if our team has a clear plan for success ...

[ ] Entrepreneurial Myth: Starting a business is easy ... well, actually, starting a new company isn't so hard ... it's making money at it that is tough ... [Thank you, Scott Shane]

[ ] Small things have been made big with advertising ...

[ ] Take a deep breath ...

[ ] Respect yourself ... this is not negotiable ...

[ ] There are few things as uncommon as common sense ... [Thank you, Frank Hubbard]

[ ] Business is competitive creativity ...

[ ] The best way to get in front of any investor is to have someone they know introduce us ... [Thank you, Rhonda Abrams]

[ ] Leave your mark when we have it in our power ...

[ ] Keep a daily diary ...

[ ] Nobody knows what is the best they can do ... [Thank you, Arturo Toscanini]

[ ] Potential venture legal issue: Promising more in the business plan than can be delivered and failing to comply with state and federal securities laws ... [Thank you, Connie Bagley]

[ ] Do not evenly divide shares between founders ... it should be equitable and that's not usually even ... [Thank you, William Bygrave]

[ ] Keep our feet on the ground but keep reaching for the stars ... [Thank you, Casey Kasem]

[ ] See what's not there ...

[ ] Web site for census data: www.census.gov ... [Thank you, US Census Bureau]

[ ] In science, progress is measured by moving the frontier of knowledge away from the core ... in engineering, progress is measured by moving the practice closer to a

commercially-interesting embodiment ... [Thank you, Will Allen]

[ ] All entrepreneurs are not created the same ...

[ ] No one is listening until we make a mistake ...

[ ] Problems can become opportunities when the right people come together ... [Thank you, Robert Redford]

[ ] We can't manage what we can't measure ... what metrics are key to the success of our venture? ...

[ ] Develop our own rituals ...

[ ] Key question for our venture: Do we have the capabilities and resources to compete in the market five to 10 years from now? ...

[ ] Obsolete ourselves or the competition will ... [Thank you, John Micklethwaite]

[ ] Focus on a particular geographic niche ... once we're big in Racine, we can expand to Milwaukee ...

[ ] Where there is money, there are monkeys, and where there are monkeys, there is monkey business ...

[ ] Do what we promised to do ...

[ ] A business model is a conceptual framework that shows how a venture creates, delivers, and extracts value ... [Thank you, Webb Smith]

[ ] Skilled innovators and entrepreneurs are flexible ...

[ ] Successful entrepreneurs have an ability to sell ... [Thank you, Timothy Butler]

[ ] Staying creative is one of the hardest things we must do ...

[ ] We can never go back ... time travel back is (so far) impossible, so saith Albert Einstein ... so let's move ahead, Fred!

[ ] Whenever we are true to ourselves, we will be true to others ...

[ ] Skilled innovators and entrepreneurs are able to make independent judgments ...

[ ] Someone else's recipe may not work for us ... [Thank you, Nelson Wang]

[ ] Figure out our why ...

[ ] If we want something changed, it's up to us to change it ...

[ ] When writing our business plan, avoid overly optimistic time frames ... ask around or do research on the Internet ... if it takes most companies 6-12 months to get up and running, that is what it will take ours ... if we think it will take 3 months to develop our prototype, double it ... we will face delays we don't know about yet--ones we can't control ... [Thank you, Kaye Vivian]

[ ] Don't be afraid to ask for what we need from investors ... be honest, be fair, be right, apply their money wisely ...

[ ] Participate ...

[ ] How to kill creativity: "We don't take any risks around here ..." ...

[ ] A good business plan has the right appearance ... not too fancy, not too plain; arranged properly with the executive summary, table of contents, and chapters in right order ... [Thank you, Conspiracy Cosmetics]

[ ] Benchmark companies ... they can help us learn a lot about our business without having to make quite so many mistakes ...

[ ] It could be a good opportunity if we have a feasible solution ...

[ ] Anticipate objections ...

[ ] Key question for our venture: What are our respective market shares? ...

[ ] Overwhelming customers with personal, unexpected service is the best way to keep them for life ... [Thank you, Seth Godin]

[ ] Business Model: a design for the successful operation of a business, identifying revenue sources, customer base, products and services, operational processes, and details of financing ... [Thank you, Yves Pigneur]

[ ] Innovators and entrepreneurs are like detectives out to solve the mystery of the hidden opportunity ...

[ ] Education is a great equalizer ...

[ ] Two types of capital: debt and equity ...

[ ] Smell the flowers, listen to the birds ...

[ ] Leadership consists of nothing but taking responsibility for everything that goes wrong and giving our colleagues credit for everything that goes well ... [Thank you, Dwight D Eisenhower]

[ ] Setting a proper "Use of Funds" strategy is a balance between asking for enough money to enable the company to achieve some meaningful milestones and preserving the founder's dilution ... for the first seed round of funding, don't sell any more than 15-20% of the company ...

[ ] Entrepreneurial Myth: It takes a lot of money to finance a new business ... it depends on the type of venture ... that's one of the key reasons to do a good job planning the new venture ... to figure out in advance how much money it will take until the venture is stable (self-funding) ... [Thank you, Scott Shane]

[ ] If we get off track, get back on as fast as we can ...

[ ] One must have sunshine, freedom, and a little flower ... [Thank you, Hans Christian Anderson]

[ ] Use secondary data that was gathered using objective, neutral processes ...

[ ] Great oaks grow from little acorns ...

[ ] Skilled innovators and entrepreneurs are independent in outlook ...

[ ] There are no great limits to growth because there are no limits of human intelligence, imagination, and wonder ... [Thank you, Ronald Reagan]

[ ] Do more with less ...

[ ] Tell them how very much they are appreciated ...

[ ] Taxes: a compulsory contribution to state revenue, levied by the government on workers' income and business profits or added to the cost of some goods, services, and transactions ...

[ ] Better to wear out than rust out ... [Thank you, Richard Cumberland]

[ ] Market Research: the action or activity of gathering information about current and prospective customer needs and preferences ... [Thank you, Google Dictionary]

[ ] Shoot for the moon ... even if we miss, we'll be among the stars ...

[ ] Absence makes the heart grow fonder ... [Thank you, McRib]

[ ] Don't sweat the petty stuff ... and don't pet the sweaty stuff! ... [Thank you, George Carlin]

[ ] Communications: the imparting or exchanging of information ...

[ ] Change things ... before they change us ...

[ ] Key question for our venture: What is the typical sales cycle between our initial customer contact and the closing of a sale? ... how can we streamline this process and shorten the time? ...

[ ] Benefit: an advantage or profit gained from something ...

[ ] Every venture has its ups and downs ...

[ ] Memorize something new each day ... could be song lyrics or the list of Islay distilleries ... never can tell when it'll come in handy ... [Thank you, James Arnold]

[ ] Elevator Pitch: a succinct and persuasive sales pitch ...

[ ] Good manners and soft words have brought many a difficult thing to pass ... [Thank you, John Vanbrugh]

[ ] Make it easy for trade show booth visitors to get information ... [Thank you, Susan Ward]

[ ] Promote our venture with direct mail and sales letters ...

[ ] Direct and Indirect ... What are two types of Price? ...

[ ] Exercise: List 10 things our competitors do better than us ... use the list to improve what we do ...

[ ] Corporate entrepreneur credo: Develop a spirited team; choose and work with only the best ... [Thank you, Gifford Pinchot III]

[ ] Travel ... it gives us new perspectives ...

[ ] Profit in business comes from repeat customers, customers that boast about our products and services and processes, and that bring their friend with them ... [Thank you, W Edwards Deming]

[ ] Our brand is our most important competitive advantage ... don't screw it up!

[ ] Limited Liability Company (LLC): a legal form of company that has many of the tax advantages of partnerships, notably the characteristic of being a pass-through entity for tax purposes ...

[ ] Promote our venture with price specials ...

[ ] Sustainable: be able to maintain something at a certain rate or level ...

[ ] Build a psychographic profile of our target customers ... needs, wants, desires, purchasing patterns, decision-making processes ...

[ ] When the chips are down, the buffalo is empty ... [Thank you, Buffalo Bill]

[ ] Creativity is a muscle that needs to be exercised regularly or it turns to mush ...

[ ] Successful teams are mutually supportive ...

[ ] Align long-term vision with short-term execution ... [Thank you, Walt Disney]

[ ] A source of opportunity for innovation are changes in perception, mood, and meaning ... [Thank you, Peter F Drucker]

[ ] Control our costs ... or they will control us!

[ ] Good design can't fix a broken business model ... [Thank you, Jeffrey Veen]

[ ] Good competitive research is critical to our success ...

[ ] Well begun is half done ... [Thank you, Horace]

[ ] Keep a camera close at hand to capture ideas, competitive products, customer problems, and other visual information ...

[ ] Beware of speedbumps and potholes ...

[ ] No shit ... further, no bullshit ... it all stinks ...

[ ] Up or Down ... what should we focus on today? ...

[ ] To see things in the seed, that is genius ... [Thank you, Lao-Tzu]

[ ] The devil's in the doing ... hopefully we can stand the heat of hell in our quest for heaven ...

[ ] Everyone gets twenty-four hours in a day ... it's all in how we use it ...

[ ] There are four types of innovation: product, process, position, and paradigm ... [Thank you, Matt Mars]

[ ] There are lots of big fat liars out there!

[ ] How to kill creativity: "If it ain't broke, don't fix it..."

[ ] Potential opportunities have perceived desirability ... [Thank you, IDEO]

[ ] Understand the value of things ...

[ ] Long-tail: ...

[ ] We can't have a light without a dark to stick it in ... [Thank you, Arlo Guthrie]

[ ] Promote our venture with fliers and circulars ...

[ ] Overcome hard luck with hard work ... [Thank you, Harry Golden]

[ ] An inventor creates a product ... an entrepreneur creates a business ...

[ ] Promote our venture with demonstrations ...

[ ] Telling the truth is always desirable, but sometimes not advisable ... [Thank you, Agatha Christie]

[ ] If we think money is limiting ... time is more so!

[ ] Choose the right co-founders ...

[ ] Entrepreneurs are often good at mathematics ...

[ ] You can never plan the future by the past alone ... but it's not a bad place to start ...

[ ] If it ain't broke, break it ... then put it back together even better than before!

[ ] Uphill or Downhill ... what should we focus on today? ...

[ ] Ask "why?" ... if that doesn't work, ask "Why not?" ...

[ ] Keep our sense of wonder ...

[ ] Let go ... mistakes happen, life isn't perfect ...

[ ] Maker: a person or thing that makes or produces something ...

[ ] We all have our own superpowers ...

[ ] Transactional Analysis: an interchange between parental (critical and nurturing), adult (rational), and childlike (intuitive and dependent) aspects of personality ... [Thank you, Eric Berne]

[ ] Muddy the waters to make them seem deep ... [Thank you, Friedrich Nietzsche]

[ ] Chance: the possibility of something happening ...

[ ] The future is never certain ...

[ ] Think and our minds will stay fresh ...

[ ] 80% of the business comes from 20% of the customers ... a common generalization ... maybe 80/20 is not quite the right ratio ... still, worth taking a look at who are our top customers and how valuable the are to our venture ...

[ ] People's minds are changed through observation, not through argument ... [Thank you, Will Rogers]

[ ] Park ourselves in the middle of the road and we'll get run over from both directions ...

[ ] It all starts with a fuzzy front-end ... [Thank you, Ken Smith]

[ ] Many ventures today consist of just a CEO with a cell phone ... everything else is outsourced! ... [Thank you, Tom Peters]

[ ] Gravity or Energy ... what should we focus on today? ...

[ ] We can fiddle with the pravda all we want ... but we can't change the istina ... [Thank you, Andrew Rosenthal]

[ ] The best burglar alarm is a dog ...

[ ] A little nonsense now and then is relished by the wisest ... gotta get goofy sometimes ... [Thank you, Roald Dahl]

[ ] Push or Pull ... what should we focus on today? ...

[ ] Key question for our venture: What do we need to know about our target market? ...

[ ] Everyday when we wake up, ask ourselves: what are we really trying to do? ...

[ ] Companies are easy to start, businesses are not ...

[ ] Skilled innovators and entrepreneurs are word fluent ...

[ ] Technology Transfer: the transfer of new technology from the originator to a secondary user ...

[ ] Success is a lousy teacher ... it seduces smart people into thinking they can't lose ... [Thank you, Bill Gates]

[ ] The world is a canvas to the imagination ... [Thank you, Henry David Thoreau]

[ ] Promote our venture with general business magazines ...

[ ] Only do business with people you trust ...

[ ] Do the very best we know how, the very best we can, and keep doing so until the end ... [Thank you, Abraham Lincoln]

[ ] Knowledge is a process of piling up facts ... wisdom lies in their simplification ... [Thank you, Martin H Fischer]

[ ] There is no status quo ... we are either getting better or worse ... [Thank you, Pat Riley]

[ ] Want to succeed ... where there's a want there's a way ...

[ ] Asset: a useful or valuable thing, person, or quality ...

[ ] Be prepared ... [Thank you, Boy Scouts]

[ ] Compensation: the pay and other incentives an organization provides to an employee in exchange for his/her services ...

[ ] How to attract new customers: highlight positive reviews and recommendations ...

[ ] T or F?: The biggest hurdle to success is me, myself, and I ...

[ ] Don't put off until tomorrow what we can do today ... if it needs doing, do it ...

[ ] Encourage people to build on the thoughts of others ... think "why not!" rather than "here's why not!" ... [Thank you, Todd Adams]

[ ] Praise accomplishments ...

[ ] Focus on our beachhead market and solution first ...

[ ] Strange signals from the sky may be signs of aliens ... potential new markets for our venture? ... [Thank you, Economist]

[ ] Mountain or molehill ... don't mix them up!

[ ] It takes genius, faith, and perseverance to create a brand ... [Thank you, David Ogilvy]

[ ] Tomorrow will be different than today ... for better, or for worse ... we're married to each and every day ...

[ ] Brainstorming does not mean narrowing down to the best idea ...

[ ] Adapt ... there are no other viable options ...

[ ] Common Stock: equity or stock ownership of a company representing owners who have the lowest-priority ...

[ ] Don't do it alone ... the first one to come along with a partner is going to beat the snot outta us!

[ ] Promote our venture with high profile publications ...

[ ] Nine Fs for entrepreneurial success: founders, focus, fast, flexible, forever innovating, flat, frugal, friendly, and fun ... [Thank you, Andrew Corbett]

[ ] Don't take any wooden nickels ... they're only good in one bar ...

[ ] Chasm: differences between the characteristics of and the ways a business markets to initial customers versus the bulk of the business's potential customers ...

[ ] Sit or Stand ... what should we focus on today? ...

[ ] Rule: principles governing conduct ...

[ ] A tried and true tradition can prevent a little sedition!

[ ] Procrastination is the thief of time ...

[ ] Ideas are like children ... our own are always wonderful, the others are little brats! ... [Thank you, Michael Harris]

[ ] Why us? Why now? ... why are we the team to do this venture? ... why is now the time to do this venture? ...

[ ] Make the commitment to make this a success ...

[ ] What makes you unafraid of failure? ... [Thank you, Frederic Premji]

[ ] If we don't know where we are going, we will probably end up somewhere else ... [Thank you, Casey Stengel]

[ ] How to kill creativity: "That's not how we do things around here ..." ...

[ ] Maintain a work environment that is challenging, rewarding, and fun ...

[ ] Know our strengths and weaknesses ... build on the strengths, mitigate the weaknesses ...

[ ] Be persistent in our vision ...

[ ] Key question for our venture: What future equity or debt financing will be necessary? ...

[ ] People usually do like to learn ... but they don't often like to be taught ... [Thank you, Winston Churchill]

[ ] If we wouldn't want to see it on the front page of the morning newspaper, don't put it in an e-mail ... [Thank you, Erika Morphy]

[ ] We won't know all the answers to all the questions, but we don't have to ... if we have the right answers to the right questions ...

[ ] Simplicity is powerful ... [Thank you, Google]

[ ] Mobilize our creative resources ...

[ ] The Balanced Scorecard describes the theory of our strategy ... if we do A, B will happen ... we should always ask the question, if I am doing A, is B happening? ... [Thank you, David Norton]

[ ] If you have an apple and I have an apple and we exchange these apples, then you and I will still each have one apple ... but if you have an idea and I have an idea and we exchange these ideas, then each of us will have two ideas ... [Thank you, G B Shaw]

[ ] Have a good memory for details ...

[ ] Delegate ...

[ ] Concise: ...

[ ] How to retain customers: loyalty and rewards programs ...

[ ] Key question for our venture: What are the major benefits of our industry? ...

[ ] Knowledge grows like a tree: slowly and on fertile ground ... [Thank you, Barbara Ann Kipfer]

[ ] Intuitive or Formulaic ... what should we focus on today? ...

[ ] Key question for our venture: How can we define our marketing plan? ...

[ ] Sometimes we have to say "no" ...

[ ] Key question for our venture: How are we better than them? ...

[ ] We can learn a lot by looking ... [Thank you, Yogi Berra]

[ ] Illusions can be more gratifying than reality ... like the billboard picture of the hamburger compared to what we really get ...

[ ] Invest in ourselves ...

[ ] Hard-boiled eggs will spin, raw eggs will wobble ... that's kind of like ventures ... the good ones have a spin, the not-so-good-ones wobble around ...

[ ] Put one dumb foot in front of the other and course-correct as we go ... [Thank you, Barry Diller]

[ ] The illiterate are not just those who cannot read and write, but those who cannot learn, unlearn, and relearn ... [Thank you, Alvin Toffler]

[ ] A web site does not equal an internet marketing strategy ... [Thank you, Ian Lurie]

[ ] Walk the customer walk, talk the customer talk ... what do we see? ... what do we hear? ...

[ ] When things go wrong, it's time to shine ... go out of our way to make it right by our customers. Often, it will become a more memorable positive experience ...

[ ] Changes will come ... but other changes will come after, wiping out each layer of change, like waves on a beach erasing the ripples in sand cast up by the previous wave ... [Thank you, John C Wright]

5280 TIPS for INNOVATORS and ENTREPRENEURS

[ ] We (usually) get what we pay for ...

[ ] Time cures all ...

[ ] Not all science is real ...

[ ] A person might be able to play without being creative, but sure can't be creative without playing ... [Thank you, Stacy Perryman]

[ ] Go where the prospects are and the prospectors aren't ...

[ ] How can we answer this Question: How will our venture create and deliver value for our customers? ...

[ ] Key question for our venture: What more should we do? ...

[ ] Whatever people think, is ... [Thank you, Otis Singletary]

[ ] No pain, no gain ... [Thank you, Benjamin Franklin]

[ ] Promote our venture with bus bench/shelter signs ...

[ ] Life cycle of a venture, a product, a service: 1] introduction, 2] growth, 3] maturity, 4] decline ...

[ ] Nothing comes easy ... Nothing is given to us. Whatever we do, we've got to work for it and earn it. Whatever reward we get we've got to know that we've had our input into that success. There's no substitute for hard work. And if we want to be well known or well liked, we have to put ourselves out for people ... [Thank you, Jack Charlton]

[ ] Skilled innovators and entrepreneurs are good leaders ...

[ ] If we look confident, we can pull off anything ... even if we have no clue what we're doing ... [Thank you, Jessica Alba]

[ ] Drink at least eight glasses of water a day ...

[ ] Over the years, the U.S. economy has shown a remarkable ability to absorb shocks of all kinds, to recover, and to continue to grow ... flexible and efficient markets for labor and

112

capital, an entrepreneurial tradition, and a general willingness to tolerate and even embrace technological and economic change all contribute to this resiliency ... [Thank you, Ben Bernanke]

[ ] Yes, we can! so, let's get up and go! ... [Thank you, Barack Obama]

[ ] Make a data sheet ...

[ ] Keep facing change ...

[ ] If the customer thinks she's right, she's right ... [Thank you, Tom Peters]

[ ] Michigan or Ohio State ... what should we focus on today? ...

[ ] Adversity is like taxes and death ... it happens to us all ...

[ ] Do it now ...

[ ] We are all part of a larger world ...

[ ] Exercise: List 10 well-established organizations that could have a vested interest in the success of our venture ...

[ ] Bureaucracy always wins over creativity and innovation ...

[ ] Common cause of venture death: lack of time ...

[ ] When writing, strike out words that aren't needed ...

[ ] Our message is complete when all relevant information is included in an understandable manner ... and there is a clear "call to action" ...

[ ] Successful Innovators and entrepreneurs know are honest with themselves and others ... [Thank you, Patricia G Greene]

[ ] SEO: abbreviation for Search Engine Optimization ...

[ ] Skilled innovators and entrepreneurs have supra-rational creative abilities ...

[ ] Beware: disclosing proprietary and trade secret information to less-than-reputable people even if they've signed a non-disclosure agreement ...

[ ] We may know their name but not their story ...

[ ] Individuals are creative, not corporations ... [Thank you, John Goulding]

[ ] Many angel investors are actually informal investors ... not high-profile sophisticated investors who mandate fancy presentations, well-coiffed business plans, and attractive 10X returns ...

[ ] Capital Structure: how a company is financed ...

[ ] Innovation never happens as planned ... [Thank you, Gifford Pinchot]

[ ] Lost time is never found again ... [Thank you, Benjamin Franklin]

[ ] Common Mistake: underestimating costs ... common, common mistake ...

[ ] The more we say, the less people remember ... [Thank you, François Fénelon]

[ ] Don't tell the "big lie" ...

[ ] Business plan competitions: Beware, the "prize money" may have strong strings ...

[ ] Put easy-to-understand information first, complicated material second ... [Thank you, Randy Accetta]

[ ] Eat well-balanced meals ...

[ ] Getting to know anyone takes time ...

[ ] Innovation is the primary driver of everything that goes on in business ...

[ ] Customer needs, wants, and desires change ... and change often, sporadically, randomly, and usually when it's least convenient for us!

[ ] 80% of the value we will receive comes from 20% of our activities ...

[ ] Minister quickly ...

[ ] Waist nothing, want nothing ...

[ ] Key question for our venture: Does the new name we're thinking about coordinate with other names used in our venture? ...

[ ] With the power of thought comes the ability to think ...

[ ] Time becomes more precious the less we have ...

[ ] Obstacles make the goal clearer ...

[ ] Entrepreneurship is a process that must be practiced in order for us to become better and better ... the more we practice, the better we become ... [Thank you, Heidi M Neck]

[ ] Common sources of new venture funding: founders, family and friends, fanatical customers, "angel" investors, venture capitalists, banks, government agencies, small business investment companies, commercial finance companies, crowdfunding ...

[ ] F-Funding: new venture funding that comes from the founders, family, friends, fanatics, and fools ...

[ ] Just imagine that ... we can, you know, just imagine that ...

[ ] Don't edit the quality of an idea when we first think of it ... capture the thought, let it rest, come back later and give it a test ...

[ ] Observation and insight ...

[ ] Real eyes realize real lies ...

[ ] A leader is a facilitator, not an order giver ... [Thank you, John Naisbitt]

[ ] Key question for our venture: How big is our market opportunity? ...

[ ] Creativity varies inversely with the number of cooks in the kitchen ...

[ ] Tell me, I forget; show me, I remember ...

[ ] The most successful entrepreneurs don't chase after money ... they find their passion and follow it and let the money come to them ...

[ ] Promote our venture with endorsements or promotion by famous personalities ...

[ ] Key question for our venture: What is the financial model of a typical company in our industry? ... use that benchmark to measure our success ...

[ ] Key question for our venture: Where is our venture based (address)? ... why there? ...

[ ] Stop trying to change other people ... change yourself instead ...

[ ] A good business plan provides a concise description of the venture's products or services ... [Thank you, UC-Berkeley Colleagues]

[ ] Never underestimate our power to change ...

[ ] How to attract new customers: offer a sample of our product or service ...

[ ] The best way to predict the future is to invent it ... [Thank you, Alan Kay]

[ ] Aim for the stars ... even if we only get to the moon, we'll have accomplished a lot!

[ ] Term Sheet: a bullet-point document outlining the material terms and conditions of a business agreement ... after a term sheet has been "executed", it guides legal counsel in the preparation of a proposed "final agreement" ...

[ ] Successful teams share a common vision ...

[ ] Be on the lookout for new ideas ... we never know where our next great inspiration will come from ... [Thank you, InsideCRM]

[ ] Know how to use at least one good financial spreadsheet program ... Microsoft Excel is a standard, Google Sheets is good, too, as are others ...

[ ] It's all in the time we spend together ...

[ ] Whatever interests is interesting ... but it it's not interesting, should it be? ...

[ ] Encourage all to do their best ...

[ ] Use our REAL Brain ... Right Brain (creative), Engaged Brain (learning), Alert Brain (attentive), Left Brain (analytical) ...

[ ] The customer always has a choice ... including the choice to not do anything ...

[ ] Complete what we begin ...

[ ] Past performance means nothing ... [Thank you, Warren Buffett]

[ ] Entrepreneurs are usually objective ...

[ ] Skilled innovators and entrepreneurs are earthy ...

[ ] Legal Issues: questions concerning the protections that laws or regulations should provide ...

[ ] Be open to new experiences ...

[ ] Sometimes we do need to say "no" ... make sure it's for the right reasons ... never say "no" in anger ...

[ ] So many things are possible just as long as we don't know they're impossible ... [Thank you, Norton Juster]

[ ] Maintain a collection of potential opportunities and ideas ...

[ ] Imagination is the beginning of creativity ... we imagine what we desire, we will what we imagine, we create what we will. ... [Thank you, George Bernard Shaw]

[ ] Success: ...

[ ] Entrepreneurship is innovation implementation ...

[ ] Innovators are often symbolistic thinkers ...

[ ] Wherever they need us, we're there ... our customers are where our customers are ...

[ ] Don't do anything that conflicts with common sense ...

[ ] Make absolute integrity the compass that guides us in all we do ... [Thank you, Karl Eller]

[ ] A good business plan stresses specifics rather than generalities ... [Thank you, Don Piper]

[ ] Entrepreneurship is not rocket science ... too bad ... it would have fewer variables and more formulas to follow for success ...

[ ] Knowing that we do not know much is already knowing a lot ...

[ ] Practice continuous improvement ...

[ ] Promote our venture with discount coupons ...

[ ] Successful entrepreneurs have an ability to manage the financial aspects of a business ... [Thank you, Janet Kraus]

[ ] Weng pups and grey hairs ...

[ ] Do not work just for the money ...

[ ] BTW EPSCPSNBC LOL ... By The Way, Earn a Profit Solving Customer Problems with Something New and Better than the Competition! (Laughing Out Loud!) ...

[ ] Promote our venture with directory advertising ...

[ ] Carry the spirit of the child with us forever ...

[ ] Eighty percent of the sales come from twenty percent of the products ...

[ ] Making money is art and working is art and good business is the best art ... [Thank you, Andy Warhol]

[ ] Evaluation: appraise, argue, assess, attach, choose compare, defend estimate, judge, predict, rate, core, select, support, value, evaluate ...

[ ] We can't live without an eraser ... [Thank you, Tom Peters]

[ ] How to kill creativity: "It's not our job ..."

[ ] The things we fear most in organizations (fluctuations, disturbances, imbalances) are the primary sources of creativity ... [Thank you, Margaret J Wheatley]

[ ] By logic and reason we die hourly, by imagination we live ... [Thank you, Jack B Yeats]

[ ] Be a good coach ...

[ ] People want to buy, they don't want to be sold ...

[ ] Storytellers seldom let facts get in the way of perpetuating a legend, although a few facts add seasoning and make the legend more believable ... [Thank you, John H Alexander]

[ ] In times like these, it helps to recall that there have always been times like these ... [Thank you, Paul Harvey]

[ ] When writing our business plan, avoid rumors about the competition ... if we know for sure one is going out of business we can allude to it, but avoid listing their weaknesses or hearsay ... stick to facts ... [Thank you, Kaye Vivian]

[ ] Limit the group of people receiving founder shares to 3 people ... [Thank you, William Bygrave]

[ ] Pack light, travel fast ...

[ ] Give it a rest ...

[ ] 'Tis not knowing much but what is useful that makes us wise ...

[ ] Never lie ... don't badmouth the competition or say negative things about their clients ...

[ ] Make quick, clean-cut decisions ...

[ ] Be on time ...

[ ] No butts about it ...

[ ] Culture drives the personality of a venture ...

[ ] Promote our venture with newsletters ...

[ ] Make visible what, without us, might perhaps never have been seen ... [Thank you, Robert Bresson]

[ ] Perfection is not obtainable ... but excellence is!

[ ] If we wouldn't be happy for everyone to see it (customers, clients, colleagues, family, or friends), keep it out of sight ... but it's important that we ask ourselves, why are we embarrassed? ... [Thank you, Joanna Roberts]

[ ] Action without thought is like shooting without aim ... a little viewfinder can go a long way in helping to hit the target!

[ ] A garden looks more beautiful from a little distance than up close ...

[ ] Capture our intuitive thoughts ...

[ ] Customer's rule ... we need to follow their orders, or their orders won't follow. ...

[ ] Delight the eye without distracting the mind ... [Thank you, Google]

[ ] Value: the importance, worth, or usefulness of something ... Value = Benefits / Price (Value divided by Price) ...

[ ] I'm mad as hell, and I'm not going to take it anymore ... (Instead, I think I'm going to be an innovator and entrepreneur and remold our world to be the place I'd like it to be!) ... [Thank you, Peter Finch]

[ ] Common cause of venture death: no market need ... with all due respect to "Field of Dreams", just because we build it doesn't mean they will come ... only in the movies ...

[ ] How can we answer this Question: What is our customer value proposition? ... what do we offer our customers that is new and better than our competition? ...

[ ] Common venture legal structures ... sole proprietorship, general partnership, C corporation, S corporation, benefit corporation, limited liability company, limited partnership, limited liability partnership, not-for-profit organization ...

[ ] Key question for our venture: Whom should we thank? ... and when? ...

[ ] Triggering Event: an event in someone's personal or professional life that starts them down the road to starting a new venture ... [Thank you, Andrew Corbett]

[ ] Do not think only in absolutes ... few things in the world are unquestionable ...

[ ] Never lie, never cheat, never steal ... never mind that you could get caught, it's just not right ... never has been, never will be ...

[ ] Don't eat anything we might see when we're at the zoo ...

[ ] Encourage active participation within our venture ... give everyone a voice and we just might find we've got a great sounding choir ...

[ ] Make sure your pronoun usage is clear to the reader ... [Thank you, Randy Accetta]

[ ] We've got two sides to our brain, use them ... but not at the same time! our right brain is the creative side ... our left brain is the analytical side ... both are important functions, but if we try to create and analyze at the same time, we'll drive ourselves (and others) crazy! ...

[ ] Don't scam anyone ... yes, of course, supposedly sophisticated investors are scammed by more-sophisticated

"entrepreneurs" every day ... but that's not how great ventures are built ... ...

[ ] Preferences: a greater liking for one alternative over another or others ...

[ ] Look at the source as well as the suggestions ...

[ ] Act quickly but correctly ...

[ ] Identify and clearly define our target market(s) ...

[ ] B-M-L (Build-Measure-Learn): the process of creating a new product, service, process, or method through continual incremental change and improvement ...

[ ] Lean Startup: a new venture formed with limited resources ...

[ ] Wisdom doesn't do desperate things ... [Thank you, Henry David Thoreau]

[ ] Never patronize ...

[ ] Switch from autopilot to manual ... a little short nose dive every now and then will keep your passengers awake, it not amused ...

[ ] Key question for our venture: Is our name easy to spell? ...

[ ] B2C: abbreviation for a Business-to-Consumer relationship ...

[ ] They who hate are lost ...

[ ] Start at the beginning and work our way through it ...

[ ] Preserve profits ... invest them in something good!

[ ] Left-brain thinking traits ... analytic, rational, objective, symbolic, math, digital, order, qualitative ...

[ ] Compound Annual Growth Rate (CAGR): the annual growth in revenues of a company, a market niche, or an industry, factoring in annual compounding ...

[ ] Good, better, best, never let it rest, until the good becomes the better and the better becomes the best ...

[ ] Wisdom means a person can see implications and draw conclusions ...

[ ] Do a few things really well rather than a lot of things poorly ...

[ ] Common cause of venture death: stronger competitors ...

[ ] Change is a challenge ... to make something new and better ...

[ ] The future belongs to those who believe in their dreams ... [Thank you, Eleanor Roosevelt]

[ ] Use good mentors ...

[ ] Good judgment comes from experience ... experience comes from bad judgment ... [Thank you, Barry LePatner]

[ ] Place the subject and main verb near each other and use strong verbs ... [Thank you, Randy Accetta]

[ ] Limitation: a restrictive rule or circumstance ...

[ ] Successful companies not only create value, they also communicate their uniqueness to customers in credible ways ... [Thank you, Michael Porter]

[ ] Choose simplicity over complexity ... complex is easy, simple is hard ... [Thank you, Warren Buffett]

[ ] Skilled innovators and entrepreneurs are able to perform "miracles" ...

[ ] Only God can make a tree ... probably because it's so hard to figure out how to get the bark on ... [Thank you, Woody Allen]

[ ] Forecast market demand ...

[ ] Product: an article or substance that is manufactured or refined for sale and can typically be defined as having a certain fit, form, function, features, and performance ...

[ ] There is no future like the present ...

[ ] Make existing products and services obsolete ... if we don't, how will we react with our competition does? ... [Thank you, Mike Morris]

[ ] Create ...

[ ] Starter or Finisher ... what should we focus on today? ...

[ ] Someone with vision can see the invisible ...

[ ] Vision, mission; goals, objectives; strategies, tactics; tasks, assignments ... levels of planning for our venture ...

[ ] Reward: something received as a result of achievement ...

[ ] A mind stretched to a new dimension never goes back to the original dimension ... [Thank you, Oliver Wendell Holmes]

[ ] Traveling up a hill is easier on a bicycle built for two than on a bicycle built for one ... [Thank you, Barbara Ann Kipfer]

[ ] Move on ... if we're not in the right place, we're not in the right place ... let's find a better neighborhood ...

[ ] Ask first: is it worth it? ...

[ ] Angels can provide entrepreneurs with experience, mentoring, monitoring, and guidance ...

[ ] Many great people were late bloomers ...

[ ] Split Testing: different versions of a product are offered to customers at the same time ...

[ ] Accept all ideas with judgment ... prioritize them later but keep all of the ideas on the list ...

[ ] Promote our venture with door hangers ...

[ ] mvp: abbreviation for minimum viable product ... mvp is often not capitalized to differentiate it from MVP (Maximum Value Product) ...

[ ] The primary mission of a venture startup team is to create an organization that will earn a profit solving customer problems with something new and better than the competition ... while this recipe for success seems straight-forward, it's not so easy to execute ...

[ ] We must always take risks when experimenting ... [Thank you, Tove Jansson]

[ ] Skilled innovators and entrepreneurs are fluent in areas of expertise ...

[ ] The future belongs to those who prepare for it today ... [Thank you, Malcolm X]

[ ] Big old bags of balderdash ...

[ ] It's "us", not "me"!

[ ] It is what it is ... how are we going to adopt and adapt? ...

[ ] If lottery odds are better than the odds of success for our business, perhaps we should go buy some lottery tickets ...

[ ] Inspiration, ideation, implementation ... the three big steps in launching an new innovative product, service, and/or process ... [Thank you, Emma L Murray]

5280 TIPS for INNOVATORS and ENTREPRENEURS

[ ] Think global, act local ...

[ ] Solve the customer's pain ... and we shall gain!

[ ] Innovation is the lifeblood of organizations ... [Thank you, Tom Kelly]

[ ] Build a great team ...

[ ] Promote our venture with Facebook ...

[ ] Link new technologies to new market needs ...

[ ] Promote our venture with radio advertising ...

[ ] If we can't ride two horses at once, we shouldn't be in the circus ... [Thank you, Ringling Brothers]

[ ] Never subtract from our character to add to our popularity!

[ ] Skilled innovators and entrepreneurs are empathetic ...

[ ] Beware: liars ... (their pants are on fire and we could get burned!)

[ ] Solve problems in parallel ... take a big problem, break it into pieces, solve for the pieces simultaneously ...

[ ] Perfection is impossible ... excellence is not ...

[ ] Learn, and unlearn, and relearn ... learning is the key ...

[ ] Elements of an elevator pitch: What the venture does; Who is making the venture happen; What is the marketing being served; How the venture will make money and when; How the venture compares to other benchmarks; Why the venture will succeed; The ultimate goals for the venture ...

[ ] Key question for our venture: How do we price our products and services? ...

[ ] Anyone can count the seeds in a melon ... it takes vision to count the melon in a seed ...

[ ] Tradition is what we resort to when we don't have the time or the money to do it right ... [Thank you, Kurt Herbert Alder]

[ ] Promote our venture with our logo on t-shirts ...

[ ] Sometimes best not to say anything ... zip our lips!

[ ] Only take money from investors you trust ...

[ ] Innovation has a revolutionary reputation but an evolutionary reality ... most innovations, even those that seem extraordinary, are incremental improvements of things that already exist ...

[ ] The Five Forces that define an industry ... 1] Supplier Power; 2] Buyer Power; 3] Barriers to Entry; 4] Threats of Substitution; 5] Degree of Rivalry ... [Thank you, Michael Porter]

[ ] Types of customers: family, friendlies, fanatics, followers, flounders ...

[ ] Beware: false labels ...

[ ] The person who says it cannot be done should not interrupt the person doing it ... [Thank you, Warren Donian]

[ ] It could be a good opportunity if there are real customers!

[ ] Experimentation is a critical skill for innovators and entrepreneurs ... [Thank you, P G Greene]

[ ] Common cause of venture death: legal issues ...

[ ] Skilled innovators and entrepreneurs are enthusiastic ...

[ ] Do not press our luck too far ...

[ ] Begin all actions with a thought ...

[ ] If we think nobody cares, try missing a couple of payments ... [Thank you, Rodney Dangerfield]

[ ] Don't let what we don't know get in the way of what we do!

[ ] Make them an offer they can't refuse ... [Thank you, Vito Corleone]

[ ] Out with the old ... in with the new!

[ ] Yin or Yang ... which one is us today?

[ ] Ninety percent of life involves drudgery ... so make the other 10 percent count ...

[ ] A good plan executed today is better than a perfect plan tomorrow ... [Thank you, George S Patton]

[ ] Beta test our new products before launching to the whole wide world ...

[ ] People like to see it, hear it, touch it, taste it, or smell it before they buy it ... [Thank you, Dean Rieck]

[ ] Invention breeds invention ...

[ ] When it comes to getting things done, we need fewer architects and more bricklayers ... [Thank you, Colleen C Barrett]

[ ] Potential business model: Provide a marketplace for the sale of products and/or services ...

[ ] Do everything for the right seasons ...

[ ] Nature gave us one tongue and two ears so we could hear twice as much as we speak ... [Thank you, Epictetus]

[ ] Common Mistake: underestimating the time it takes to generate sustainable revenue ...

[ ] If we always do what we have always done, we'll always get what we have always gotten ... [Thank you, Tom Peters]

[ ] Due or Dew or Do ... what should we focus on today? ...

[ ] Complex Customers: an acknowledgment that customers needs, wants, and desires are continuously changing ...

[ ] Check our egos at the door ...

[ ] Creative people collaborate ... [Thank you, Emma L Murray]

[ ] Skilled innovators and entrepreneurs are resourceful ...

[ ] It's work time, team! so let's go do it ...

[ ] The truth is often hidden and hard to find ... [Thank you, New York Times]

[ ] Each profession talks to itself in its own language ... [Thank you, Leonardo da Vinci]

[ ] Become better than we were ... continuous improvement!

[ ] Don't play games ... someone always loses!

[ ] Play the game we're most likely to win ...

[ ] Teaching is easier than learning ...

[ ] Assure everyone is compensated fairly ...

[ ] Good people attract other good people ... [Thank you, Robert Ruiz]

[ ] The success of an advertisement or product, just like a business or a career, depends upon the skillful combination of association and differentiation ... [Thank you, Dale Dauten]

[ ] Customer success is our mission ... [Thank you, Raytheon Missile Systems]

[ ] It pays to test first ... [Thank you, Otis Singletary]

[ ] Exercise: List 10 new potential products and services our venture could develop in the next year ...

[ ] Don't make our customers think ... at least not very hard or very long ...

[ ] If something can go wrong, it will ... and at the most inopportune time! ... [Thank you, Murphy]

[ ] An A team with a B opportunity is better than a B team with an A opportunity ...

[ ] What we don't know we can learn ...

[ ] We are what we do ... let's do it well ...

[ ] Guess, fail, pivot, repeat ...

[ ] Instead of asking for money, ask for advice ... let the prospective investors get to know us and help us mold our venture so it better fits their investment interests ...

[ ] We see things and you say 'Why?' instead, dream things that never were and say 'Why not?!' ... [Thank you, George Bernard Shaw]

[ ] Word of Mouth: gossip spread by verbal communications ... the "grapevine" ...

[ ] Design our products for people ...

[ ] We cannot improve the past ... but we can improve the future ...

[ ] What puts a smile on your face? ... [Thank you, Frederic Premji]

[ ] Keep our feet on the ground ... even if (especially if!) our heads are in the clouds!

[ ] Skilled innovators and entrepreneurs are able to keep an open mind ...

[ ] Focus on improving benefits and lowering costs ...

[ ] Tastes differ ... [Thank you, Napoleon Bonaparte]

[ ] Simple will always be in style ...

[ ] Use our own best judgment at all times ... [Thank you, Nordstrom]

[ ] Entrepreneurship or Entrepreneur-shit ... what should we focus on today? ...

[ ] Momentum is hard to change ... the world keeps turning, the moon keeps rising, the sun keeps setting ... put our energy and efforts where we can actually make an impact ...

[ ] Big or little ... which do we need to be with our venture? ...

[ ] Fearless or Fearful ... what should we focus on today? ...

[ ] Advisor: someone who is expert in a particular field who gives guidance or recommendations ...

[ ] It is not the employer who pays the wages ... it is the customer when they are satisfied with what we have done! ... [Thank you, Henry Ford]

[ ] The deeper the color of the honey, the stronger the flavor ... [Thank you, Andrea F Siegel]

[ ] Share (noun): one of the parts into which the capital of a company is divided ...

[ ] Share (verb) ... enjoy jointly.

[ ] Promote our venture with referral incentives ...

[ ] Give every member of our organization a chance to dream, and tap into the creativity those dreams embody ... [Thank you, Walt Disney]

[ ] Clear, crisp, clean ... a guide for our communications ...

[ ] The cover page of a venture plan should have a product picture, the venture name, the logo and tagline, and contact information ...

[ ] Everything we can imagine is real, or will be ... [Thank you, Pablo Picasso]

[ ] Intrapreneur: an innovator and/or entrepreneur working within an established organization ...

[ ] Working with limited resources means entrepreneurs must carefully choose where to allocate their scarce resources ... [Thank you, Andrew Zacharakis]

[ ] Change requires tolerating failure ... [Thank you, Roger Kirkham]

[ ] Comparable: a company in the same or a similar industry, and/or at the same or similar stage of development, to which a startup can compare itself regarding various key operating ratios and valuation metrics ...

[ ] Emphasize ... give special importance, like the benefits our products have in solving our customer's problems!

[ ] The first step to getting what we want is to decide what we want ... [Thank you, Ben Stein]

[ ] Long term profit equals revenue from continuously satisfied customers minus cost ...

[ ] Potential venture legal issue: Hiring a lawyer not experienced in dealing with entrepreneurs and venture capitalists ... [Thank you, Connie Bagley]

[ ] Don't be a NoBird ... that person that says "No!" to most everything ... an antithesis to innovation and entrepreneurship!

[ ] Promote our venture with radio advertising spots ...

[ ] Say please and thank you ... being polite doesn't cost anything but the rewards are infinite ...

[ ] Modular: standardized parts or independent units that can be used to construct a more complex item ... [Thank you, Google Dictionary]

[ ] Successful teams are balanced ...

[ ] Wicked Problem: a problem that is difficult or impossible to solve because of incomplete, contradictory, and changing requirements that are often difficult to recognize ... [Thank you, C West Churchman]

[ ] Improvise ... make due with what we have

[ ] Evolutionary or Revolutionary ... what should we focus on today? ...

[ ] Guerrilla marketing: activities that are non-traditional, grassroots, and captivating, that gain consumers' attention and build awareness of the company ... [Thank you, Andrew Corbett]

[ ] Change is a challenge to make things better ... are we up to the challenge? ...

[ ] Male or Female ... what should we focus on today? Try thinking from the other side, or in-between ...

[ ] Loose lips sink ships ... keep our trade secrets secret!

[ ] If we can't find the right word, invent a new one ...

[ ] Be kind ... why in the world wouldn't we be?

[ ] The world can never be learned by trying to learn all its details ... [Thank you, Ralph Waldo Emerson]

[ ] Skilled innovators and entrepreneurs are able to express themselves ...

[ ] Do the groundwork first ...

[ ] Always be ready to take an order ... whenever our customers are ready to do business with us ... [Thank you, Susan Ward]

[ ] The more we know the more we know we know so little ...

[ ] Promote our venture with mailing labels ...

[ ] Industry tries to make the complex simple ... universities try to make the simple complex ... government tries to make the complex even more so ... [Thank you, Andy Rooney]

[ ] Protect our brand at (almost) all costs ...

[ ] To imagine is everything ... [Thank you, Anatole France]

[ ] I stopped believing in Santa Claus when I was six ... my mother took me to see him in a department store and he asked for my autograph ... [Thank you, Shirley Temple]

[ ] Do everything we do well ...

[ ] Three o'clock is always too late or too early for anything we want to do ... [Thank you, Jean-Paul Sartre]

[ ] Promote our venture with developing a sales slogan ...

[ ] First funding from founders, family, friends, fans, fanatics, and fools ...

[ ] Time flies [Tempus fugit] ... [Thank you, Ovid]

[ ] Making a great presentation: Make visuals big enough to see ... [Thank you, Ian McKenzie]

[ ] Pick funding sources that are right for our venture ...

[ ] Conventional wisdom might actually work sometimes ...

[ ] Skilled innovators and entrepreneurs are good judgment.

[ ] You can't force people to do anything ... we can urge, push, entice, but ultimately, people do what they want to do ... [Thank you, Dean Rieck]

[ ] A lie can never fix the truth ... a truth can break a lie ...

[ ] If the cow doesn't give milk, sell her ... [Thank you, John Peers]

[ ] A good business plan explains and justifies the level of product development required ... [Thank you, Carlos Alsua]

[ ] Asking dumb questions is easier than correcting dumb mistake ... [Thank you, Spreuk van Laubengayer]

[ ] Make sure what we're writing or saying is accurate ... bad information doesn't help anybody ...

[ ] It ain't necessarily so ... that's why objective research is so important ... [Thank you, George Gershwin]

[ ] Courage doesn't always roar ... sometimes courage is the little voice at the end of the day that says "I'll try again tomorrow." ... [Thank you, Mary Anne Radmacher]

[ ] If we can't define it, we can't control it ... if we can't control it, it will go where it wants to go, not where we'd like it to go ...

[ ] Verbal agreements lead to verbal disagreements ... don't necessarily have to be super-legalistic about it, but make some notes that all agree convey the agreement ...

[ ] Entrepreneurship is like a giant jigsaw puzzle ... we've got all the pieces and we know they fit together, we just don't yet know how ...

[ ] Reward hard work ... even if it can only be a "Thank you, that's really nice!" ...

[ ] There will be times with everything goes well ... don't be frightened, it won't last ... [Thank you, Jules Renard]

[ ] It's the planning, not the plan ... [Thank you, Jan Konstanty]

[ ] Waiting for everything to be perfect before we launch is a mistake ... first, it will never be perfect ... second, perfection is not a prerequisite for success ... the best way to know if we're ready to start is to start ... [Thank you, Tony Clark]

[ ] A venture plan is a living document ... we won't have all the answers right away ... keep refining as we go ... [Thank you, Luis Palomares]

[ ] Let our minds play ...

[ ] A good business plan addresses how the venture will develop and sustain a distinct competitive advantage ... [Thank you, Gary Libecap]

[ ] Skilled innovators and entrepreneurs are able to control and direct ...

[ ] It's not the idea that has value, it's acting on it! there are some 7,000,000,000 people on this planet ... whatever unique idea we think we may have, there are likely a thousand other people with exactly the same idea ... but the vast majority won't do anything with it ... that's our competitive advantage: not the idea itself, but acting on it!

[ ] To cut distractions and stay focused at work, practice returning to our key task through persistent refocusing ... [Thank you, Nando Pelusi]

[ ] Our minds are made up ... don't confuse us with facts!

[ ] Promote our venture with stickers ...

[ ] Total Available Market (or Total Addressable Market), abbreviated TAM: the total number of customers or revenue potential for a venture, product or service ...

[ ] Describe the intensity of the competitive environment in our industry ...

[ ] Just because we know doesn't mean they know ... if we want them to know, we've got to tell them ...

[ ] We cannot do everything at once ... but we can do something at once ... [Thank you, Calvin Coolidge]

[ ] Focus on quality opportunities, not quantity ...

[ ] Nothing is simple ... if it was, everyone would do it ...

[ ] Promote our venture with television advertising ...

[ ] Build a fanatical customer base ... be the very best that we can be ...

[ ] Separate the vital few from the trivial many ... [Thank you, Joseph Juran]

[ ] Write everything down ...

[ ] Wonder begins everything new ... [Thank you, Barbara Ann Kipfer]

[ ] Identify who is responsible for taking an idea from generation to assessment ... is it you, is it me, or is it we? ...

[ ] Learn from the mistakes of others ... we can't live long enough to make them all ourselves ...

[ ] Promote our venture with sales calls ...

[ ] Customers decide who offers the better value! let's make sure it's us ...

[ ] Validation: demonstrate or support the truth or value of something ...

[ ] There are no secrets to success: it is the result of preparation, hard work, learning from failure ... [Thank you, Colin Powell]

[ ] Know how to use at least one good slide presentation program ... Microsoft PowerPoint is a standard, Google Slides is very good, too, as are others ...

[ ] Write first, edit second, format last ... (I wish I had taken that to heart when I started writing this book! -jj)

[ ] Innovation is most often more evolutionary than revolutionary ... even small incremental improvements can make a big difference ...

[ ] Promote our venture with PR ...

[ ] Here or There or Everywhere ... what should we focus on today? ...

[ ] Delaying can be dangerous ... the time it takes can't be recovered ...

[ ] Skilled innovators and entrepreneurs are basically knowledgeable of their target area ...

[ ] Key question for our venture: What gives our venture a competitive advantage? ...

[ ] We win by innovation, by being better than our competition ... [Thank you, Vince Lombardi]

[ ] Encourage anyone trying to improve ...

[ ] A source of opportunity for innovation is the incongruity between reality as it actually is and how reality is perceived ... [Thank you, Peter F Drucker]

[ ] Intuition isn't always intuitive ...

[ ] Key question for our venture: Are we making it harder than it really is? ...

[ ] Time Value of Money (TVM): the principle that a certain currency amount of money today has a different buying power than the same currency amount of money in the future ...

[ ] Create demand ... [Thank you, Charles Revson]

[ ] Smile ... then smile again!

[ ] Nearly everything looks like a failure in the middle ...

[ ] Nothing recedes like success ... if we don't keep at it, it may go away ... [Thank you, Bryan Forbes]

[ ] Key question for our venture: Are there any product liability risks? ...

[ ] I love deadlines ... I love the whooshing sound they make as they go by! ... [Thank you, Douglas Adams]

[ ] Not everything can be defined ...

[ ] Daring ideas are like chessmen moved forward ... they may be beaten, but they may start a winning game ... [Thank you, Johann Wolfgang von Goethe]

[ ] Mountaintops inspire leaders but valleys mature them ... [Thank you, Winston Churchill]

[ ] The most compelling reason for large companies to become more entrepreneurial is to spot opportunities in their own markets before someone else does ... [Thank you, Edward Russell-Walling]

[ ] Key question for our venture: What is unique about our venture? ...

[ ] The inefficiency and stupidity of the staff corresponds to the inefficiency and stupidity of the management ...

[ ] Honesty is the best policy ...

[ ] Beware: enterprises that require new clothes ...

[ ] Have patience ...

[ ] Key question for our venture: Does the name suggest what our business venture, product, or service does? ...

[ ] Entrepreneurs create businesses, businesses create customers ...

[ ] Say no to long meetings ...

[ ] People resist even the most trivial change ... [Thank you, Roger Kirkham]

[ ] Performance: the act of accomplishing a task ... [Thank you, Robert Lorber]

[ ] Startup Company: a new business venture that is about to launch, or has recently launched but has not yet achieved sustainable sales revenue ...

[ ] It only looks hard until we understand it ...

[ ] Careless hurry may cause endless regret ... [Thank you, Barbara Ann Kipfer]

[ ] Encourage self-sufficiency ...

[ ] Corporate entrepreneur credo: Circumvent any orders aimed at stopping the dream ... [Thank you, Gifford Pinchot III]

[ ] Entity: a thing with distinct and independent existence ...

[ ] Successful innovators and entrepreneurs have a strong work ethic ...

[ ] Details create the big picture ... [Thank you, Sanford I Weill]

[ ] When writing our business plan, avoid long documents ... keep it under 25 pages total ... write whatever we want to write, but keep it at home ... if they want details, they will ask ... [Thank you, Kaye Vivian]

[ ] Instead of writing, draw pictures ...

[ ] Implementation: putting something new and better to work ...

[ ] Software gets slower faster than hardware gets faster ... [Thank you, Niklaus Wirth]

[ ] Price: the amount of money expected in payment for something ...

[ ] The secret of getting ahead is getting started ... [Thank you, Samuel Clemens]

[ ] Focus on an industry that is likely to grow in the foreseeable future ...

[ ] We have to earn our wings every day ... [Thank you, Frank Borman]

[ ] Everything comes to her who hustles while she waits ... [Thank you, Thomas A Edison]

[ ] Don't be satisfied with the status quo ...

[ ] The highest form of courage is the courage to create ... [Thank you, Rollo May]

[ ] Always have a Plan B ... and maybe a Plan C, D, E, and F ... just in case!

[ ] Common popular social media outlets: Facebook, Instagram, Twitter, YouTube, Instagram, LinkedIn, blogs ...

[ ] When speaking, tell the audience where it's going ...

[ ] Just because we get up early doesn't mean we like to get up early ...

[ ] The odds that a start-up company will get VC money are about one in 4,000 ... [Thank you, Scott Shane]

[ ] Common cause of venture death: lost focus ...

[ ] If we can persuade our customers to tattoo our name on their chests, they probably will not switch brands ... [Thank you, Harley-Davidson]

[ ] If we don't do it, how will we feel when our competition does? ...

[ ] Successful teams are individually team players ...

[ ] Bu l s hi! ... buy low sell high! ... a core business model!

[ ] What makes us think that someone wants to hear what we want to say? ...

[ ] Return phone calls and emails ...

[ ] Sales: the exchange of a product or service for money; the action of selling something; the organization within a venture responsible for the selling activities ...

[ ] Sweet Spot: an optimum point or combination of factors or qualities ...

[ ] Surprise: something unexpected, but pleasant (usually) ...

[ ] A brand is more than just a logo and a name ... they may create a way of identifying a company, product, or service, a brand is the way of experiencing it ... [Thank you, Leslie Bromberg]

[ ] Whatever hits the fan will not be evenly distributed ...

[ ] When the fruit is ripe, it falls ... when it's fall, the fruit is usually ripe ...

[ ] The only way to discover the limits of the possible is to go beyond them into the impossible ... [Thank you, Arthur C Clarke]

[ ] Don't just try to hit hard home runs ... we can win the games by consistently hitting singles ...

[ ] It's only superstitious if it doesn't work ... Warriors win when we wear white woolies ... [Thank you, Michael J Jindrick]

[ ] How to kill creativity: "It would take too long ..." ...

[ ] An entrepreneur is someone who perceives an opportunity and creates an organization to pursue it ... [Thank you, William Bygrave]

[ ] Define: mark out boundaries or limits ...

[ ] Learn one new thing every day ...

[ ] Corporate entrepreneur credo: Build a network of good people to assist ... [Thank you, Gifford Pinchot III]

[ ] Promote our venture with messages pulled by airplane ...

[ ] X: a commonly used reference for "experimental" ...

[ ] A gift to an opponent: tolerance ... [Thank you, Oren Arnold]

[ ] Just because we don't know doesn't mean they don't know ...

[ ] Successful companies are nimble, aggressive, adaptable, speedy, and innovative ... [Thank you, Richard Branson]

[ ] Integrity is doing the right thing knowing nobody is going to know whether we did or didn't ... [Thank you, Oprah Winfrey]

[ ] Being an entrepreneur is like standing naked on a street corner in Sparta, Wisconsin in the middle of the winter ... got nothing but cold and we're shaking all over, but we're having fun!

[ ] Key question for our venture: What key additions to our team are needed in the short term? ...

[ ] Use strong verbs ... [Thank you, Randy Accetta]

[ ] The young know the rules ... the old know the exceptions! ... [Thank you, Oliver Wendell Holmes]

[ ] Worry gives us something to do ... but so does hitting our thumbs with a hammer and that's a lot more obvious that it's a stupid thing to do ...

[ ] Clean up after ourselves ... mommy and daddy aren't around anymore!

[ ] Customers applaud what they like best ... (Thank you, Mitch Miller)

[ ] Angel Investor: an affluent individual who provides capital for a business start-up, usually in exchange for convertible debt or ownership equity ...

[ ] Buy off the rack ... don't buy custom components if we possibly avoid it! ... [Thank you, Buck Crouch]

[ ] Practice makes perfect ...

[ ] Patience is a virtue ... but often even stresses a saint!

[ ] If we do right by our customers, we'll do right all around ... [Thank you, Spencer Johnson]

[ ] We can't be afraid to take advantage of change ... [Thank you, Eric Schmidt]

[ ] Leadership is about growing others ...

[ ] Persona: the aspect of someone's character that is presented to or perceived by others ...

[ ] Flag: marked for attention, usually because there is a problem ...

[ ] Beware: some "investors" want to take a cut of the money you raise ...

[ ] Nothing is more dangerous than an idea when it's the only one we have ... [Thank you, Emile Chartier]

[ ] The cover page of a business plan should include: company name, tag line, contact information, venture address, telephone number, fax number, email address, the date of the venture plan, a legal disclaimer and copyright notice, and a copy number ...

[ ] Make it look like the real thing ...

[ ] Key question for our venture: how do we make it all legal, moral, and ethical? ...

[ ] Effective executives start with their time ... [Thank you, Peter F Drucker]

[ ] If a picture is worth a thousand words, a prototype is worth a thousand pictures!

[ ] Less than 1 in every 1000 companies will be attractive to VCs for investment ... [Thank you, Andrew Zacharakis]

[ ] Skilled innovators and entrepreneurs are analytical ...

[ ] Strategy: a plan of action or policy designed to achieve a major or overall aim ...

[ ] Use consistent verb tenses, and find the single most correct word ... [Thank you, Randy Accetta]

[ ] They'll do as we do, not as we say ...

[ ] Better an hour too soon than a minute too late ... [Thank you, William Shakespeare]

[ ] Don't rely on just one marketing vehicle ... build a complete internet marketing strategy that includes, at a minimum, paid search, organic search, email and online PR ... [Thank you, Ian Lurie]

[ ] Earn: obtain money or other value in return for products or services ...

[ ] Care about our community ...

[ ] If all we have is a hammer, everything looks like a nail ...

[ ] Create a multiple revenue models ...

[ ] Face adversity with a smile ... if nothing else, you'll confuse it ...

[ ] Where there is no vision, the people perish ... [Thank you, Steve Jobs]

[ ] A lot of discoveries are made by mistake ... the invention of the home smoke detector was almost accidental ... [Thank you, Cindy Pearsall]

[ ] Dumb and dumber ... it happens ...

[ ] Make it clear and concrete ...

[ ] Knowledge needs to be acquired to be had ...

[ ] Identify our biggest threat ...

[ ] People don't plan to fail ... but they do fail to plan ... [Thank you, John Beckley]

[ ] Stress happens ... be forewarned, be prepared ...

[ ] The pessimist sees difficulty in every opportunity ... the optimist sees the opportunity in every difficulty! ... [Thank you, Winston Churchill]

[ ] Common bootstrapping strategy: negotiate payment terms with suppliers ...

[ ] Knowledge needs a strong foundation on which to grow ...

[ ] Needs, wants, and desires can be met if understood ...

[ ] One of the secrets of success for companies that demonstrate high rates of innovation is that they simply try more things ... [Thank you, Rosabeth Moss Kanter]

[ ] 10-slide business plan pitch: 1] Cover page including the venture name, logo, tagline, a picture of the product, a short (10 words) summary of the venture, and contact information ... 2] A description of the opportunity identifying the customer problem or need that we solve ... 3] An illustration of how our product or service solves the customer's problem ... 4] Some details (as needed) to describe our product, and any potential intellectual property ... 5] An overview of the competition and strategies for differentiating our venture ... 6] Entry and growth strategies showing how we enter the market and grow ... 7] An overview of our business model ... how we will make money and how much it will cost to support those sales ... 8] Team summary including the core and key advisors ... 9] Current status with timeline and financial objectives ... 10] Summary including resources we need and how they will be used ... [Thank you, William Bygrave]

[ ] Develop and maintain a strong relationship between marketing and solution development technical expertise ... [Thank you, K A Zein]

[ ] One-third of American entrepreneurs are dyslexic ... entrepreneurs are hands-on people who push a minimum of paper, do lots of stuff orally instead of reading and writing, and delegate authority, all of which suggests a high verbal facility ... compare that with corporate managers who read, read, read ... [Thank you, Julie Logan]

[ ] Financial future fell into a freefall ...

[ ] Key question for our venture: Is everyone in our venture pulling their weight? ... who might we do without? ...

[ ] Four key elements of a business model ... the customer value proposition, customer profile, venture infrastructure, and financial viability ...

[ ] Skilled innovators and entrepreneurs are colorful ...

[ ] Winning means we're doing better than we've ever done before ...

[ ] Often failure comes from within ...

[ ] A thought precedes an action ... make it a good thought ...

[ ] Hang around people that are encouraging ...

[ ] Give it a name ... even before it's born ... it will give it the first breath of life ...

[ ] Promote our venture with computer data service ...

[ ] Be committed, passionate, and persistent ...

[ ] We must make our opportunity as often as we find it ...

[ ] Embrace our own uniqueness ...

[ ] Keep our customers close and our competitors even closer ...

[ ] SPLUCK! a very critical success factor for innovators and entrepreneurs: Skills, Passion, and LUCK ... successful

innovators and entrepreneurs have all three ... Skill from education and experience, Passion to do what they do even when what they do is really hard, and they capitalize on fortuitous circumstances or they make their own luck ...

[ ] Do not complain about the boat that carries us safely from shore to shining shore ...

[ ] Sometimes little ideas need to incubate to become big ideas ... [Thank you, Anita Bell]

[ ] To achieve great things, we must dream as well as act ... [Thank you, Anatole France]

[ ] Entrepreneurs are often detail-oriented ...

[ ] Avoid dumb people ... but keep in mind that dumb people one day may well be brilliant people the next ... [Thank you, J D Watson]

[ ] Key question for our venture: How are our benefits better than the competition? ...

[ ] Sources of inspiration: previous experiences; personal interests; someone else's idea; systematic research; an "aha" moment ... [Thank you, Rhonda Abrams]

[ ] Have fun at what we do ... or it will become hard work!

[ ] People or Places or Things ... what should we focus on today? ...

[ ] There's no such thing as bad press ... it's what we do with it if and when it happens ...

[ ] Key question for our venture: How did we arrive at the sales of our industry and its growth rate? ...

[ ] Adhocracy is the direct opposite of bureaucracy ... unstructured, decentralized, and responsive ... in a bureaucracy, the structure is more important than the person

... an adhocracy, on the other hand, is designed to bring out the best in them ... [Thank you, Edward Russell-Walling]

[ ] Experience is not what happens to us, it's what we do with what happens to us ... [Thank you, Aldous Huxley]

[ ] Exploration and ideation, vision and mission, goals and objectives, strategies and tactics, tasks and assignments

... five levels of venture planning ... "

[ ] Beware: accredited investors are a perfect target for scammers posing as entrepreneurs ... don't get sucked in ...

[ ] Pitch: a form of words used when trying to persuade someone to buy or accept something ... [Thank you, Google Dictionary]

[ ] Key question for our venture: What are typical metrics for companies in our industry and market? ...

[ ] To reach a port, we must sail; sail, not tie at anchor; sail, not drift ... [Thank you, Franklin Delano Roosevelt]

[ ] Perform more than promised rather than promise more than perform ...

[ ] How to attract new customers: have a sale ... everyone loves to save a little money ...

[ ] The future ain't what it used to be ... [Thank you, Yogi Berra]

[ ] Dream it, see it, do it ...

[ ] Mind Map: a diagram used to visually outline and organize information ... (one of my personal favorite tools for capturing and organizing my thoughts, for taking notes, for outlining, for doodling thoughts, for making connections, for having a little fun) ...

[ ] Great leaders earn their money when times are tough ...

[ ] We can, should, and must add value to everything we do ...

[ ] Adversity reveals genius ... prosperity conceals it ...
[Thank you, Quintus Horatius Flaccus]

[ ] We can't tell how deep a puddle is until we step into it ...
[Thank you, Gene Kelly]

[ ] Promote our venture with window signs ...

[ ] Always be nice to bankers ... [Thank you, John Gotti]

[ ] How to start a new venture, start with TRIM: Team,
Resources, Idea, Mission ...

[ ] When promoting our game, promote our game ... don't
compare it to another ... [Thank you, Robert Bowling]

[ ] Common Mistake: underestimating the length of time to
secure financing ... and underestimating the level of financing
needed to become a self-sustaining venture ... [Thank you,
Andrew Corbett]

[ ] Look for ways to be more useful to our customers ...

[ ] We don't meet the competition, we crush them! ... [Thank
you, Charles Revson]

[ ] Keep our motor running ... [Thank you, Jerry Lee Lewis]

[ ] Follow the yellow brick rubric ... what are the standards
we need to meet or beat?

[ ] Time flies like an arrow, fruit flies like a banana ... [Thank
you, Groucho Marx]

[ ] Clearly identify our primary competition ...

[ ] Skilled innovators and entrepreneurs are open-minded ...

[ ] A little bait can catch a large fish ...

[ ] Contribute more than just our product ... provide our customers with industry news updates, creative ideas, and business advice as part of the services we offer ...

[ ] Have some wild and crazy ideas ... the more the merrier ... some might actually lead us somewhere new and better!

[ ] Put the surprise where you want the attention ... [Thank you, Marty Neumeier]

[ ] Innovating is hard work ...

[ ] Education is not the filling of a pail ... it's the lighting of a fire ... [Thank you, William Butler Yeats]

[ ] An idea cannot be jailed ... it will seep out through the cracks and crevices ...

[ ] Make friends, not enemies ...

[ ] Promote our venture with attention getters ...

[ ] Promote our venture with point-of-purchase signs ...

[ ] Write a song ...

[ ] Use personal observations to gather primary research data ...

[ ] Skilled innovators and entrepreneurs are aware and empathetic of the needs of others ...

[ ] Imitate the successes of the wise ... not the mistakes of the fools ...

[ ] New ideas hurt some minds like new shoes hurt some feet ... [Thank you, Marv Dobkin]

[ ] Monitor our environments ... see the rain coming before it gets here!

[ ] Creativity is allowing ourselves to make mistakes ... art is knowing which ones to keep ... [Thank you, Scott Adams]

[ ] You break it, you bought it ...

[ ] Tomorrow is another day ... [Thank you, Scarlett O'Hara]

[ ] If we want to be a writer, we gotta write ...

[ ] Every stumble is not a fall, and every fall does not mean failure ... [Thank you, Oprah Winfrey]

[ ] Less is more ... more or less ...

[ ] Match function to form ...

[ ] Our gift to a customer: exceptional service ... [Thank you, Martin Reed]

[ ] We're only getting older ... and hopefully wiser with the years!

[ ] Maybe give them a little sample of our goods? ... if they like them, they'll buy more?

[ ] Ideas are a dime a dozen ... value comes from working the idea to become something useful ...

[ ] Skilled innovators and entrepreneurs are resistant to closure ...

[ ] Sometimes it takes a long time to get somewhere ...

[ ] Promote our venture with billboards ...

[ ] Ideas won't work unless we do ...

[ ] Average Selling Price: the average price at which a particular product or commodity is sold across channels or markets ...

[ ] Pixar Pitch: "Once upon a time ... Every day ... Then, one day ... Because of that ... Because of that ... Until finally ... " ... use it to tell a story ... [Thank you, Pixar]

[ ] Trademark: identifying name or graphical mark that is uniquely identified with a specific product, service or company ...

[ ] Praise loudly, blame softly ... [Thank you, Catherine the Great]

[ ] When it comes to policies, the fewer the better ... [Thank you, Dale Dauten]

[ ] GDP measures everything except that which makes life worthwhile ... [Thank you, Robert Kennedy]

[ ] Potential opportunities have potential novelty or newness ... [Thank you, IDEO]

[ ] Keep your inner open ...

[ ] As we learn this from that, we learn that from this ...

[ ] Cap Table: abbreviation for Capitalization Table ... a capitalization table lists who owns what in a startup ... it calculates how the option pool shuffle and seed debt lower the Series A share price ...

[ ] The trouble with being an optimist is that people think we don't know what's going on ... [Thank you, Johnny Carson]

[ ] Actions make history ...

[ ] An average McDonald's generates about $2.5 million revenue per year ... how many McD's is our venture? Or what fraction of one McD? ...

[ ] The future is made in the present ... [Thank you, Kelly Andrews]

[ ] Credible or Incredible or Uncredible ... which do we need to be? ...

[ ] Give it our best shot ...

[ ] 1N73LL1G3NC3 15 7H3 4B1L17Y 70 4D4P7 70 CH4NG3 ... [Thank you, Nathan Christensen]

[ ] Keep your writing simple ... [Thank you, Randy Accetta]

[ ] Be an Angel Advocate ... build on new ideas, not tear them down ... [Thank you, Tom Kelly]

[ ] Think neatness and visibility when putting a trade show display together ... [Thank you, Susan Ward]

[ ] Assume rapport ...

[ ] Be the best that we can be ... [Thank you, US Army]

[ ] Amplify our strengths ... attenuate our weaknesses ...

[ ] The fatal law of gravity: when we are down, everything falls down on us ... [Thank you, Sylvia T Warner]

[ ] Set a target date to reach break-even ...

[ ] Brand: a type of product manufactured by a particular company under a particular name; an identifying name and/or mark ...

[ ] We have to know what our personal core competencies are ... then go with them! ... [Thank you, Louise Francesconi]

[ ] Marketing: the action or business of identifying, promoting and selling products or services to selected markets ...

[ ] Have a philosophy for our venture ...

[ ] Get to the point quickly ...

[ ] Don't talk about people behind their backs ... if we wouldn't say it when they're standing in front of us, why would we say when they're not? ...

[ ] Scale it up ... scope it out ...

[ ] Lead by example ... the best way to get a point across is to be the model to emulate ... [Thank you, InsideCRM]

[ ] Right-brain thinking traits ... instinct, art, emotion, imagination, memory, creative, music, qualitative ...

[ ] Bait the hook well and the fish will bite ...

[ ] Grey hairs: slang for experienced individuals ...

[ ] Skilled innovators and entrepreneurs are able to elaborate ...

[ ] Everybody thinks differently ... variety is the spice of life!

[ ] Input: a contribution of work, information, money, or material ...

[ ] Set goals ...

[ ] When we make a mistake, don't look back at it long ... take the reason of the thing into our mind and then look forward ... mistakes are lessons of wisdom ... the past cannot be changed ... the future is yet in our power ... [Thank you, Hugh White]

[ ] In God we trust, all others bring cash or a valid credit card!

[ ] Explore more ...

[ ] When innovation stops, the end is near ...

[ ] When eating an elephant, take one bite at a time ... [Thank you, Creighton W Abrams]

[ ] Try to see things from a different angle ... [Thank you, Gloria Gaynor]

[ ] People will find a complicated means to perform a simple task ... [Thank you, Rube Goldberg]

[ ] It's the law of demand and supply, not the other way around ... [Thank you, Rick Kash]

[ ] Successful teams are experienced ...

[ ] Love will find a way ... like will not ...

[ ] Light tomorrow with today ... [Thank you, Elizabeth Barrett Browning]

[ ] Today or Tomorrow ... what should we focus on today? ...

[ ] Go with the flow ... or swim upstream? ...

[ ] Skilled innovators and entrepreneurs are emotionally appealing ...

[ ] How we say something is as important as what we say ...

[ ] Promote our venture with send a thank you note after a new purchase ...

[ ] Embrace our champions ... along the way, we'll find people that genuinely believe in us and our mission; they will cheer us on, root for us, stand by us when things are tough ... we need to embrace them, thank them, keep them close ... they may be all we have at times ... [Thank you, Nelson Wang]

[ ] Ideas are cheap and plentiful ... it's that hard work of putting ideas into action that makes the difference ...

[ ] There is always competition ...

[ ] Don't give up our goals ...

[ ] Simple or Complex ... what should we focus on today? ...

[ ] Everybody who gives us money for our venture wants something in return ... [Thank you, Rhonda Abrams]

[ ] Quantity: the amount or number of a material or immaterial thing not usually estimated by spatial measurement ...

[ ] Beware: stealers ...

[ ] The more choices, the longer the decision ... why the idiot in front of us in the drive-through lane takes so long to place an order ...

[ ] Common cause of venture death: inferior solutions ...

[ ] Stop, look, listen ...

[ ] Get the facts first ...

[ ] Gravity sucks, energy blows ... four word physics summary ...

[ ] Promote our venture with tape or ribbon ...

[ ] The future belongs to creative right-brain thinkers ... [Thank you, Daniel H Pink]

[ ] Do what we like and it's not work ... [Thank you, Holly Joubert]

[ ] Common Mistake: underestimating the time it takes to make a sale ...

[ ] In the middle of difficulty lies opportunity ... [Thank you, Albert Einstein]

[ ] Beware: liars, cheaters, and stealers ...

[ ] Keep questioning ...

[ ] If we can't measure it, we can't management it ...

[ ] Freeze or Boil ... which one describes what we should be doing today? ...

[ ] Entrepreneurship is a continually iterative process ...

[ ] Ask questions and learn ...

[ ] Any road will do if we don't know where we're going ...

[ ] Strive for excellence ... not perfection ... [Thank you, H Jackson Brown]

[ ] Ignorance can be educated and crazy can be medicated, but there's no cure for stupid. ... [Thank you, Steven Stralser]

[ ] Share ideas ...

[ ] Good logos are simple, memorable, positive, reproducible, useable, clear, and broad enough to use as our venture grows ...

[ ] Train extensively and constantly reinforce the venture culture ... [Thank you, Walt Disney]

[ ] Thank people who refer prospects to us ... if the referral results in business, send a small, business-related thank-you gift, too ...

[ ] When writing a business plan, avoid superlatives and strong adjectives ... words like major, incredible, amazing, outstanding, unbelievable, terrific, great, most, best, and fabulous don't have a place in a business plan ... avoid "unique" unless we can demonstrate with facts that the product or service is truly "one of a kind" ... our opportunity is probably not unique ... [Thank you, Kaye Vivian]

[ ] Stay in direct contact with our customers ... they are a very important part of our family ... [Thank you, Mike Dell]

[ ] Buy used ... when we can get a better deal, but don't cut corners on quality ...

[ ] Don't try to change what cannot be changed ... make what's good and already there even better ...

[ ] Give them something unexpected ... (a sandwich shop I like always gives a chocolate chip cookie as an added bonus to every order) ...

[ ] Any press can be good press, even if it isn't ... but if it isn't, address it quickly and honestly ... win points with the public by taking responsibility, fixing mistakes, and doing what's right ...

[ ] Promote our venture with local business magazines ...

[ ] Elements of a marketing mix ... product, place, position, price, and promotion ...

[ ] Skilled innovators and entrepreneurs need to be in good health ... if the body starts to go, the mind may go with it ...

[ ] Dream a little dream ... of me, customers, the future, et al ... and just maybe it should be a big dream, too ...

[ ] Treat the name of our venture as if it was our own ... because it is our own!

[ ] Information is easy to come by, inspiration is not ...

[ ] The end of one thing is the beginning of something else ... exit the old as gracefully as we can ... [Thank you, Anne Stringfellow]

[ ] Arrange things differently ... a little change here and there can make for a big difference in perspective ...

[ ] "What's in it for me?" ... crass as that may be, it's often the top motivating force for many decisions, particularly by customers! ... [Thank you, Chuck Bolotin]

[ ] Whatever the mind of a person can conceive and believe, it can achieve ... (within the laws of physics ... but it is fun to push them to the limits) ... [Thank you, Napoleon Hill]

[ ] Always be curious ... keep asking, "Why?!" ... if that doesn't work, ask, "Why not?!" ...

[ ] Failure is the opportunity to begin again more intelligently ... the key point here is to learn from our mistakes, not repeat them ... [Thank you, Henry Ford]

[ ] There's many a good tune played on an old fiddle ...

[ ] If at first we don't succeed ... try something else! But before we do, let's make sure we understand why what we just tried didn't work ... [Thank you, Laurence J Peter]

[ ] Our get up and go got up and went ... so get up and go make another pot of coffee ...

[ ] Test our assumptions ...

[ ] Every morning, make a list of things that need to be done that day ... then do them! ... [Thank you, J P Morgan]

[ ] Time is the most valuable and the most perishable of all our resources ... [Thank you, John Randolph]

[ ] A strong conviction that something must be done is the parent of many bad measures ... but doing something for the right conviction can lead to many good treasures! ... [Thank you, Daniel Webster]

[ ] How can we answer this Question: Can we sell subscriptions? ...

[ ] Key question for our venture: What is our serviceable addressable market? ...

[ ] Skilled innovators and entrepreneurs have good judgment ...

[ ] Make our own heaven and enjoy it ...

[ ] Beware: far-out projections ...

[ ] Meet more people ...

[ ] Maximum Value Product (MVP): a product, service, process, or method designed and developed to deliver a high level of benefits, features, and functionality to customers ...

[ ] Silent gratitude isn't much use to anyone ... [Thank you, Gertrude Stein]

[ ] Promote our venture with symbols ...

[ ] Let people know the topic to be explored before the meeting ... [Thank you, Todd Adams]

[ ] To learn we must pay attention ...

[ ] A flow will have an ebb ... a high tide will have a low ... don't get stuck in the mud in the middle ...

[ ] Understand our role ... play our part well ...

[ ] Get it in writing ...

[ ] A new venture may be feasible if it solves a big problem ...

[ ] Make something special our specialty ...

[ ] A business venture plan must establish an opportunity worth exploiting ... and detail how to accomplish it ... [Thank you, Andrew Corbett]

[ ] Deliver: provide something promised ... if we don't deliver the goods, we won't reap the rewards ...

[ ] Incremental change is not the same as incremental improvement ...

[ ] Promote our venture with share costs with event sponsors ...

[ ] Beware of myths that sound good but might not be so true ... and there are lots and lots of myths in the worlds of innovation, entrepreneurship, and venture startups!

[ ] Stand tall ...

[ ] To solve a big problem, break it into pieces, then solve for each of the smaller pieces ...

[ ] Employers don't pay the wages, customers do ... [Thank you, Henry Ford]

[ ] Don't drift at sea ... if the sharks don't get us, the pirates will ...

[ ] Have an exit strategy ... for investors, for the venture, for the future ...

[ ] Don't bite the hand that feeds us ... treat our customers with the utmost respect ...

[ ] There are 5280 feet in a mile ... the first step is the longest ...

[ ] The only time we don't fail is the last time we try something and it works ... [Thank you, William Strong]

[ ] Judgment: the ability to make considered decisions or come to sensible conclusions ... there is no other single skill we can have as important as good judgment ...

[ ] Parent or Adult or Child ... what one should we focus on today? ...

[ ] Potential business model: consult or provide expertise ...

[ ] Successful teams are competent in their individual fields ...

[ ] There are moments when everything goes well ... don't be frightened, it won't last! ... [Thank you, Jules Renard]

[ ] Don't be a macro-boss ... let your people go!

[ ] Demand: customer needs, wants, and desires for particular products and services ...

[ ] Never rely on one or two clients/customers ... [Thank you, Ryan Ginstrom]

[ ] Be consistent ... it's the foundation of trust ...

[ ] Industry averages can be used to calibrate our numbers, be they good or be they bad ... it is highly unlikely that our venture is going to be an exception to the rule ...

[ ] We can't expect to hit the jackpot if we don't put a few nickels in the machine ... [Thank you, Flip Wilson]

[ ] A good business plan has facts rather than opinions ... [Thank you, ChangeOver]

[ ] If we run out of wood, the fire goes out ... [Thank you, Proverbs 26]

[ ] No matter where we are ... we are there, not somewhere else, so make the best of it we are no matter where ... [Thank you, Buckaroo Bonzai]

[ ] The eraser disappears before the pencil ... is that an opportunity to make bigger erasers or shorter pencils or fewer mistakes? ...

[ ] Someone who is appreciated will always do more than expected ... if you appreciate someone, try saying thank you ...

[ ] If we don't give people information, they'll make up something to fill the void ... [Thank you, Carla O'Dell]

[ ] Improve constantly, and forever ... [Thank you, W Edwards Deming]

5280 TIPS for INNOVATORS and ENTREPRENEURS

[ ] Skilled innovators and entrepreneurs are able to imagine ...

[ ] Focus on an industry that is not dominated by just a few players ...

[ ] Know what to remember as well as what to forget ...

[ ] Use it or lose it ...

[ ] Brainstorm ... It's a team sport; support our team members! No criticism; no "devil's advocates" allowed! Anything goes; wild, crazy, impractical, ingenious ideas encouraged! Go for quantity, not quality, of ideas! All ideas encouraged! Piggyback, improve, combine ideas ... be an "angel advocate" for our colleagues! Record all ideas so nothing gets lost! Filter ideas later, not during the brainstorming session! et a time limit for the session, then stick to it!

[ ] A sale isn't a sale until the check clears the bank ... even then, the customer could still come back for a refund ...

[ ] Buy land: they've stopped making it! ... [Thank you, Mark Twain]

[ ] Those who won't fill our pockets will fill our ears ... yibidee, yibidee, yibidee ... [Thank you, Warren Buffett]

[ ] Quality is everyone's responsibility ... [Thank you, W Edwards Deming]

[ ] Our achievements will live longer than us ... let's make sure they're worth that kind of longevity ...

[ ] Business has two basic functions: innovation and marketing ... [Thank you, Peter F Drucker]

[ ] We should want little ideas as much as big ideas ...

[ ] Anyone can say they are an entrepreneur ... not everyone can can deliver on that promise ...

[ ] Anything is possible if we've got the time and money ...

[ ] Things that matter most must never be at the mercy of things that matter least ... unfortunately, so many priorities in life are set by what is easier rather than what is best ... [Thank you, Johann Wolfgang Goethe]

[ ] Focus on what values our product can bring to its target customers ... [Thank you, Ching Lee]

[ ] Investors will seek anywhere from a 40% to 60% annual rate of return ...

[ ] Mental Error: "We don't have any competition!" ... Yes, we do! If we think we don't, we haven't done all of our homework!

[ ] Entrepreneurship is a habit ... a good one at that ... make it a habit every day of our lives ...

[ ] Happy, happy, happy ... happy customers, happy employees, and happy suppliers ...

[ ] Start now ...

[ ] Work with the right people ...

[ ] Beauty is only skin deep ... but it does attract some attention ...

[ ] Emphasize the convenience and exclusivity of what we want to sell ... [Thank you, Dean Rieck]

[ ] Failure is just another chance to start over ... [Thank you, Bob Morrison]

[ ] Static or Dynamic ... what should we focus on today? ...

[ ] It can take many words to describe a simple thing ... the real trick is to use simple words to describe many things ...

[ ] Earnings: the excess of revenues over outlays in a given period of time ...

[ ] Self-trust is the first secret of success ... [Thank you, Ralph Waldo Emerson]

[ ] Reduce our waste ... and reduce our waist, too, if we can ...

[ ] How can we answer this Question: How will the valuation or our venture at the exit point be determined given current market comparables? ...

[ ] Entrepreneur: someone who organizes and operates a new venture to the point where that venture becomes stable ... an entrepreneur puts something new and better to work ...

[ ] Take care of our customers and our business will take care of itself ... [Thank you, Ray Kroc]

[ ] Our imagination needs nourishment and exercise ...

[ ] Be genuine ... never false or flaky ...

[ ] See it, do it, teach it ... [Thank you, Cody Nicholls]

[ ] Having common enemies makes for strong alliances ...

[ ] Silence can be beautiful ...

[ ] Dig deeper ...

[ ] Grunt work, ok, but ... someone has to do it ... (Jim Note: Unfortunately, I know too many "important" people who have to have someone else answer their phone, write their emails, schedule their meetings, while they sit in their offices and read nonsense news!) ...

[ ] The only way to do great work is to love what we do ... [Thank you, Steve Jobs]

[ ] TAM: abbreviation for Total Available Market ...

[ ] Depreciation: a reduction in the value of an asset with the passage of time ...

[ ] The proof is in the pudding ... even if it's not, it'll taste good looking for it!

[ ] State the problem, show the solution, clarify the benefits ...

[ ] The efforts of any employee must generate 3 to 5 times what the company pays that person ... [Thank you, Dan Miller]

[ ] Skilled innovators and entrepreneurs are able to visualize the future ...

[ ] We forget what we read, we remember what we see, we learn what we do ...

[ ] Respect ... Give it, expect it ...

[ ] Get all our ducks in a row ... now just try to keep them there ...

[ ] If we don't give people information, they'll make up something to fill the void ...

[ ] Be a class act ... [Thank you, Jimmy Carter]

[ ] There is no great genius without some touch of madness ... [Thank you, Woody Allen]

[ ] Entrepreneurs are usually quite good at analytical thinking ...

[ ] There are many crooks running around disguised as "entrepreneurs", but real entrepreneurs are not crooks ... entrepreneurs may make mistakes, they may lose their investor's money in the process ... but they don't do it intentionally ... crooks do ...

[ ] Venture Plan: a detailed proposal for a venture, usually a formal document or slide presentation ...

[ ] Learn a new culture ... what can we learn that we can apply to our situations ...

[ ] People respond to their perceptions in spite of reality ... [Thank you, Roger Kirkham]

[ ] Contribute to the success of others ...

[ ] Entrepreneurial Myth: Most business angels are rich ... actually, most investors in new ventures are not rich and do not meet SEC accreditation requirements ... but they are willing to take a risk on our venture, just because we are we ... [Thank you, Scott Shane]

[ ] We need a lean, mean marketing machine ...

[ ] Don't confuse comfort with happiness ...

[ ] Focus on markets that can be affordably reached ...

[ ] Have a healthy breakfast every day ...

[ ] We must do the thing we think we cannot do ... in order to accomplish the thing we think we cannot ...

[ ] Promote our venture with statement stuffers ...

[ ] No one can make us feel inferior without our consent ... [Thank you, Eleanor Roosevelt]

[ ] How to kill creativity: "We don't have time ..."

[ ] Just because something doesn't do what we planned it to do doesn't mean it's useless ... [Thank you, Thomas Alva Edison]

[ ] Customers decide who offers the better value ... it better be us!

[ ] Rely on our common senses ... [Thank you, Alton Brown]

[ ] Don't overanalyze ... just figure out what makes sense and get on with it ...

[ ] Whine less, breathe more ... but every now and then, wine more ... [Thank you, Barbara Ann Kipfer]

[ ] Back to the future ... what do we see when we look there? ...

[ ] Pigs get fed ... hogs get slaughtered ...

[ ] Key question for our venture: Are all our employees trained in customer service because all our employees are in customer service? ...

[ ] Effective listening requires suspending judgment ... [Thank you, Roger Kirkham]

[ ] Any fool can make a rule ... and any fool will mind it! ... [Thank you, Henry David Thoreau]

[ ] Are we a "Yes" or are we a "No"? [Jim's 2 cents: I have a friend, a nice person, a smart person, but a "no" person. Everything is "no" to her. No, don't change anything, just because. A total left-brainiac. Regimented. No innovations there. What a shame.] ... Do we look for ways to get things done, or do we look for excuses to keep things undone? ...

[ ] Make or buy? ... what should we focus on today? ...

[ ] The squeaky wheel doesn't always get the grease ... sometimes it gets replaced! ... [Thank you, Vic Gold]

[ ] Skilled innovators and entrepreneurs are able to visualize ...

[ ] Making a great presentation: Present one key point per visual ... presenting more than one main idea per visual can detract from the impact ... [Thank you, Ian McKenzie]

[ ] Sometimes our customer doesn't know what they want until we show them ... [Thank you, Steve Jobs]

[ ] Very few angel investors are actually accredited ... and many of these investors don't call themselves "angels" either ...

[ ] Price is what we're asking ... cost is what the customer actually pays ...

[ ] For outstanding performance, a company has to beat the competition ... the trouble is that the competition has heard the same message ... [Thank you, Mark Peterson]

[ ] Nobody's gonna leave this rock alive ... [Thank you, Chris Sorbe]

[ ] Don't presuppose ... don't assume we already know the answer when we know there is not data to back it up ...

[ ] Provide motivation ...

[ ] Entrepreneurship: the process of starting a business venture or other organization ...

[ ] There's no such thing as a free lunch ...

[ ] Good humor makes all things tolerable ... [Thank you, Henry Ward Beecher]

[ ] Peak or Poke ... what should we focus on today? ...

[ ] "Let me be a devil's advocate" ... that's the code for "I think your idea sucks, but I'm going to smile while I pick it apart!" ... easy to tear down, not so easy to build up ...

[ ] Founder, Friends, Family, Fanatics, and Fools Funding: a form of startup funding in which the entrepreneur asks friends, family members, and people that are fanatical about the new venture products and services for investments in an early-stage business venture ... "Fools" is a semi-humorous

reference to individuals that fund a startup venture based highly on emotion rather than logic ...

[ ] Market research is nowhere near perfect ...

[ ] Fire bad customers ...

[ ] We gotta do what we gotta do ... so let's go and do it ...

[ ] Promote our venture with national cable TV ...

[ ] The purpose of education is to replace an empty mind with an open one ... [Thank you, Malcolm Forbes]

[ ] Stay fresh ...

[ ] Turbulence is an opportunity ... [Thank you, William Ramsey Clark]

[ ] Any sufficiently large problem can be solved in parallel ... break it into pieces, then solve for the pieces ... [Thank you, John Gustafson]

[ ] Exercise: List 3 things we are going to accomplish today ...

[ ] Define new market segments ...

[ ] Have everyone in the management team get in front of customers on a regular basis ...

[ ] Successful teams are cohesive ...

[ ] Look it up on Google ...

[ ] Amortization: the process by which the loan principal decreases over the life of the loan ...

[ ] Nothing we can't spell will ever work ... keep this in mind every time we are naming a new product or service or venture ... [Thank you, Will Rogers]

[ ] Skilled innovators and entrepreneurs are tactful ...

[ ] How to kill creativity: "Yes, but ..." ...

[ ] Forty thousand wishes won't fill our bucket with fishes ...

[ ] Knowledge comes by taking things apart; wisdom comes by putting them back together ... don't throw away any left-over pieces, either ...

[ ] Common cause of venture death: pricing-cost issues ...

[ ] They say time changes things, but we actually have to change them ourselves ... [Thank you, Andy Warhol]

[ ] Creative people focus on small actions together to make a big impact ... inch by inch, bit by bit, it all comes together in something bigger ...

[ ] We're prudent if we're patient ...

[ ] If we change the way we look at things, the things we look at change ... [Thank you, Wayne Dyer]

[ ] Do all we can to turn ordinary customers into fanatical fans of our venture ... go above and beyond to keep our customers happy ...

[ ] Leadership is the ability to translate vision into reality ... [Thank you, Warren Bennis]

[ ] It's not a product, it's a service ... our customers are buying a gizmogadget, they're buying what the gizmogadget does to make their lives better, beneficial, rewarding, valuable ... [Thank you, Bob Lusch]

[ ] AEIOU Framework: Activities, Environments, Interactions, Objects, Users ... use AEIOU to trigger observations when doing field research ... [Thank you, Emma L Murray]

[ ] Engage our customers ... interactive, part of our family ...

[ ] Democratic leadership style ... draws on people's knowledge and skills, and creates a group commitment to the resulting goals ... [Thank you, Daniel Goleman]

[ ] Start a revolution ... stay in the lead ...

[ ] A good target market is definable, meaningful, sizable, and reachable ...

[ ] There is nothing more frightful than ignorance in action ... [Thank you, Johann Wolfgang Goethe]

[ ] The simplest solution tends to be the best ...

[ ] Do what we love and success will follow ...

[ ] Positioning: strategies for marketing a product, service, or business within a particular sector of a market to fulfill that sector's specific requirements ...

[ ] A thoughtful benefits plan can have huge impact on employee satisfaction and loyalty ... [Thank you, Andrew Zacharakis]

[ ] What we do makes a difference ... and we have to decide what kind of difference we want to make ... [Thank you, Jane Goodall]

[ ] Common cause of venture death: failure to pivot ...

[ ] Elements of a customer profile ... age, gender, sex, nationality, income, location, education, profession, level of acceptable risk, type of buying process, traditionalist or trend-setter ...

[ ] Inspiration is all around us ... pay attention!

[ ] If we know where we are and what we have to do, then it is easier to figure out how to do it ... [Thank you, Barbara Ann Kipfer]

[ ] A luxury, once experienced, becomes a necessity ... smart phones, computers, automobiles, fast-food hamburgers, et al ...

[ ] First tell them what they already know ... then tell them what they're missing ... [Thank you, Roone Arledge]

[ ] Common bootstrapping strategy: handle own legal matters ...

[ ] Make a list of what was done today ...

[ ] Stay humble ... nobody likes a braggart ... [Thank you, Nelson Wang]

[ ] Skilled innovators and entrepreneurs are able to see inside-out ...

[ ] Invent solutions, not problems ...

[ ] Create a compelling challenge that will allow people to become committed emotionally to the project ... [Thank you, Don Treffinger]

[ ] Forgive and let go ... move on to the future, not cling to the past ... [Thank you, Mahatma Ghandi]

[ ] Work or Relax ... what should we focus on today? ...

[ ] Make things easy on our customers ...

[ ] It is better to delay than to do it wrong right away ...

[ ] Time is our most valuable asset ... it's the only one that can't be replaced ...

[ ] Creativity often starts where language ends ... [Thank you, Arthur Koestler]

[ ] Life is an echo; what we send out comes back ... [Thank you, Martha Novy]

[ ] When in doubt, check for rules of grammar and usage with a handbook ... [Thank you, Randy Accetta]

[ ] Start where the last person left off ... [Thank you, Thomas Alva Edison]

[ ] We are not alone ... there are some 7,000,000 people on this planet, what are the odds we're the only one with this great idea? Pretty low, but ... most others will not act on it!

[ ] There are two kinds of companies: those that work to charge more, and those that work to charge less ... [Thank you, Jeff Bezos]

[ ] Never send a chicken to bring home a fox ...

[ ] Reason is a harmonizing, controlling force rather than a creative one ... [Thank you, Bertrand Russell]

[ ] It's easy to suggest solutions if we don't know too much about the problem ... [Thank you, Malcolm Forbes]

[ ] Skilled innovators and entrepreneurs have a positive attitude ...

[ ] No goals, no problem ... no head, no headache ... no expectations, no failure ... [Thank you, John Dale]

[ ] Goodness is the only investment which never fails ... [Thank you, Henry David Thoreau]

[ ] Jack or Jill ... what should we focus on today? ...

[ ] Explore the world ...

[ ] We can't change the cards we are dealt, just how we play the hand ... [Thank you, Randy Pausch]

[ ] Goals and objectives ... goals are 5 years, objectives are 5 months (or 5 weeks) ...

[ ] Tolerance levels ... they are different for different customers ... some customers will tolerate a tepid cup of tea, some will not ...

[ ] Discover: become aware of a fact or situation ...

[ ] Advice is like snow ... the softer it falls, the longer it dwells upon and the deeper it sinks into the mind! ... [Thank you, Samuel Taylor Coleridge]

[ ] An idea is salvation by imagination ... [Thank you, Frank Lloyd Wright]

[ ] Shark Tank: bane or boon? ... while the TV show has certainly piqued the interest in entrepreneurship, it's also over-simplified the process of creating a healthy, sustainable venture ...

[ ] Tip for creating a good venture plan: Include profiles of each of our venture founders, partners, and advisors, and what kinds of skills, qualifications and accomplishments they bring to the table ...

[ ] Time is money, but money isn't time ...

[ ] Great people do great things ...

[ ] Website: a location connected to the Internet that maintains one or more pages on the World Wide Web ...

[ ] Do what the competition does but do it better ...

[ ] Build quality in right from the start ...

[ ] Start something new today ...

[ ] Sell good products, make appealing offers, treat people fairly ... the surefire formula for success ... [Thank you, Dean Rieck]

[ ] We won't always have the answers ... sometimes we will have to make decisions with just what we have ...

[ ] Whatever we're thinking of doing has already been done ... so let's look out there and learn from their mistakes!

[ ] In what industry (or industries) is our venture? ...

[ ] There's always room for one more ...

[ ] Beware of project creep ...

[ ] Include people with different cognitive styles ...

[ ] Mediocrity knows nothing higher than itself, but talent instantly recognizes genius ... [Thank you, Arthur Conan Doyle]

[ ] Worrying is using our imagination to create something we do not want ... [Thank you, Jerry Hicks]

[ ] Key question for our venture: What are our primary core competencies? ...

[ ] It's not "me", it's "we" ...

[ ] Make it personal ... customize to individual customers to make it theirs ...

[ ] It takes time to make money, but money can't make time!

[ ] Stay alert ...

[ ] How to kill creativity: (Yawn) ...

[ ] Beware: levels of lies ...

[ ] A pint of sweat will save a gallon of blood ... [Thank you, George S Patton]

[ ] It is not the strongest of companies that survive, nor the most intelligent, but the ones most responsive to change ... [Thank you, Charles Darwin]

[ ] It is of equal importance with the discovery of facts to know what to do with them ... [Thank you, Mary Parker Follett]

[ ] We can only make a difference if we get out of bed ... [Thank you, Cathy Guisewite]

[ ] Reward ourselves for doing good ... there are days when things go well and days when they don't ... celebrate the good ones so the bad ones are more tolerable ...

[ ] The only way to last is to be better ...

[ ] Accomplish small tasks as if they were great and noble ... [Thank you, Helen Keller]

[ ] No rule of thumb will work if we don't ...

[ ] Alternative Value: other positive results (aside from the products and services we deliver to our customers) from the activities within a venture ...

[ ] Successful Innovators and entrepreneurs know how to build on their learning ... [Thank you, Patricia G Greene]

[ ] Tolerate ambiguity ... it happens ...

[ ] Promote our venture using folders with our trademark ...

[ ] Remember stories have a beginning, a middle, and an end ... Don't leave the reader, viewer, listener, customer dangling ... [Thank you, Randy Accetta]

[ ] Our customer's attitude will be based on how we treat them ...

[ ] We must accept finite disappointment but never lose infinite hope ... [Thank you, Martin Luther King]

[ ] It could be a good opportunity if we can build barriers to entry ...

[ ] Key question for our venture: How can we market our venture with social media? ...

[ ] Time changes all ...

[ ] Seek the good and build on it ...

[ ] SAM: abbreviation for Served Addressable Market ... the customers we can really get to!

[ ] Reinvent our world ... make it a better place ...

[ ] Focus on our core competencies, outsource everything else ...

[ ] There is potential in every mistake we make ... the potential to make the same mistake again, or never again ...

[ ] Having another bidder in the mix will add 10% to the sales price ... [Thank you, Yves Smith]

[ ] Would-be entrepreneurs who cannot readily name prospective customers are not ready to start a venture ... [Thank you, Gary Smith]

[ ] The future is embedded in the present ... the challenge is finding it! ... [Thank you, John Naisbitt]

[ ] Wise people make more opportunities than they find ... [Thank you, Francis Bacon]

[ ] Skilled innovators and entrepreneurs maintain good interpersonal relations ...

[ ] A gift to a friend: your heart ... [Thank you, Oren Arnold]

[ ] The end doesn't always justify the means ... pick and choose carefully the direction we take ...

[ ] If we want people to understand, we've got to explain ... show, tell, demonstrate ...

[ ] Better to remain silent and be thought a fool, than to speak out and remove all doubt … (Jim note: been there, done that, more often than I care to admit!) … [Thank you, Abraham Lincoln]

[ ] Change is the only thing that's permanent … tomorrow will be different than today …

[ ] Keep our costs low and our value high …

[ ] Skill: the ability to do something well; expertise …

[ ] Gotta love someone who smiles …

[ ] Innovators are usually good at big-picture thinking …

[ ] Promote our venture with free or low-cost samples …

[ ] If we want to achieve greatness, stop asking for permission … [Thank you, Google]

[ ] It takes all the running we can do to keep in the same place … if we want to get somewhere else, we must run at least twice as fast as that! … [Thank you, Red Queen]

[ ] Wisdom: the quality of having experience, knowledge, and good judgment …

[ ] Potential business model: Create and sell information …

[ ] Key question for our venture: What are our major product development milestones? …

[ ] How can we answer this Question: Is our venture in a growth market? …

[ ] Don't count our chickens before they are hatched … [Thank you, Aesop]

[ ] The past is the only part of our history that we cannot change …

[ ] People like to buy, but they don't usually like to be sold ...

[ ] Headings for a Feasibility Study ... A. Market / Industry Attractiveness: Problems to Be Addressed; Industry and Environment; Potential Competitive Advantages ... B. Product Market Fit: Prospective Customers; Potential Solutions ... C. Go To Market / Customer Acquisition Strategy: Marketing; Sales ... D. Operating Plan; Production Operations; Team ... E. Financial Viability; Financial Objectives; Funding Proposal ... F. Business Model: Business Model Canvas; Status Timeline; Additional Venture Values; Scope and Scale ... [Thank you, Joe Broschak]

[ ] Think ...

[ ] Successful innovators and entrepreneurs possess a willingness to embrace ambiguity, paradox, and uncertainty ... [Thank you, Michael J Gelb]

[ ] The truth isn't so obvious ... [Thank you, New York Times]

[ ] Motives are behind everything customers do ...

[ ] It is impossible to teach without learning as well ...

[ ] It takes a team ... one can do so little, many can do so much!

[ ] Use plain English even on technical subjects ...

[ ] Left brain thinking ...

[ ] Funding Proposal: a plan or suggestion for providing money for a particular purpose, especially a formal or written one, put forward for consideration or discussion by others ...

[ ] Gift: a present given willingly without expectation of payment ... give gifts to our customers to say "thank you"!

[ ] Don't make things worse ... [Thank you, Dennis Page]

[ ] Money is limitless, time is not ... money is unlimited, time is not ...

[ ] Six key qualities of an idea that is made to stick: Simplicity, Unexpectedness, Concreteness, Credibility, Emotional, Stories ... [Thank you, Chip Heath & Dan Heath]

[ ] A target is something we aim to hit ... our weapons include our products and services, our processes and methods of doing business, our relationships and benefits ...

[ ] Spend a lot of time spying on our customers, looking for tip offs to new trends ... [Thank you, Rachael Ray]

[ ] Believe in their potential ...

[ ] We can say what we like about long dresses, but they cover a multitude of shins ... [Thank you, Mae West]

[ ] Free! the number one most powerful word in the English language ... "Sale" is second ...

[ ] People usually "geek out" on something in their life ... for some people, it's beer or music or football, and for other people it's direct-to-customer fulfillment ... [Thank you, Jeff Wilkins]

[ ] Find our niche in life ...

[ ] Separate opinion from fact ...

[ ] Falling is a part of learning ... learning how to fall can make it less painful ...

[ ] Stay in the bounds of integrity ...

[ ] Successful teams are comfortable with disagreements ...

[ ] Reading is to the mind what exercise is to the body ... [Thank you, Richard Steele]

[ ] Allow sufficient time for people to think ideas through before having to act ... [Thank you, Charlie Prather]

[ ] Choose our teammates wisely ...

[ ] If the automobile had followed the same development cycle as the computer, a Rolls-Royce would today cost $100, get a million miles per gallon ... and explode once a year, killing everyone inside! ... [Thank you, Robert X Cringely]

[ ] Work smarter and harder than the competition ...

[ ] Entrepreneur's slang dictionary ...

[ ] Beware: jumping in bed with the first investor we meet ...

[ ] Trying putting it in our catalog; if it doesn't sell, take it out!

[ ] Lies are the hardest things to forgive ...

[ ] Curly or Moe or Larry ... which one should we follow? ...

[ ] If we're going to think big, think BIG ...

[ ] Key question for our venture: Is the name descriptive of the benefits offered by the product, service, or business venture? ...

[ ] An original thought is not always readily understood ...

[ ] Fit or Fat ... which one's where we're at? ...

[ ] Be responsible ...

[ ] The purpose of life is a life of purpose ... the purpose of a venture is a venture of purpose ... [Thank you, Barbara Ann Kipfer]

[ ] Better to turn back and start over than to lose our way forever ...

[ ] Thank the people who made it all happen ...

[ ] How to kill creativity: "It's good enough already ..."

[ ] Promote our venture with skywriters ...

[ ] Wisdom does not come by chance ... it does come by choice ...

[ ] Don't be discouraged by our mistakes ... unless we keep making the same ones over again ...

[ ] People justify decisions with facts ... [Thank you, Dean Rieck]

[ ] Innovating and entrepreneuring is an iterating, sometimes irritating, jumping from here to there and back again, activity ... it's rarely as simple as going from A to B ...

[ ] The Six C's of Credit: character, capacity, capital, collateral, conditions, confidence ... [Thank you, SCORE]

[ ] Fix the faults first ...

[ ] Add a human touch ... [Thank you, Sue Factor]

[ ] If nothing went wrong, life would be great ... unfortunately, it ain't necessarily so ...

[ ] Don't acquire the next resource until there is an equivalent amount of recurring, bankable revenue to support the associated costs ... [Thank you, Scott Miller]

[ ] GAAP: abbreviation for Generally Accepted Accounting Principles ... follow the rules ...

[ ] Strategies are the right things to do ... tactics are the right way of doing them ... [Thank you, Clay Tatum]

[ ] Making a great presentation: Make text and numbers legible ... if we can't read everything, make it larger ... highlight areas where we want the audience to focus ... [Thank you, Ian McKenzie]

[ ] Successful teams challenge each other ...

[ ] Brainwriting ... Similar to brainstorming, brainwriting is a where ideas are recorded on paper by each individual who thought of them; they are then passed on to the next person who uses them as a trigger for their own ideas ...

[ ] Promote our venture with video commercials in stores ...

[ ] Listen exceptionally well ...

[ ] This or That ... what should we focus on today? ...

[ ] Put others first ...

[ ] Beachhead: the first test market for our new products and services ... the term originated in World War II when the allies stormed Normandy ...

[ ] The reward of a thing well done is to have done it ... [Thank you, Ralph Waldo Emerson]

[ ] Do something unexpected ... something unexpected good .. surprise our customers when they may least expect it ... give them a nice surprise ...

[ ] If appearance isn't everything ... but it's still in first place! ... [Thank you, Gina Lee]

[ ] Sometimes we lead, sometimes we follow, sometimes we get left behind ...

[ ] There is good and bad in everything ... pros and cons, highs and lows ...

[ ] Beware: pseudo-scientists ...

[ ] People don't want to be managed ... they want to be led ... [Thank you, Ewing M Kauffman]

[ ] Nice guys finish fast ... and nice gals, too ... the audience is getting bored after the first 30 seconds ...

[ ] Skilled innovators and entrepreneurs are sensible ...

[ ] Good or Bad or Evil ... what should we focus on today? ...

[ ] Skilled innovators and entrepreneurs are willing to accept responsibility ...

[ ] A patent is really a license to sue and be sued ... [Thank you, Arthur C Clarke]

[ ] Say what we mean but don't say it mean ...

[ ] Call things by their right names ... or we'll really confuse our suppliers!

[ ] Opportunity comes often ... it knocks as often as we have an ear trained to hear it, an eye trained to see it, a hand trained to grasp it, and a head trained to use it ... [Thank you, Charles Kemmons Wilson]

[ ] We're a nut until you succeed ...

[ ] Creativity starts when we cut a zero from our budget ... [Thank you, Jaime Lerner]

[ ] Smell the roses ...

[ ] Key question for our venture: How are we going to work together? ...

[ ] The SLATE mentoring process ... Suspend judgment; Listen and Learn; Assess and Analyze; Test ideas and Teach with Tools; set Expectations and Encourage the team to build their dream ... [Thank you, SCORE]

[ ] Use first names a bit more than most people would during conversation ... without overdoing it!

[ ] Rearrange, reverse ... what can be rearranged in some way? ... interchange components? ... another pattern? ... another layout? ... another sequence? ... transpose cause and

effect? ... change the pace? ... change the schedule? ... "I can rearrange ... like this ... such that ..."

[ ] A business plan brief is typically just about 6 pages in length ...

[ ] Promote our venture with free trials ...

[ ] We can never guard against chance ...

[ ] Skilled innovators and entrepreneurs are adept with numbers ...

[ ] A designer know she has achieved perfection not when there is nothing left to add, but when there is nothing left to take away ... [Thank you, Antoine de Saint-Exupéry]

[ ] Try to irrelevantize our competition ... [Thank you, Bob Carter]

[ ] Build on our strengths ... mitigate our weaknesses ...

[ ] It takes a team to raise a venture ...

[ ] Strive for excellence always ...

[ ] Three key lender questions: 1] how much money is needed?; 2] how will the money be used?; 3] how will the money be paid back? ...

[ ] Slow and steady ...

[ ] A good business plan shows how and when the venture will generate sustainable profit ... [Thank you, Bill Quiroga]

[ ] Realize that there are other points of view ... our customer may not necessarily see things the same way as us ...

[ ] Great things in life are achieved with passion ...

[ ] Is that piece of information a WAG, TWAG, SWAG, or science ...

[ ] Mistakes are inevitable ... they are a necessary part of learning and skill building, a sign we are active and curious and doing something!

[ ] Profit and Loss (P&L): abbreviation for a Profit and Loss statement, an alternative name for an income statement ...

[ ] Equity Funding: exchanging an ownership share of a venture for a cash or resource investment ...

[ ] The quality of an organization can never exceed the quality of the minds that make it up ... [Thank you, Harold R McAlindon]

[ ] Live by our word ... [Thank you, Adam Engst]

[ ] Skilled innovators and entrepreneurs are able to find order in chaos ...

[ ] Say it and mean it ... if we don't mean it, don't say it ...

[ ] The customer is a rear-view mirror, not a window to the future ... [Thank you, George Colony]

[ ] Key question for our venture: On what basis can we compete? ... on what basis should we compete? ...

[ ] Most people follow the crowd ... why testimonials and case histories are so influential ... [Thank you, Dean Rieck]

[ ] Accidents happen with creativity and innovation ... and sometimes we're better off when they do ... [Thank you, Robert Austin]

[ ] People will buy anything that is one to a customer!

[ ] Key question for our venture: Do we take advantage of our competitors' weaknesses? ...

[ ] Distribution Channel: the mechanism or method by which a business brings its products to market, or distributes its products to its target customers and generates sales ...

[ ] Skilled innovators and entrepreneurs generally are not status seekers ...

[ ] Beware "consultants" that ...

[ ] What's done is done ... we cannot go back, we can only go forward ...

[ ] Skilled innovators and entrepreneurs are able to solve collision conflicts for which there are no readily apparent solutions ...

[ ] Promote our venture with special events ...

[ ] How much equity and debt has our venture raised? ... is it enough to carry us through until we are a stable (consistently breaking even) venture? ...

[ ] Hire people smarter than us ...

[ ] Traits of leaders who are good at influencing: activation, commanding, communications, competitive, maximizer, self-assured, significance, ability to win over others ... [Thank you, Gallup]

[ ] A venture must thrive, not just survive ... we must keep looking for new ways to grow ...

[ ] Every picture tells a story ...

[ ] Feel or Smell or See or Hear or Taste ... try them all ...

[ ] Respect others ... this is not negotiable ...

[ ] No one can be right all of the time ... but it helps to be right most of the time ... [Thank you, Robert Half]

[ ] Mind over matter ...

5280 TIPS for INNOVATORS and ENTREPRENEURS

[ ] Plan, but adapt ... don't be stubborn. Listen to what our customers tell us in their response ...

[ ] GizmoGadget: a small device or tool, especially an ingenious or novel one ...

[ ] Business in not just about deals, business is about doing great things ... [Thank you, Ross Perot]

[ ] Key question for our venture: What hats are we all going to wear in our venture? ...

[ ] I fear regret more than I fear failure ... [Thank you, Taryn Rose]

[ ] Drive out fear so everyone may work effectively ... [Thank you, W Edwards Deming]

[ ] Good market research is critical to our success ...

[ ] Do little things well ... it's the little things that can make a big difference ...

[ ] Skilled innovators and entrepreneurs have a good sense of timing ...

[ ] Analyze the data, but not while we're still collecting it ...

[ ] Think big ...

[ ] A source of opportunity for innovation is process need ... [Thank you, Peter F Drucker]

[ ] Opening a new business is easy ... keeping it open is not!

[ ] Even if you're the owner, you don't have to be the CEO ... [Thank you, Andrew Corbett]

[ ] Skilled innovators and entrepreneurs are ethical ...

[ ] Engage beginners and attract experts ... [Thank you, Google]

[ ] Everyone is the architect of their own future ...

[ ] Recognition is often more important than money ...

[ ] Trust them ...

[ ] The great benefit of the business planning process is that it allows the entrepreneur to articulate the business opportunity to various stakeholders in the most effective manner ... [Thank you, William Bygrave,]

[ ] Lager or Ale? ... what should we focus on today? What process did we use to make our decision? What process will our customers use to make their decision? ...

[ ] What the eyes see can change what the mind believes ... but sometimes the eyes don't see what they think they see, and that can be a problem ...

[ ] Spell their name correctly ... get their name wrong and they will naturally assume everything else you have to say or write is wrong, too ...

[ ] Define our market ...

[ ] Key question for our venture: Can the name of our venture, product, service, or process be legally protected? ...

[ ] Time is a great teacher ... unfortunately, it kills all its pupils ... [Thank you, Hector Berlioz]

[ ] Customer: a person or organization that pays for goods or services ...

[ ] We win more votes by energizing our base than by trying to persuade undecided voters ... so be it with current customers versus prospective customers! Repeat orders are typically easier to capture than new orders ... [Thank you, John McCain]

[ ] Don't worry, be happy ... [Thank you, Bobby McFerrin]

[ ] Embrace failure and learn from it ...

[ ] If it's easy, everyone will do it ... even if it is easy, maybe we might not want to show the world ...

[ ] Promote our venture with moving billboards on trucks ...

[ ] If we're not better, why bother? ...

[ ] Successful teams communicate clearly continuously ...

[ ] When will our venture achieve profitability? ...

[ ] A gift to yourself: respect ... [Thank you, Oren Arnold]

[ ] Passion is energy ... feel the power that comes from focusing on what excites us ... [Thank you, Oprah Winfrey]

[ ] Always keep our spurs on ... get up and go when we gotta go!

[ ] The greater the risk, the greater the reward should be ... but often, it is not that way at all. ...

[ ] Promote our venture with samples of product ...

[ ] Entrepreneurs are not their own boss ...

[ ] Sit! Stay! Don't bark at anyone!

[ ] Position: the state of being placed where one has an advantage over one's rivals in a competitive situation ...

[ ] Long or Short ... what should we focus on today? ...

[ ] Set aside 15 minutes for community building at every meeting ... [Thank you, Todd Adams]

[ ] Focus on people, their lives, their work, their dreams ... [Thank you, Google]

[ ] Common Mistake: top-down forecasting versus setting bottom-up objectives ...

[ ] Inventing is a combination of brains and materials ... the more brains we use, the less material we need ... [Thank you, Charles Kettering]

[ ] Let's ask our customers: "Would you recommend our products to your friends and acquaintances?" ... it the answer isn't a fast and automatic "YES", we've got work to do!

[ ] Common cause of venture death: burn-out ...

[ ] These soon will be the good old days ...

[ ] Over or Under ... what should we focus on today? ...

[ ] Skilled innovators and entrepreneurs are creative in a particular domain ...

[ ] It's always worthwhile to make others aware of their worth ... [Thank you, Malcolm S Forbes]

[ ] Bad company corrupts good character ...

[ ] The timing has to be right ... all the parties involved in the transaction have to be ready to move together ...

[ ] Good corporate governance should provide incentives for the board and management to pursue objectives that are in the interest of the company and its shareholders ... [Thank you, Organisation for Economic Co-operation and Development]

[ ] Set aside quiet time every day ...

[ ] Accounting is an exact science ... finance is not ... [Thank you, Mary Durham-Pflibsen]

[ ] If our actions inspire others to dream more, learn more, do more, and become more ... we are leaders! ... [Thank you, Dolly Parton]

[ ] The lack of money is the root of all evil ... [Thank you, George Bernard Shaw]

[ ] Seek advice ...

[ ] Pay commissions instead of salaries ...

[ ] Let our creative work be our inner friend ...

[ ] Live or Die ... what should we focus on today? ...

[ ] The majority of patents don't make any money ... the inventions simply aren't better that the alternatives ...

[ ] How to retain customers: refund their money if they are not completely satisfied ...

[ ] Key question for our venture: Do we regularly track our competitors' moves? ...

[ ] Projections: an estimate or forecast of a future situation or trend based on a study of present ones ...

[ ] Beware: investors that only want to talk about the financials of a business ...

[ ] Projections are passive ... objectives are active ... set objectives for our venture and responsibilities for making them happen ...

[ ] Trust only those who stand to lose as much as us if things go wrong ...

[ ] If it's to be, it's up to me ... or us, as is much more likely the case, but us doesn't rhyme so nicely with be as me!

[ ] Money comes and goes ... knowledge comes and grows ...

[ ] Work never hurt anybody ...

[ ] Sometimes we just can't worry about what someone else thinks about us ... as long as we're doing the right things for the right reasons, we'll be ok ...

[ ] Make it simple to understand ... hard is easy, easy is hard!

[ ] Innovators and entrepreneurs are leaders ...

[ ] Be professional ...

[ ] How can we answer this Question: Can we really execute our venture concept? ...

[ ] Know there's always room for improvement ...

[ ] Use PowerPoint (or Google Slides, or similar) as the homebase for a business plan and backup supporting information ... while the first 20 to 30 slides in the deck will be the core of the business plan presentation, the "backup slides" can contain all the supporting information that might come up in the question-and-answer part of a presentation or discussion ... create an index of the slides with the title, content, and slide number ... jump to the desired slide by entering the slide number on the keyboard and pressing enter.

[ ] We learn 10% of what we read; 20% of what we hear; 30% of what we see; 50% of what we see and hear; 70% of what we discuss with others; 80%of what we experience personally; and 95% of what we teach to someone else ... [Thank you, William Glasser]

[ ] Don't use words too big for the subject ... [Thank you, C S Lewis]

[ ] Go with our strengths, mitigate the weaknesses ...

[ ] It's not about the service, it's about the experience ... [Thank you, Howard Schultz]

[ ] The best products are those that people don't yet know they want ... [Thank you, Roxanne Quimby]

[ ] Focus our attention ... practice this critical skill everyday ... [Thank you, R A Baron]

[ ] Innovation is creative destruction ... [Thank you, Adam Smith]

[ ] Prepare, and work hard ...

[ ] Explain things as we would to a close friend or relative who's perfectly intelligent but isn't familiar with our business ... would we tell this person we were, for example, trying to 'incentivise' our staff? ... [Thank you, Giulia De Cesare]

[ ] Give it a good SWOTT: Strengths, Weaknesses, Opportunities, Threats, and Trends ... a great tool for analyzing the competition, our venture, our new products, our customers ...

[ ] Do onto others as we would have them do onto us ... do for others as we would like them to do for us ... [Thank you, Luke]

[ ] Be sincere, be brief, be seated ... [Thank you, F D Roosevelt]

[ ] The great tragedy of science: the slaying of a beautiful hypothesis by an ugly fact ... [Thank you, Thomas H Huxley]

[ ] A revenue model identifies how the venture will earn income and generate profits ...

[ ] Feel ...

[ ] The winner of the war writes the history books ...

[ ] Our idea doesn't have to be big ... it just has to change the world ... [Thank you, Spence Silver]

[ ] We do not all think the same way ...

[ ] Obliterate obfuscation! ... [Thank you, William Zinsser]

[ ] A disruptive innovation is a technologically simple innovation in the form of a product, service, or business model that takes root in a market segment that is not attractive to the established leaders in an industry ... [Thank you, Clayton M Christensen]

[ ] Successful innovators and entrepreneurs recognize the interconnectedness of all things and phenomena ... [Thank you, Michael J Gelb]

[ ] When talking to people smarter than us, something is bound to rub off ...

[ ] There is nothing more difficult to carry out, nor more doubtful of success, nor more dangerous to handle than to initiate a new order of things ... the innovator has enemies in all who profit by the old order, and only luke warm defenders in all those who profit by the new order ... this lukewarmness arises partly from the incredulity of mankind, who do not truly believe in anything new until they actually experience it! ... [Thank you, Niccolò Machiavelli]

[ ] Skilled innovators and entrepreneurs are driven ...

[ ] Customer acquisition cost ...

[ ] Fantasize for fun ...

[ ] No exchange takes place unless both parties benefit ... [Thank you, Milton Friedman]

[ ] Skilled innovators and entrepreneurs are magical ...

[ ] Potential venture legal issue: Disclosing inventions without a nondisclosure agreement, or before the patent application is filed ... [Thank you, Connie Bagley]

[ ] Not everything can be put in order ... but like leaves on a tree, it can still look beautiful ...

[ ] Time out, Green Bay ... let's make sure we've got the right play ready to make the next first down ...

[ ] Victory often comes only after many struggles and defeats ... [Thank you, Og Mandino]

[ ] Dysfunctional teams will fail ...

[ ] If people are offered something which gives them a reason to act according to their beliefs, they will accept it even on the slightest evidence ... [Thank you, Bertrand Russell]

[ ] The customer is always right ... even when they're not. If they think they are right, they are right. Either we change or we find new customers ...

[ ] Illuminate the fog that surrounds us ... [Thank you, Henri Matisse]

[ ] Improve our skills ... now and forever ...

[ ] Break down the revenue model by many categories in order to understand how the firm can increase each source of revenue ... [Thank you, Andrew Zacharakis]

[ ] Continuously solicit feedback from our customers ...

[ ] It is simple to make something complex, and complex to make it simple ... [Thank you, Thomas A Edison]

[ ] Formal or Loose ... what should we focus on today? ...

[ ] How can we answer this Question: Can we lease our products? ...

[ ] Mistakes will teach us a lesson ... but maybe not the right one ...

[ ] Ready or not, here comes change ...

[ ] Learn: gain or acquire knowledge or skill ... [Thank you, Google Dictionary]

[ ] Friendships should never be painful to keep up ... make it easy for our customers to consider us friends ...

[ ] Stakeholder: a person with an interest or concern in something, especially a business venture ...

[ ] Fit: the right shape and size ...

[ ] Vision and mission ... what we see in the future, what we do to get there ...

[ ] Management: the responsibility and process of applying and controlling resources to achieve particular objectives ...

[ ] If we dream big enough, anything can come true ... just kidding ... get back to work! ... [Thank you, Drew Ellis]

[ ] Key question for our venture: What are we fighting for? ...

[ ] When we're green, we're growing ... when we're ripe, we're not ... [Thank you, Ray Kroc]

[ ] Learning keeps us young ...

[ ] The way to succeed is to double our failure rate ... [Thank you, Thomas Watson]

[ ] Meanness, hardness, and coldness are unforgivable sins ... [Thank you, C Benson]

[ ] The supreme accomplishment is to blur the line between work and play ... [Thank you, Arnold J Toynbee]

[ ] Defy time ...

[ ] Barrier: an obstacle that prevents movement or access ...

[ ] Hail, Mary ... the game ain't over 'til it's over! ... [Thank you, Aaron Rodgers]

[ ] The Internet allows us to find the precise point of view that matches our own biases, no matter what they may be!

[ ] Adventure: daring and exciting activity calling for enterprise and enthusiasm ... innovators and entrepreneurs are constantly creating new venture adventures ...

[ ] Accredited investor: a term defined by securities laws that delineates investors permitted to invest in certain types of higher risk investments including seed money, limited partnerships, hedge funds, private placements, and angel investor networks ... [Thank you, Google Dictionary]

[ ] Free advice is worth every cent ...

[ ] String our pearls on a very strong string ...

[ ] Key question for our venture: What are the barriers to future competition? ...

[ ] Always be legal, moral, and ethical ...

[ ] Skilled innovators and entrepreneurs are not risks ...

[ ] Always keep a pad and pen nearby so we can capture ideas, solutions, and thoughts as they occur ...

[ ] Entrepreneurship is a life skill ...

[ ] Start where we are ... it's easier than trying to move somewhere else ... [Thank you, Edgar Cayce]

[ ] People who fight fire with fire often end up with ashes ...

[ ] We will be out of cash much sooner than we think ... never enough time or money ... [Thank you, Jeffry A Timmons]

[ ] Follow chance wherever it takes us! ... [Thank you, Amanda Congdon]

[ ] Lead and they will follow ...

[ ] Nothing is so infectious as example ... Give our customers samples of our work!

[ ] Luck: success or failure apparently brought by chance rather than through one's own actions ... [Thank you, Google Dictionary]

[ ] Never be idle ...

[ ] Supplement our strengths with advisors ...

[ ] Entrepreneurship can be taught and learned ... critical is the desire to learn ... the teacher cannot force the student to learn ... [Thank you, Heidi M Neck]

[ ] Actions speak louder than words ...

[ ] Traits of leaders who are good at strategic thinking: analytical, contextual, futuristic, idea generation, input seeking, intellectual, learner, strategic overview ... [Thank you, Gallup]

[ ] Do it right the first time ... so we don't have to do it again ...

[ ] Who, What, Where, When, Why, How? ... the six most powerful questions in the world! Keep asking around ... [Thank you, Journalism 101]

[ ] Skilled innovators and entrepreneurs have superior conceptual abilities ...

[ ] Machines should work, people should think ... [Thank you, IBM]

[ ] When writing an ad, use sentences of no more than twelve words ... [Thank you, David Ogilby]

[ ] There are two things that people want more than sex and money: recognition and praise ... [Thank you, Mary Kay Ash]

5280 TIPS for INNOVATORS and ENTREPRENEURS

[ ] A source of opportunity for innovation is the unexpected success or failure of some outside event ... [Thank you, Peter F Drucker]

[ ] Improvement always pays ...

[ ] I haven't failed ... I just found 1,000 ways that don't work ... [Thank you, Thomas Alva Edison]

[ ] As we think, so shall we be ... [Thank you, Wayne Dyer]

[ ] I yam what's I yam and that's all what's I am ... [Thank you, Popeye]

[ ] Entrepreneurial Myth: the growth of a start-up depends more on an entrepreneur's talent than on the type of business ... both are important, but we'll be less likely to succeed if we're in the wrong business ... [Thank you, Scott Shane]

[ ] Give rewards for referrals ...

[ ] Aim at nothing and we'll hit it every time ...

[ ] Balance centers us ...

[ ] Great team members have complementary skills and collaborative styles ...

[ ] When nothing is sure, everything is possible ... [Thank you, Margaret Drabble]

[ ] Develop: cause to become more mature, advanced, or elaborate ...

[ ] Reserve ignorance for the things we know nothing about ...

[ ] Be clear ...

[ ] Clowns to the left of us ... jokers to the right! ... [Thank you, Gerry Rafferty]

[ ] It is the best of times to start a new business ... [Thank you, Joann MacMaster]

[ ] An alpha version of a new product is typically in the lab and just seen by venture insiders ...

[ ] Research is the process of going up alleys to see if they are blind ... [Thank you, Marston Bates]

[ ] Seek to learn from the best practices in our industry ...

[ ] It ain't work if we like it ...

[ ] Want to get rich quick? ... buy some lottery tickets ...

[ ] Have a plan to deal with the unexpected ...

[ ] Stay cool ...

[ ] Show we're interested ...

[ ] Promote our venture with specialty items ...

[ ] Key question for our venture: Do we take advantage of competitive opportunities? ... How? ...

[ ] Skilled innovators and entrepreneurs are lively ...

[ ] If we tell the truth we don't have to remember anything ... [Thank you, Mark Twain]

[ ] Put everything we've got in a catalog ... let our customers pick what they want ... next catalog, take out the stuff that doesn't sell and replace it with new stuff ...

[ ] Everything is good for something ...

[ ] Successful entrepreneurs often prefer to operate in a more established and structure business environment ... [Thank you, Lynda Applegate]

[ ] Success is based on partnerships ... [Thank you, Bill Gates]

[ ] Promote our venture with charitable volunteerism ...

[ ] And you ask "What if I fall?" Oh but my darling, what if you fly? ... [Thank you, Erin Hanson]

[ ] There's a sucker born every minute ...

[ ] Entrepreneurs have a knack for looking at the usual and seeing the unusual ... [Thank you, D G Mitton]

[ ] Skilled innovators and entrepreneurs possess a vivid imagination ...

[ ] Life is not fair ... [Thank you, Paris Hilton]

[ ] Focus on what we want to have happen ... [Thank you, Bob Parsons]

[ ] Go where our customers are and our competitors aren't ...

[ ] Ignorance is the root of misery ...

[ ] Solution: products, services, or processes designed to meet particular need, wants, and desires ...

[ ] Successful entrepreneurs have an ability to develop and execute a business vision and strategy ... [Thank you, Lynda Applegate]

[ ] An effective brand provides a shortcut for our customers ... it helps customers quickly understand who we are, what we do, and our place in the marketspace ... [Thank you, Leslie Bromberg]

[ ] The only people who find what they are looking for in life are the fault finders ... [Thank you, Robert Foster]

[ ] Ants make a big hill one grain at a time ... [Thank you, Vera Shury]

[ ] Buzz marketing: using high-profile entertainment or news to get people to recognize a brand ... [Thank you, Andrew Corbett]

[ ] Don't go over someone's head without talking to them first ... don't be a jerk, it's not becoming ...

[ ] Beware the charming narcissist ... [Thank you, Nina W Brown]

[ ] Always smile ... smiles are contagious ...

[ ] Respect the rules ... break them if needed ...

[ ] Sometimes we become so enchanted with new customers we forget our old friends ... [Thank you, Dorothy Gaiter]

[ ] Good wares make good markets ... [Thank you, Nicholas Breton]

[ ] Product, place, price, promotion ... the "P's of Marketing"

[ ] Spring forward, fall back ...

[ ] It takes twenty years to build a good reputation and five minutes to ruin it ...

[ ] How to kill creativity: "Well, maybe tomorrow ..." ...

[ ] Promote our venture with gifts and premiums ...

[ ] Promote our venture with city/regional magazine advertising ...

[ ] Praise a job well done ...

[ ] Wish or Work ... what should we focus on today? ...

[ ] Skilled innovators and entrepreneurs are intense ...

[ ] Not every new start-up venture is going to be a home run.

[ ] Promote our venture with event sponsorship ...

[ ] Characteristics of successful business ventures: compelling, executable venture concept; significant market potential; growth markets and industry; scalable concept; capable team; incrementally innovative concept ...

[ ] Two steps forward, one step back ... we'll still make it home ...

[ ] Tell powerful stories that reinforce the principles and practices of innovation in our venture ... [Thank you, S A Buckler]

[ ] Science: the intellectual and practical activity encompassing the systematic study of the structure and behavior of the physical and natural world through observation and experiment ...

[ ] Beware of all enterprises that require new clothes ... let's go where we are comfortable going dressed as we are ... [Thank you, Henry David Thoreau]

[ ] Garbage to one, treasure to another ...

[ ] If we think we're going beat the established competition with a lower price, think again ... the competition has been around for a while. If they feel threatened, they'll just lower their price and squish us like a bug. But if we do something new and better, something innovative, they'll have a much harder time keeping up!

[ ] It takes an army to win a war ... [Thank you, Dan Janes]

[ ] Low-hanging fruit: a thing or person that can be won, obtained, or persuaded with little effort ...

[ ] What we read, see, and hear ain't necessarily so ...

[ ] Give a positive push ... a smile, a kind word, appreciation.

[ ] Negotiation: Discuss issues on which we're pretty sure we'll agree first ... [Thank you, William N Yeomans]

[ ] Trust is something earned ... and that is usually hard work to do ...

[ ] One adventure will lead to another ...

[ ] Forecasting is very difficult, especially it it's about the future ... [Thank you, Niels Bohr]

[ ] Don't be content being average ... average is as close to the bottom as it is to the top! ... [Thank you, David Smith]

[ ] School: taught a lesson, given a test ... Life: given a test, taught a lesson ...

[ ] Entrepreneurs are motivated by the five C's: challenge, creativity, control, celebrity, and cash ...

[ ] Describe the buying process by customers in this industry ... How strong is buyer power? ... [Thank you, Patty Sias]

[ ] Have passion, build our skills, and luck will find us ...

[ ] Imitate other successful ventures ... do what they do right ...

[ ] Finance: monetary support for an enterprise ...

[ ] We must not rust ... [Thank you, Clara Barton]

[ ] Never outgrow fun ...

[ ] People find fault with things they don't understand ...

[ ] Small things make perfection, but perfection is no small thing ... [Thank you, Henry Royce]

[ ] Learning from from the past helps eliminate mistakes in the future ...

[ ] Be careful what we show ... keep the dirty laundry hidden away ...

[ ] Fanatic: someone filled with obsessive and single-minded zeal ... do what we can to create our own fanatic customers ...

[ ] Make them feel really special ...

[ ] Competitor, or potential collaborator? ...

[ ] Chart our own course ... but that doesn't mean we can look at how those that went before us got there ...

[ ] Common Mistake: not understanding our key revenue drivers ...

[ ] A new venture may be feasible if it is competitively unique.

[ ] Logic will get us from A to B ... imagination will take us everywhere ... [Thank you, Albert Einstein]

[ ] How to attract new customers: offer something free ...

[ ] Embrace our naysayers ... use their doubt as a source of motivation ... [Thank you, Nelson Wang]

[ ] It's amazing what we can do when we put our mind to it ... [Thank you, R Buckminster Fuller]

[ ] Use the most reliable sources to get the most reliable information ...

[ ] Key question for our venture: Why do we need to develop financial objectives and budgets? ...

[ ] Things can always get better ... or not. It's up to us ...

[ ] Genius is the ability to reduce the complicated to the simple ... [Thank you, C W Cerar]

[ ] Top 10 way to fail: be overconfident ...

[ ] Always be true and truthful ...

[ ] Focus on an industry that is economically healthy ...

[ ] Tell it like it is ...

[ ] Don't let words get in the way of action ...

[ ] There is no happiness without action!

[ ] There are three parts to every good solution: the product, the service, and the process ...

[ ] Coaching leadership style ... a one-on-one style that focuses on developing individuals, showing them how to improve their performance, and helping to connect their goals to the goals of the venture ... [Thank you, Daniel Goleman]

[ ] Series A: the first round of financing given to a new business once seed capital has already been provided ...

[ ] Options make employees think like owners ...

[ ] Web site for small business help and information: www.sba.gov ... Small Business Administration ...

[ ] Innovate or die ... if we don't keep creating something new and better, how will we survive when our competition does? ...

[ ] Spend less money than we have ...

[ ] Spend only when it's necessary ...

[ ] Have some wine and cheese ... savor the combination ... describe what you're tasting, trigger new word combinations.

[ ] C Corporation: the most common legal form of organization for a company ...

[ ] Free Cash: the cash generated beyond what is needed to purchase assets and keep the company growing ...

[ ] Don't worry about winning awards ...

[ ] Go with the odds ... nothing is for certain, go where the getting is good ...

[ ] Continuous innovation is our most important competitive advantage ...

[ ] Change the way someone does something ... for the better!

[ ] Changing momentum takes power ...

[ ] How we spend our days is how we spend our lives ... [Thank you, Annie Dillard]

[ ] Key question for our venture: Are we confident that our intellectual property does not violate the rights of a third party? ...

[ ] R – E – S – P – E – C – T ... earn it, give it ... [Thank you, Aretha Franklin]

[ ] Common Mistake: top-down rather than bottom-up objectives ... [Thank you, Andrew Zacharakis]

[ ] Successful teams have a collective sense of humor ...

[ ] Promote our venture with letterhead ...

[ ] When we lose, learn a lesson ...

[ ] Create new products ...

[ ] How to improve our financial bottom line: lower our expenses ...

[ ] Breadth: wide range or extent ...

[ ] Key question for our venture: What is our social media strategy? ...

[ ] Look for ways to profit from change and disruption ...

[ ] Learn by doing ... eventually we'll get it right, hopefully sooner than later ...

[ ] Pleasure in the job puts perfection in the work ... [Thank you, Aristotle]

[ ] Tell them a story ... our prospective customers will listen to a friendly story longer than a hard-sell pitch ...

[ ] Ideas are like rabbits ... we get a couple and learn how to handle them, and pretty soon we have a dozen! ... [Thank you, John Steinbeck]

[ ] Set priorities ...

[ ] List our core competencies ...

[ ] Top 10 ways to fail: be overconfident ...

[ ] Mission: something important carried out for a particular purpose ...

[ ] Rather than being truly novel, most new businesses are built on a product that has improved performance, price, distribution, quality or service ... [Thank you, William Bygrave]

[ ] Everyone is a genius at least once a year ... the real geniuses simply have their bright ideas closer together ... [Thank you, Georg C Lichtenberg]

[ ] It too shall pass ...

[ ] Tip for creating a good venture plan: Establish the market opportunity ...

[ ] We can resist an invading army ... we cannot resist an idea whose time has come ... [Thank you, Victor Hugo]

[ ] Just getting going is a great first step ...

[ ] Strike while the iron is hot ... the opportunity may not last very long ...

[ ] Promote our venture with two-for-one offers ...

[ ] Choose business partners who are strong where we are weak ...

[ ] To know, we must do ...

[ ] Skilled innovators and entrepreneurs are willing to take calculated risks ... carefully evaluated risks, not wild-ass jumps into space ...

[ ] Plan: detailed proposal for doing or achieving something.

[ ] Charm is the ability to create extraordinary rapport that makes others feel exceptional ... [Thank you, Brian Tracy]

[ ] If we really believe in what we're doing, we should put our name on it ... [Thank you, James Dyson]

[ ] Scientific Method: a method or procedure consisting of systematic observation, measurement, and experiment, and the formulation, testing, and modification of an hypotheses ...

[ ] Angel investors and venture capitalists would (ideally) like a 5 to 20 times return on their money in five years ...

[ ] It takes two to tango ...

[ ] Making a great presentation: Use visuals pictorially ... graphs, pictures of equipment, flow charts give the viewer an insight that would require many words or numbers ... [Thank you, Ian McKenzie]

[ ] Key question for our venture: Does our advertising grab viewer/reader/listener attention? ...

[ ] Key question for our venture: Do we know the myths and realities of entrepreneurship? ...

[ ] Tact is the knack of making a point without making an enemy ... [Thank you, Isaac Newton]

[ ] Make the best of a bad situation ...

[ ] Gross margin is the most important number on the income statement ... [Thank you, Norm Brodsky]

[ ] Keep moving forward! ... [Thank you, Walt Disney]

[ ] Just because the monkey is off our back doesn't mean the circus has left town ...

[ ] What customers look for in a product or service: recognizable brand; wanted features; desired benefits; competitive price; purchase and delivery convenience; relationship with the venture; social impact of the purchase; durability; maintenance requirements; product and service quality; perceived value; delivery time; image and style; product performance ...

[ ] Leadership: hold by the hand, show how it is done ...

[ ] Key question for our venture: Who is going to wear which hats in our venture, and for how long? ... common hats in a startup venture: general manager, product development manager, marketing and sales manager, operations manager, finance manager ...

[ ] Opportunity comes, sooner or later ... so that it doesn't get lost in the forest, we often have to go find it ...

[ ] Equity: common and preferred stocks, which represent a share in the ownership of a company ...

[ ] A river begins with a drop of water ... a fortune with the first dollar ...

[ ] Business Model Canvas Checklist: The Offering: 1] Value Proposition ... The Customer: 2] Customer Segments; 3] Channels; 4] Customer Relationships ... The Infrastructure Portion: 5] Key Activities; 6] Key Resources; 7] Key Partners ... The Financial Viability Portion: 8] Cost Structure; 9;

Revenue Streams ... [Thank you, Alexander Osterwalder and Yves Pigneur]

[ ] Innovate ... we have no choice ...

[ ] It always takes more time and money ...

[ ] We must take risks when experimenting ... [Thank you, Tove Jansson]

[ ] Keep improving our customer experience ... the best way to win loyal customers is to become their best friend and not screw up once we do ...

[ ] Focus only on the present ... stop regretting the past; stop worrying about the future! ... [Thank you, Nelson Wang]

[ ] Common cause of venture death: lack of customers ...

[ ] Locate our business where there are industry-specific resources gathered together in one "cluster" that can lead to a competitive advantage ... think Silicon Valley or the Napa wine country ... [Thank you, Michael Porter]

[ ] A race horse that can run a mile a few seconds faster is worth twice as much ... [Thank you, John Hess]

[ ] Beta Test: a trial of machinery, software, or other products, in the final stages of its development, carried out by a party unconnected with its development ...

[ ] Compare similar data from multiple sources to see the data converges, or not ...

[ ] Striving for excellence puts wind in our sails ... but striving for perfection takes it out! ... [Thank you, Harriet Braiker]

[ ] Beware: there are lots of fake "investors" out there ...

[ ] Put to another use ... how can we put our something to different or other uses? ... new ways to use it as is? ... other uses if it is modified? ... "I can reuse ... in this way ... by ..." ...

[ ] Innovation is finding new possibilities in old situations ... [Thank you, J G Saxe]

[ ] EBITDA is what counts the most ...

[ ] If we dare to fail, we won't fail to dare ...

[ ] We remember giving longer than we remember getting ...

[ ] Past, present, and future ...

[ ] Share, share alike, and share differences ...

[ ] Key question for our venture: Do our promotional efforts and messages provide a clear path to action by the viewer/reader/listener? ...

[ ] I don't know anything about Chevys, but I can tell you all about this Ford ... [Thank you, Jim Click]

[ ] Be aware of our situations ...

[ ] Key question for our venture: What is written without effort is generally read without pleasure ... [Thank you, Samuel Johnson]

[ ] When trying to create something new we have to do something different to get it to happen ... don't make life too comfortable for our creative colleagues; keep them on the edge ... [Thank you, Paul Robertson]

[ ] Problems cannot be solved by thinking within the framework in which the problems were created ... [Thank you, Albert Einstein]

[ ] Readiness is it ...

[ ] High expectations are the key to everything ... [Thank you, Sam Walton]

[ ] The only limits are those of vision ... [Thank you, James Broughton]

[ ] Be worthy of people's trust ... [Thank you, Google]

[ ] Many great thoughts come while walking ...

[ ] Window of Opportunity: the length of time in which a problem exists without a viable solution ...

[ ] Will existing investors participate in future investments?

[ ] Take the right perspective ... Rather than telling a colleague, "You look good in that suit," tell them, "That suit looks good on you." ... [Thank you, Dale Carnegie]

[ ] Timing sets the tone ...

[ ] Use humor but not at someone else's expense ...

[ ] Everyone has a purpose ... we are not here by mistake ... [Thank you, Ben Morrow]

[ ] We are always representing our venture to the public ... careful we're not caught with our pants down ...

[ ] She who has a why can endure any how ... [Thank you, Friedrich Nietzsche]

[ ] Time is our most precious possession ...

[ ] Beware: big talkers ...

[ ] Alpha Test: a trial of machinery, software, or other products carried out by a developer before a product is made available for beta testing ...

[ ] To estimate the revenues of a company, multiply the number of full-time employees by $150,000 ... while this is a

gross estimation, it is useful for providing a quick order-of-magnitude guess ... [Thank you, Guy Hagan]

[ ] Employees tend to rise to their level of incompetence ...

[ ] The internal combustion engine is a hard act to follow ...

[ ] Listen as if we are wrong ... [Thank you, K Weick]

[ ] How can we answer this Question: Would we pay good money to use our products or services? ... If not, why would we expect anyone else to? ...

[ ] Key question for our venture: How do we plan to scale our venture in the next 12 months? ...

[ ] Just because someone says they are a something doesn't make them a something ...

[ ] Successful business ventures continually introduce new product, service, process, and positioning innovations; they keep improving internal and external transformation methodologies; and they continually monitor goal and objective achievements ... innovators and entrepreneurs are wise to closely follow these core concepts ...

[ ] Key question for our venture: Does our venture possess a uniqueness that easily separates it from my competitors? ... What, specifically, is it? ...

[ ] 80% of the effects come from 20% of the causes ... let's be sure to focus on that 20% that will have the most effect on our venture ... [Thank you, Vilfredo Pareto: The Famous 80/20 Rule of Thumb]

[ ] Life is short: break the rules, forgive quickly, kiss slowly, love truly, laugh uncontrollably, and never regret anything that made us smile! ... [Thank you, Anna Robinson]

[ ] Types of risks: competition, market, technology, product, execution, opportunity costs ...

[ ] Green flag ...

[ ] Laughter is an instant vacation ... [Thank you, Bob Hope]

[ ] Make sure that our message is typo free ...

[ ] Easy to suggest solutions when we don't know too much about the problem ... [Thank you, Malcolm Forbes]

[ ] While creativity is the generation of new ideas, which we have in abundance, innovation is the successful exploitation of them ... [Thank you, George Cox]

[ ] A little knowledge is a dangerous thing ... it's not the complete story ...

[ ] Skilled innovators and entrepreneurs are loaded with energy ...

[ ] Competitors help validate the market ... they can make a path through a dense jungle which we can follow with a lot less fear than they who go first!

[ ] Key question for our venture: What is the cost of acquiring a new customer? ... the cost of retaining an old customer? ...

[ ] Leadership is the art of getting others to do something we want done because they want to do it ... [Thank you, Dwight D Eisenhower]

[ ] Gaining someone's trust is an awesome feeling ... don't blow it ...

[ ] Nothing beats cute animals ... [Thank you, L C Bensinger]

[ ] There is no elevator to success ... only stairs ...

[ ] Dream or Doze ... what should we focus on today? (Personally, I like to do both ... dream in a nice deep sleep

sometimes, other times just take a little doze and see what happens! Quite often, there is a nice reward at the end of the siesta ... a little idea, a big idea, perhaps something humorous to laugh at, sometimes something scary to hide away!) ...

[ ] Enclose our business card with every letter and note ...

[ ] Get out of debt ... and stay there ...

[ ] Treat other people's money as if it were our own ... if we're not willing to put in our own money, why should we expect anyone else to put in theirs? ... [Thank you, Ray Anderson]

[ ] Acceleration takes a whole lot more energy than steady-state ...

[ ] Customer Characteristics Profile: Decision maker, Purchasing agent, New/Repeat customer, Saboteur, Tire-kicker ...

[ ] Don't throw spitballs at big, ugly lions ... [Thank you, Sherry Hoskinson]

[ ] Dry or Wet ... what should we focus on today? ...

[ ] We don't see things as they are, we see things as we are ... [Thank you, Anais Nin]

[ ] Schtuff happens ... [Thank you, Holly Joubert]

[ ] Journalism: gathering, processing, evaluation, and dissemination of information ...

[ ] Sometimes help comes from unusual sources ...

[ ] Skilled innovators and entrepreneurs are able to translate ideas into action items ...

[ ] Perceive alternatives ...

[ ] One day at a time ... a basic law of physics ...

[ ] The world is flat and getting flatter ... [Thank you, Thomas L Friedman]

[ ] Deliver quality ...

[ ] Be as useful as we can to our colleagues ...

[ ] Self-observe, self-reflect ...

[ ] Key question for our venture: Does our name reinforce customer expectations? ...

[ ] Nothing is free ... but some things are cheap, at least ...

[ ] During the first 30 seconds, our light is green ... that means our listener is listening and not thinking we talk too much. During the next 30 seconds, our light is yellow ... that means the risk is increasing that our listener is bored, overwhelmed, or dying to respond. After the one-minute mark, our light is red ... yes, occasionally, we can go beyond a minute, for example, when telling an interesting story, but generally we should stop or ask a question ... [Thank you, Marty Nemko]

[ ] Promote our venture with business breakfasts/lunches ...

[ ] Avoid verbal instructions ...

[ ] Look for ways to create better business models ...

[ ] Tell me and I forget; teach me and I remember; involve me and I learn ... [Thank you, Benjamin Franklin]

[ ] When writing our business plan, avoid form over substance ... if it looks good but doesn't have a solid basis in fact and research, we might as well save our energy ... [Thank you, Kaye Vivian]

[ ] We can't play in dirt without getting dirty ...

[ ] It's objectives, not projections ...

[ ] Successful teams share leadership and ownership of team tasks ...

[ ] Don't buy anything until we must ... and then, could be just rent it for some time, or borrow it from a friend? ...

[ ] Successful teams have integrity ...

[ ] Key question for our venture: What have we learned from early versions of our products or services? ...

[ ] "Yes, and..." not "Yes, but..." ... it's not how we can pick apart someone else's idea, it's how we help them mold it and grow it and make it better ... [Thank you, Bernie Saboe]

[ ] Price is more than money ... the price includes convenience, related expenses, et al. Customers will often look beyond the posted price and consider their other expenses as well before purchasing from us or from our competition ...

[ ] Time heals all wounds ...

[ ] Our efforts and attitudes are everything ... [Thank you, Reid Wilson]

[ ] Those who succeed are those who have been given opportunities and have the strength and presence of mind to seize them ... [Thank you, Malcolm Gladwell]

[ ] Promote our venture with bulletin board signs ...

[ ] Innovators are often good at art ...

[ ] Don't go mountain climbing over mole hills ...

[ ] Cost of Sales: the carrying value of goods sold during a particular period ...

[ ] Fuzzy or Firm ... what should we focus on today? ...

[ ] Often we have to rely on our intuition ... [Thank you, Bill Gates]

[ ] Time doesn't change things ... we have to do the changing ourselves ...

[ ] WAG: abbreviation for Wild Ass Guess ...

[ ] Indecision is often worse than the wrong action ... [Thank you, Gerald R Ford]

[ ] Never live a quiet ordinary life ...

[ ] If we can't say something good, don't say anything at all ...

[ ] Key question for our venture: How much of a stock option pool is being set aside for employees? ...

[ ] People don't like to be sold, but they do like to buy!

[ ] Nobody roots for Goliath ... but they don't necessarily buy from David, either!

[ ] Finish what we start ...

[ ] Deliver more than we promise ...

[ ] Promote our venture with free information ...

[ ] Rent instead of buy ...

[ ] If we don't tell them ... they won't know ...

[ ] Become a little more expert ... [Thank you, Bill Murphy, Jr]

[ ] Mental Error: "People can have the Model T in any color they want, as long as it's black." ... oh, we've come a long way since Henry Ford was around! ... [Thank you, Henry Ford]

[ ] The problem with beauty is that it's like being born rich and getting poorer ... [Thank you, Joan Collins]

[ ] Controlling waste is like bailing a boat ... we have to keep at it! ... [Thank you, Lyndon Johnson]

[ ] Healthy, wealthy, and wise ... two outta three ain't bad, but nothing beats a trifecta ... 1, 3, 2, in that order ...

[ ] Confirm commitments ... then do them ...

[ ] Grant: a sum of money given to an organization for a particular purpose and not requiring repayment.

[ ] Learn to unlearn and relearn ...

[ ] A good read: Innovator's Dilemma (Clayton Christensen)

[ ] The defeat of habit by originality overcomes everything ... [Thank you, George Lois]

[ ] There are five forces that define an industry: supplier power, buyer power, the barriers to entry, the threats of substitution, and the degree of rivalry ... [Thank you, Michael Porter]

[ ] Communications is critical ...

[ ] Toto, I don't think we're in Kansas anymore ... so where the heck are we and how do we get to where we're going? ... [Thank you, Dorothy]

[ ] Do it big or stay in bed ... [Thank you, Barbara Ann Kipfer]

[ ] Be willing to change the way we play the game ... even if we're at the top of our league ...nothing lasts forever ...

[ ] If it doesn't fit, try on something else ... it it still doesn't fit, try a different style ...

[ ] We are not in a position in which we have nothing to work with ... we already have capacities, talents, direction, missions, callings ... [Thank you, Abraham Maslow]

[ ] Just because a rose smells better than a cabbage doesn't mean it will make better soup ... [Thank you, H L Mencken]

[ ] Science can amuse and fascinate us all, but it is engineering that changes the world ... [Thank you, Isaac Asimov]

[ ] What we have here is a failure to communicate ... how can we assure our customers will "get it" when we introduce a new product, service, or process? ... [Thank you, Strother Martin]

[ ] Potential venture legal issue: Waiting to consider international intellectual property protection ... [Thank you, Connie Bagley]

[ ] Circumstances are the instruments of the wise ...

[ ] Today will soon become a yesterday, too ... with a little bit of luck, we just might have a tomorrow to start all over again.

[ ] The burden is on us to validate a potential investor is accredited ...

[ ] Promote our venture with bumper stickers ...

[ ] If it doesn't sell, it isn't creative ... [Thank you, David Ogilvy]

[ ] Don't waste time wishing for things we don't have ...

[ ] Problem solving process: Perceive; Define; Analyze; Generate alternative solutions; Evaluate the alternatives; Decide; Implement; Evaluate; Iterate; Do it all over again ...

[ ] Method: a particular form of procedure for accomplishing or approaching something, especially a systematic or established one ...

[ ] Skilled innovators and entrepreneurs are willing to invest in the future ... there is nowhere else to go but the future ...

[ ] Phases of innovation: 1] Preparation; 2] Exploration; 3] Stimulation; 4] Incubation; 5] Illumination; 6] Selection; 7] Planning; 8] Implementation; 9] Evaluation; 10] Iteration ...

[ ] Creativity: the use of imagination or the making of original ideas ...

[ ] Key question for our venture: What are the trends? ...

[ ] Improve our grammar ...

[ ] Follow up promptly ...

[ ] Me or We ... what should we focus on today? ...

[ ] Mission Statement: a statement of the purpose of a venture or organization, and its reason for existing; the mission statement should guide the actions of the organization, spell out its overall goal, provide a path, and guide decision-making ...

[ ] Promote our venture with classified advertising ...

[ ] We cannot spoil a rotten egg ... and we shouldn't try to serve it for breakfast ...

[ ] SMILE when picking a name for a venture, product, or service ... Simple: one easy-to-understand concept ... Meaningful: customer instantly "get it" ... Imagery: visually evocative, creates a mental picture ... Legs: carries the brand, lends itself to wordplay ... Emotional: empowers, entertains, engages, enlightens ... [Thank you, Wall Street Journal]

[ ] Lead, follow, or get out of the way ... [Thank you, Ted Turner]

[ ] Say what we want and they won't care ... say what they want and they will ...

[ ] People are naturally suspicious ... they seek to avoid risk ... back up claims with evidence, testimonials, survey results, endorsements, test results, scientific data ... [Thank you, Dean Rieck]

[ ] Get regular feedback ...

[ ] Key question for our venture: Are other new ventures likely to enter this industry or our market, and why? ...

[ ] We often ask for advice when we already know the answer but wish we didn't ...

[ ] Successful entrepreneurs are team-oriented ... [Thank you, Timothy Butler]

[ ] If we want the rainbow, we gotta put up with the rain ... [Thank you, Dolly Parton]

[ ] To be is to do, to do is to be ... do be do be do ... [Thank you, Socrates, Sartre, and Sinatra]

[ ] It is better to solve problems than crises ... [Thank you, John Guinther]

[ ] Competition: relationship in which two parties compete to gain customers ...

[ ] Promote our venture with talks and presentations ...

[ ] It's not work, unless we'd rather be doing something else ... [Thank you, James Barrie]

[ ] Perfection is not attainable, but if we chase perfection we can catch excellence ... [Thank you, Vince Lombardi]

[ ] Scope: the extent of the area that a venture deals with or to which it is relevant ...

[ ] A source of opportunity for innovation is change in industry structure or market structure that catches everyone unaware ... [Thank you, Peter F Drucker]

[ ] A good business plan shows how investors can cash out in three to seven years, with an appropriate return on their investment ... [Thank you, Sandy Klausa]

[ ] CAGR: abbreviation for compound annual growth rate ...

[ ] Key question for our venture: What is our specific strategy for success? ...

[ ] Let us be thankful for the fools ... but for them, the rest of us could not succeed! ... [Thank you, Mark Twain]

[ ] Trivial matters take up more time because we know more about them than important matters ... [Thank you, Ed Steiner]

[ ] It is a characteristic of wisdom not to do desperate things ... [Thank you, Henry David Thoreau]

[ ] Creative people start with what they already have ... they start by putting it together in new and different ways and see what happens ... [Thank you, Christopher P Neck]

[ ] Do not follow where the path may lead ... go instead where there is no path and leave a trail ... [Thank you, Robert Frost]

[ ] Key question for our venture: Does our ad hold viewer/reader/listener interest? ...

[ ] Go on a venture adventure ...

[ ] Successful teams have members that get along with each other ...

[ ] Four basic steps of idea multiplication: 1) Gather stimuli (Beware the leading question), 2) Multiply stimuli (Build upon the input of others), 3) Create customer concepts (Build prototypes), and 4) Optimize practicality (Add/remove features) ... [Thank you, William Bygrave]

[ ] We can tell if we get butterflies ... and we will ... it's how we handle them that will make us great, or not ...

[ ] Promise less, deliver more ...

[ ] Stay away from wicked people ... [Thank you, King Solomon]

[ ] Logic and common sense can sometimes deter creativity ... sometimes wild and crazy rule!

[ ] The rearview mirror is always cleaner than the windshield ... [Thank you, Warren Buffett]

[ ] Skilled innovators and entrepreneurs need feedback on a regular basis ...

[ ] The highest entrepreneurship rates generally occur among 25-34 year olds ... [Thank you, Andrew Corbett]

[ ] How to kill creativity: "We don't have resources ... "

[ ] Everything is always in state of flux ... including (or especially) the status quo! ... [Thank you, Robert Byrne]

[ ] A Beta version of a new product is one that is starting to look nice; it a version that we're not afraid to show it to some of our friendly customers for feedback ...

[ ] Be eccentric ... to a point!

[ ] Skilled innovators and entrepreneurs are able to synthesize or combine ...

[ ] In journalism, it takes three events of a similar nature to constitute a trend ... but in this wilderness called the internet all we really seem to need is two, if that! ... [Thank you, Todd Hill]

[ ] Immediate gratification isn't fast enough!

[ ] Much of what we learn is by trial and error ...

[ ] Now or Never ... what should we focus on today? ...

[ ] Key question for our venture: Who are our primary competitors? ... make a list ...

[ ] Circumstances: an event or fact that causes or helps to cause something to happen ... [Thank you, Google Dictionary]

[ ] Renovation innovation ... tear down the old to make room for the new and better ...

[ ] How can we answer this Question: Is there significant market potential for our products and services? ...

[ ] Don't ask ourselves what the world needs; ask what makes us come alive ... then let's go out and do that, because what the world needs is people who are alive ... [Thank you, Howard Thurman]

[ ] Choose the right investors ... it isn't just the money, it's the relationship ...

[ ] Right brain thinking: creativity at work ...

[ ] Don't promise more than we can deliver ... but deliver more than we promised!

[ ] Give a little, take a little ...

[ ] There is a remedy for everything, except death ...

[ ] We rather than me ... [Thank you, Charles Garfield]

[ ] The main thing is to keep the main thing the main thing ... [Thank you, Stephen R Covey]

[ ] The greatest compliment that was ever paid me was when someone asked me what I thought, and actually paid attention to my answer ... [Thank you, Henry David Thoreau]

[ ] Reiterate, restate, recap, rerun, repeat ... keep our message in front of our customers ...

[ ] No amount of money can cure an unhappy mind ...

[ ] Too many fingers spoil the pie ... but not too many blueberries; can never have too many blueberries in the pie ... [Thank you, Martha Novy]

[ ] Anybody can cut prices ... it takes brains to make a better value ... [Thank you, Alice Hubbard]

[ ] Creative people tolerate the unknowable ... [Thank you, Emma L Murray]

[ ] Stick to our aims to accomplish our goals ...

[ ] How to kill creativity: "I don't like it ..." ...

[ ] The truth pulls no punches ... sometimes it hits very hard, too ... [Thank you, New York Times]

[ ] Successful innovators and entrepreneurs know how to network with others ... [Thank you, Candida G Brush]

[ ] Make a wish list ... then go do them!

[ ] Change our minds when we know we must ...

[ ] Snap, Crackle, Pop ... three of the best product mascots ever! ... [Thank you, Kellogg's]

[ ] Key question for our venture: Do we have the skills, passion, and luck that it will take to make this venture survive and thrive? ...

[ ] The most successful companies are nimble, aggressive, adaptable, speedy, and innovative ... they don't just welcome change, they make change happen ... [Thank you, Richard Branson]

[ ] Optimism is medicinal ... and contagious!

[ ] A good business plan focuses on market-driven opportunities ... [Thank you, OneBlock]

[ ] Do what we cannot do in order to learn how to do it ... [Thank you, Pablo Picasso]

[ ] When we thoroughly enjoy what we're doing, we'll thoroughly enjoy what we're doing ...

[ ] Give ourselves plenty of time to play ...

[ ] Characteristics of successful entrepreneurs ... dreamers, decisive, do-ers, determined, dedicated, devoted, detail-oriented, destiny, dollars, distributive ... [Thank you, Andrew Zacharakis]

[ ] Admit misteaks ... (Ok, ok, so I misspelled mistakes!)

[ ] Discuss ...

[ ] What we are thinking about, we are becoming ... is it good, is it bad, is it ugly, is it wonderful? ...

[ ] Life is not a dress rehearsal ... [Thank you, Howard Lester]

[ ] Have an agenda ...

[ ] A leader leads by example, not by force ... [Thank you, Sun Tzu]

[ ] Key question for our venture: What is the scope of products and activities for our venture? ...

[ ] Keep helpful advice ... get rid of the rest ...

[ ] Pay our bills on time ... keep our vendors happy and they'll do extra nice things for us!

[ ] When branding our venture, keep it simple and memorable!

[ ] Customer problems are our friends ... problems are opportunities if only we see them so ...

[ ] Promote our venture with magnetic holders ...

[ ] There are two kinds of people: those who finish what they start and so on ... [Thank you, Robert Byrne]

[ ] Do not confuse motion and progress ... a rocking horse keeps moving but does not make any progress. ... [Thank you, Alfred A Montapert]

[ ] Founder Funding: funding for a venture that comes from the venture founders ...

[ ] When we're up to our nose, keep our mouth shut ... [Thank you, Henry Fonda]

[ ] The truth doesn't take sides ... [Thank you, New York Times]

[ ] Open our eyes, open our ears, don't open our mouth ...

[ ] Be ruthless when proofreading ... cut whatever you can ... [Thank you, Randy Accetta]

[ ] Key question for our venture: What key intellectual property does our venture have (patents, patents pending, copyrights, trade secrets, trademarks, domain names)? ...

[ ] It seems most people want the facts to fit the preconceptions ... when they don't, it is easier to ignore the facts than to change the preconceptions ... [Thank you, Jessamyn West]

[ ] People gossip about things they are interested in ... let's make them interested in us ...

[ ] 90/10 Rule ... it's sort of like the 80/20 Rule except more pronounced. One example is what many angel investors say about their investments ... no significant payoff 9 times out of 10, but the one that does pay off may well be a doozy!

[ ] They say the world has become too complex for simple answers ... they are wrong ... [Thank you, Ronald Reagan]

[ ] Promises, schedules, and estimates are important instruments in a well-run business ... [Thank you, William H Swanson]

[ ] Start off every day with a smile ... and get it over with! ... [Thank you, W C Fields]

[ ] In Hollywood, nothing beats cute animals ... [Thank you, Ken Bensinger]

[ ] Dreaming permits each and every one of us to be quietly and safely insane every night of our lives ... [Thank you, William C Dement]

[ ] Match our solutions to our markets ...

[ ] Celebrate progress ... even the baby steps ...

[ ] I-T-O: abbreviation for Inputs-Transformation-Outputs ... that's what an organization does ... it takes inputs and transforms them into outputs ...

[ ] Knowing how to find knowledge is a critical skill ...

[ ] Skilled innovators and entrepreneurs are self-sufficient ...

[ ] Make our house a home ... warm, comfortable, easy, friendly, cozy ... make our customer guests feel welcome ...

[ ] Give them something extra ... (A sandwich shop I like always includes a free chocolate chip cookie with every sandwich, a little bonus for the customer) ...

[ ] Creativity, challenge, control, cash, and celebrity ... the motivators for innovators and entrepreneurs ...

[ ] How to kill creativity: "It's not my job ..."

[ ] Co-creation: new product concepts are 'co-created' with target customers ...

[ ] Height ...

[ ] EBITDA: abbreviation for Earnings Before Interest, Taxes, Depreciation, and Amortization ...

[ ] Make customer service an integral part of our venture ...

[ ] Look for the circumstances we want ...

[ ] Develop new products for the same markets, develop new markets for the same products, but don't do both at once ...

[ ] Kind words can be short and easy to speak ...

[ ] It is useless to be a creative, original thinker, unless we can also sell what we create ... [Thank you, David Ogilvy]

[ ] Sometimes we're the dog ... sometimes we're the hydrant ...

[ ] People are always looking for something ... love ... wealth ... glory ... comfort ... safety ... show how our particular product, service, or cause fulfills one or more of their needs, wants, or desires ... [Thank you, Dean Rieck]

[ ] Key question for our venture: What are the features, functions, and forms of our solution, and how do they fit our customers? ...

[ ] Successful teams are inspirational ... yes we can, together ...

[ ] Do not count our chickens before they hatch ... but we can set some objectives for how many we want to hatch, and when ...

[ ] Promote our venture with videos ...

[ ] It's not over until it's over ...

[ ] Find inspiration wherever we are ...

[ ] Experienced mentors can help us effectively and efficiently move our venture concept through the research,

ideation, test, and planning stages to resourcing, launch, stability, sustainability, and growth ...

[ ] Promote our venture with take-one racks ...

[ ] Skilled innovators and entrepreneurs possess a sense of urgency ...

[ ] We will never stub our toes standing still ... the faster we go, the more chance we'll stub our toes, but the more chance we have of getting somewhere! ... [Thank you, Charles Kettering]

[ ] Work with the best ...

[ ] Every why has a why not ...

[ ] Beware of what we wish for ... we may well get it, and then what? ...

[ ] Give them something special ... a little reward for our customers just for being our customers ...

[ ] Short and sweet, succinct and neat ...

[ ] Give them something to talk about ... [Thank you, Jim Koch via David Molite]

[ ] Patent: a grant by the United States federal government or a foreign government to an entity (individual inventor, company or organization) giving the entity the exclusive right to produce and sell an invention for a given period of time ...

[ ] Build morale, encourage teamwork, create enthusiasm, lead!

[ ] The truth can't be glossed over ... [Thank you, New York Times]

[ ] There is nothing either good or bad, but thinking makes it so ... [Thank you, Anne Hathaway's husband]

5280 TIPS for INNOVATORS and ENTREPRENEURS

[ ] Skilled innovators and entrepreneurs are self-confident ...

[ ] Everyone has 168 hours per week, no less, no more ... what are we going to do with the time we've got? ...

[ ] Keep a daily log of our venture adventure together ...

[ ] Skilled innovators and entrepreneurs are good at timing ...

[ ] E-nnovations are new things electronically-based ... (I love made-up words!) ...

[ ] Don't just be the best of the best, be the only ones who do what we do ... [Thank you, Jerry Garcia]

[ ] It's five o'clock somewhere ... if the time is not right where we are, let's go somewhere where it is ... [Thank you, Jimmy Buffett]

[ ] Don't just be a better game in town, be the only game in town ... take the competition out of play ...

[ ] It takes $10 of revenue to put $1 on the bottom line ... 10% earnings is not atypical, but we can do better!

[ ] There are two ways to achieve change ... through crisis or through leadership ...

[ ] Promote our venture with local cable ...

[ ] It's easier to ask forgiveness than it is to get permission ... [Thank you, Grace Hopper]

[ ] The past can only be re-lived in the mind, not undone ... the past does not exist, but only in our memories ...

[ ] Promote our venture with decals ...

[ ] People look for value ... [Thank you, Dean Rieck]

[ ] Key question for our venture: What else do we have to do?

[ ] Always keep our word ...

[ ] Typical new venture business plans are from 15 to 35 pages in length ...

[ ] Be open to constructive criticism ...

[ ] Common evaluation criteria for new concept selection: market (size, growth, drivers, access, potential share); competency (business infrastructure, customer familiarity, core competencies); competitive issues (proprietary position, leadership position, cost position, key competitive advantages, sustainability of position); time factors (sales cycle, first mover or fast mover, time to break-even); technology (availability, readiness, skill base); financial (potential income, break-even, upside potential) ... [Thank you, P A Koen]

[ ] Politics is the art of looking for trouble, finding it everywhere, diagnosing it incorrectly, and applying the wrong remedies ... [Thank you, Groucho Marx]

[ ] Sit up straight ... we're no slouches!

[ ] Pleasure or Pain ... what should we focus on today? ...

[ ] Promote our venture with free calendars ... what could be finer than to have our customers look at our logo every day of the year ...

[ ] Entrepreneurs create new technology, products, processes, and services that become the next wave of new industries ... [Thank you, Jeffry A Timmons]

[ ] In the beginning, an innovator created something new and better ...

[ ] When in the vicinity of any microphone, whether it's a lavaliere, a handheld, or a boom, always assume it's "hot" ... [Thank you, Jesse Jackson]

[ ] Action Item: something that needs to be accomplished ...

[ ] Evaluate and accommodate ...

[ ] It's everyone's job to innovate ...

[ ] There's a great future in plastics ... Think about it. Will you think about it? ... [Thank you, Mr McGuire]

[ ] Bootstrap: launch and build a startup business without using outside funding ...

[ ] Beware strangers with candy ... remember what we learned about talking to strangers!

[ ] A venture operations manual becomes a training tool for employees ...

[ ] Being a corporate entrepreneur is like standing on a street corner in Gila Bend, Arizona wearing six layers of wool clothing in the middle of summer ... hot as all get out, but we're having fun!

[ ] The easy stuff doesn't teach us much ...

[ ] Common bootstrapping strategy: be own accountant ...

[ ] Listen ... carefully!

[ ] Any plan is bad which is not susceptible to change ... [Thank you, Bartolomeo da San Concordio]

[ ] Mistakes lead little by little to the truth ... [Thank you, Jules Verne]

[ ] Surround ourselves with beauty ...

[ ] Slay a beautiful hypothesis with ugly facts ... [Thank you, Thomas H Huxley]

[ ] Key question for our venture: Compared to our competition, how do we compete with respect to price and benefits? ...

[ ] Key question for our venture: Do we think our venture has high growth potential? ... Why? ...

[ ] Wonder or Thunder ... what should we focus on today? ...

[ ] Innovators and entrepreneurs should have experience in their venture industry or a similar one ... [Thank you, Andrew Corbett]

[ ] Key question for our venture: What big problem does our venture solve? ...

[ ] Put our new ideas to work ...

[ ] Angels ... or devils in disguise? ...

[ ] If we're coasting, we're going downhill ...

[ ] A good business plan is more quantitative than qualitative ... [Thank you, LOOP]

[ ] If we want to catch fish, we can't mind getting wet ...

[ ] Own each day ...

[ ] Types of customers ... the user, influencer, recommender, buyer, decision maker, saboteur ...

[ ] Make or break? ... what should we focus on today? ...

[ ] Promote our venture with multiple purchase offers ...

[ ] The only people who never experience failure are those who are not pushing the envelope of what mankind is capable of doing ... [Thank you, John Preston]

[ ] Potential venture legal issue: Thinking any legal problems can be solved later ... [Thank you, Connie Bagley]

[ ] A majority of entrepreneurs developed their ideas within the field or industry in which they were working prior to starting the new business ... [Thank you, William Bygrave]

[ ] Seeing is believing ... let's make sure our customers see what we want them to believe ...

[ ] Opportunity is missed by most people because it looks like work ... [Thank you, Thomas A Edison]

[ ] Many new venture startup management teams consist of three key people ... the general manager (administration, money, general health of the venture) ... the innovator (new product and service development, operations) ... the entrepreneur (marketing, sales, customer relationships, problems and solutions) ...

[ ] Nothing takes the place of persistence and determination ... [Thank you, Calvin Coolidge]

[ ] Plans get us into things ... but we have to work our way out ... [Thank you, Will Rogers]

[ ] Be ourselves ... everyone else is already taken ... [Thank you, Oscar Wilde]

[ ] Potential venture legal issue: Negotiating venture capital financing based solely on the valuation ... [Thank you, Connie Bagley]

[ ] Beware that the remedy might be worse than the disease ... [Thank you, Francis Bacon]

[ ] AIDA ... An acronym for Attention, Interest, Desire, Action ... a short checklist for evaluating communications ...

[ ] A chain is no stronger than its weakest link ...

[ ] Choose the right angels ... don't just jump because someone says they have money ... make sure they have a good

understanding of what we want to do and the tolerance to go for the ride with us ... the top is down and they're going to get their hair messed up ...

[ ] The next move is always ours ... [Thank you, Forbes]

[ ] Beware: lots of talk, not much walk ... amazing how many "experts" have little if any expertise ... before we hitch our wagon, let's make sure the ass has been there before and knows the way to and fro ...

[ ] Label things so we all know what they are ...

[ ] Don't burn bridges ... we might need them for a retreat ...

[ ] Not every new idea needs our personal input ...

[ ] Skilled innovators and entrepreneurs are good communicators ...

[ ] Entrepreneurial Myth: Startups can't be financed with debt ... actually, debt is more common than equity ... [Thank you, Scott Shane]

[ ] Even old bodies can have young minds ...

[ ] Simple is good ... very good ... yes, very good indeed!

[ ] Creativity comes in waves ... when it comes, surf!

[ ] How to improve our financial bottom line: change suppliers ...

[ ] Effective: successful in producing a desired result ...

[ ] Integrity is all we've got ... [Thank you, Karl Eller]

[ ] We never know for sure ... we just have to go with what we know ...

[ ] Four domains of leadership: strategic thinking, relationship building, influencing, executing ... [Thank you, Gallup]

[ ] TEAM: Together Everyone Achieves More ...

[ ] We are in control ... even if we're backwards on the horse, grab the tail and pull real hard ...

[ ] Until we actually do, many may think we can't ... fie on them!

[ ] Save costs where they matter the most ... save money by improving quality ...

[ ] Do our homework ... get as many right answers as we can before the big test comes ...

[ ] Clear: easy to perceive, understand, or interpret ...

[ ] Corporate entrepreneur credo: Come to work each day willing to be fired ... [Thank you, Gifford Pinchot III]

[ ] As long as we can start, we're all right ... [Thank you, Ernest Hemingway]

[ ] And that's the way it is ... but is that the way we want it to be? Tomorrow is another day ... [Thank you, Walter Cronkite]

[ ] Every firm's business model consists of two base components; a revenue model and a cost model ... [Thank you, Andrew Corbett]

[ ] Create multiple paths to success ... [Thank you, Doug Goodman]

[ ] Anyone can say anything, doesn't make it true ... we need to be careful about what we do and don't believe ...

[ ] Skilled innovators and entrepreneurs are charismatic ...

[ ] Key question for our venture: Who are our customers? ... Where are they? When do they want to shop? What do they need, want, desire? Why should they buy from us? How are we going to capture their business? ...

[ ] The fewer the choices, the quicker the decision ... the quicker the decision, the more likely the sale ...

[ ] Energy, knowledge, and persistence conquers all ... [Thank you, Benjamin Franklin]

[ ] Ask, listen, and observe ...

[ ] Don't do anything we don't understand ... if we really think we need to do it, let's make sure we understand how to do it right ...

[ ] Identify our strongest strength ... go with it ...

[ ] Pivot: structured course correction designed to test a new fundamental hypothesis about the product, strategy, and engine of growth ...

[ ] Choose the right VC ...

[ ] Product development is about adding value to the product ... marketing is about adding perceived value ... [Thank you, James Latham]

[ ] Life is a little of this and a little of that ... sometimes too little of this and too much of that ...

[ ] Know or Need to Know ... what should we focus on today?

[ ] Industry: the aggregate of manufacturing or technically productive enterprises in a particular field, often named after its principal product: the software industry ...

[ ] Excellence is to do a common thing in an uncommon way ... [Thank you, Booker T Washington]

[ ] Necessity-driven entrepreneurs are those who are pushed into starting businesses because they have no other work options and need a source of income ... [Thank you, Andrew Zacharakis]

[ ] Talk low, talk slow, and don't talk too much ... [Thank you, John Wayne]

[ ] The wrong name and it's soon forgotten ... the right name can do no wrong ...

[ ] If people aren't talking about our products and services and processes, they're not good enough ...

[ ] Do what we do better ... our aim is always high, to be better than anyone else at what we know best ...

[ ] How to retain customers: offer rewards for continuing purchases ...

[ ] Collaborate and communicate ... the basis of a solid team.

[ ] Promote our venture with balloons ...

[ ] Have fun doing it ... or live a long and boring life ...

[ ] The longer it takes to make a sale, the less likely we'll be able to make the sale ...

[ ] The commercialization process is not linear ... it moves more like the balls in a pinball machine, taking off in one direction until it hits a snag, then bouncing off in another direction ... this chaotic process continues until the technology or venture either goes to market or fails ... [Thank you, Kathleen Allen]

[ ] A source of opportunity for innovation is demographic and population changes ... [Thank you, Peter F Drucker]

[ ] In school, we're taught a lesson and then given a test ... in life, we're given a test that teaches us a lesson ... [Thank you, Tom Bodett]

[ ] List the things we need, and need to do ...

[ ] We are all explorers, each sailing out on a voyage of discovery, guided each by a private chart, of which there is no duplicate ... the world is all gates, all opportunities! ... [Thank you, Ralph Waldo Emerson]

[ ] The things which hurt, instruct ... [Thank you, Benjamin Franklin]

[ ] We gotta get out there and learn ...

[ ] Skilled innovators and entrepreneurs take pride in what they do ...

[ ] Speed is useful only if we're pointed in the right direction ... [Thank you, Joel Barker]

[ ] "New! Improved!" (box) ... the Tide is not new and improved, but the box it comes in is ...

[ ] Avoid the concrete promise and cultivate the delightfully vague ...

[ ] The only limit to our realizations of tomorrow are our doubts of today ... [Thank you, Franklin Delano Roosevelt]

[ ] Ask followup questions ... not likely to get a full answer with a first question ...

[ ] Promote our venture with searchlights ...

[ ] Be self-starters ...

[ ] Never give up our right to be wrong ...

[ ] Do not do what already exists, it is already done ... either do it a whole bunch better, or don't do it at all ...

[ ] Key question for our venture: Why are we here? ... sad answer if it's because there's nowhere else to go ...

[ ] If we don't say it, they can't repeat it ... [Thank you, Wilbur C Munnecke]

[ ] Newco: a common placeholder name for a new venture ... Newco is a combination of "new" and "company" ...

[ ] It could be a good opportunity if the risks can be mitigated.

[ ] Experience creates knowledge ... knowledge creates new experiences ...

[ ] Don't assume we know the answer ... ass u me ...

[ ] Key question for our venture: What are the major threats to a new entrant in our industry? ...

[ ] Learning can be a significant competitive advantage ...

[ ] Dream as big as we can dream ... we can always chop it into little bits later ... [Thank you, Michael Phelps]

[ ] Mistakes happen ... it's how we handle them that matters.

[ ] The odds of creating the next "big thing" are about 14,354 to 1 ... more like getting hit by lightning or winning the lottery! ... [Thank you, Loveable Pliable Statistics]

[ ] Common cause of venture death: lack of passion to succeed ...

[ ] Raising money is a waste of time ... it's time away from running and growing the venture ... not that money doesn't have to be obtained, it's just that the actual process of raising money is not advancing the venture, per se ... [Thank you, Tom Brown]

[ ] Brand happens ... customer experiences create the perceptions that form a brand image in customer minds ... [Thank you, Leslie Bromberg]

[ ] Beware: one-dimensional investors ... if an investor isn't willing or able to discuss all aspect of the venture, they aren't likely to be willing or able to contribute to its success ...

[ ] Call old friends ...

[ ] It takes perseverance ... venture building is not an easy task ...

[ ] We are what we eat ...

[ ] The emotional tail wags the rational dog ... explains why some customers buy things that really don't make much sense ... [Thank you, Jonathan Haidt]

[ ] Resisting change has a price ... is it worth it? ...

[ ] Complete three simple tasks every day ... break down complex tasks into simple, logical steps ... dedicate ourselves to completing 3 simple steps everyday that bring us closer to our goal ... it may only be 3 steps today, but we'll complete 21 steps by this time next week and 84 steps by this time next month ... the more we get done, the faster we'll go, the easier it will get, and the closer we will be to our desired end result ... [Thank you, Marc & Angel]

[ ] We must shift our sail with the wind ... where are our customers going now? ...

[ ] Plant our roots deep ...

[ ] Exercise: Describe 10 new potential market segments for our venture and its products and services ...

[ ] Find out what people are willing and able to pay for, then give it to them ...

[ ] A new product usually starts with a prototype, then an alpha version, next a beta version, and finally the first public release (version 1.0) ...

[ ] Keep our heads up and give a big smile ... [Thank you, George W Bush]

[ ] Promote our venture with package inserts ...

[ ] If it moves, tax it; if it keeps moving, regulate it; if it stops moving, subsidize it ... [Thank you, Politicians Everywhere]

[ ] Key question for our venture: What are the two or three key features we plan to add in the next 3 months? ... how about the next six months? ...

[ ] Letter of Intent: a brief, temporary, pre-contract document between two or more entities that outlines the parties' intention regarding a future contractual or business arrangement ...

[ ] Share profits with everyone on our team ... make everyone responsible for success ...

[ ] Promote our venture with tours ...

[ ] 72.6% of all statistics are made up ... ok, ok, so maybe a bit of an overstatement ... the point here is that statistics can be readily manipulated ... let's make sure they accurate for our use ... (I once saw an entrepreneur tell his potential investor audience that 1% of the population was affected by a particular issue. For his particular product, that was a very large number and his product could be very successful serving that size market. Problem was, the real number was 0.01% ... but the spreadsheet program he was using had converted his raw 0.01 entry to 1.0% when he changed the units on the spreadsheet cell from raw number to percentage. Yes, his

actual market was 0.01% ... 1/100th of what his venture plan had detailed! It was not a feasible venture! Beware, statistics!)

[ ] Remove or bypass the barriers to our success ... if there's a wall, dig a tunnel ...

[ ] Eight ways to expand globally: Technology Transfer (joint venture, Technology Licensing, Outsourcing, Exporting, Foreign Direct Investment (FDI), Franchising, Venture financing, Mergers and acquisitions (M&A) ... [Thank you, Andrew Zacharakis]

[ ] Create a better business model ...

[ ] How to build an elevator pitch ... figure out what is unique about what we do, make it exciting, keep it short and simple, write it down, then practice and practice some more ... [Thank you, Steve Strauss]

[ ] Failures are divided into two classes ... those who thought and never did, and those who did and never thought ... [Thank you, John Salak]

[ ] We cannot be smarter than everyone ... but it helps if we're smarter than someone!

[ ] Always do our best ...

[ ] Build a solid team ...

[ ] Encourage word-of-mouth ... give rewards for referrals ...

[ ] One data point does not make a trend ...

[ ] Make change happen ...

[ ] Customers will tell us one thing, then do another ...

[ ] Promote our venture with product exhibitions ...

[ ] What would you regret not having tried? ... [Thank you, Frederic Premji]

[ ] Leadership is the heart and soul of business management ... [Thank you, Harold Geneen]

[ ] People rise to their level of incompetence ... [Thank you, Laurence J Peter]

[ ] A good listener is popular everywhere ...

[ ] Never discuss employee matters with their co-workers ...

[ ] It is better to be roughly right than to be precisely wrong ... [Thank you, John Maynard Keynes]

[ ] A single thought can revolutionize our lives ... evolutionize our strife!

[ ] Put old information first, new information second ... [Thank you, Randy Accetta]

[ ] Promote our venture with on-line computer services ...

[ ] We must be willing to lose a battle in order to win the war ...

[ ] In skating over thin ice, our safety is in our speed ... [Thank you, Ralph Waldo Emerson]

[ ] Skilled innovators and entrepreneurs are willing to take a chance ...

[ ] Product diffusion curve ... innovators, early adopters, early majority, late majority, and laggards ...

[ ] Chance happens ... get ready, or not ...

[ ] Make someone feel good ... what goes around comes around ...

[ ] Snowflakes are one of nature's most fragile things ... but just look what they can do when they stick together ... [Thank you, Vesta M Kelly]

[ ] Start where we're most likely to succeed ...

[ ] It's not just what we've got, it's what we do with what we've got ... [Thank you, Rhonda Abrams]

[ ] A good business plan provides a clear, rational explanation of why the venture concept is better than anything else already available ... [Thank you, University of Oregon Colleagues]

[ ] Knowledge: facts, education, skills, experience ...

[ ] The way to make a friend is to be one ... [Thank you, Dale Carnegie]

[ ] The difference between the right word and the almost right word is the difference between lightning and the lightning bug ... [Thank you, Mark Twain]

[ ] When the going gets tough, the tough get going ...

[ ] Successful teams coordinate activities ...

[ ] Do onto our customers before our competition does ...

[ ] Lazy people get bored ...

[ ] Take the initiative ...

[ ] Better a good conscience without wisdom than wisdom without a good conscience ... ethics over money ...

[ ] Focus on customers that must have our types of products and services ...

[ ] Like seeks like ... dislike doesn't care ...

[ ] The Devil's Advocate is toxic ... encouraging idea-wreckers to see only the downside, to smother a fragile new idea in negativity ... [Thank you, Tom Kelly]

[ ] Skilled innovators and entrepreneurs are able to build new structures ...

[ ] Good or Bad ... what should we focus on today? ...

[ ] Presume that anything we put on the internet will be out there forever and ever, whether we want it to be or not ...

[ ] Reward success ...

[ ] Identify obstacles and knock them down ...

[ ] Confidence begets confidence ...

[ ] Served Available Market or Serviceable Available Market (SAM): the part of the total addressable market (TAM) that can actually be reached ...

[ ] Let us be guided by the vision of what our venture can become ...

[ ] Have a clear vision ... if it's not, maybe time to clean our glasses ...

[ ] The truth isn't red or blue ... [Thank you, New York Times]

[ ] Equity creation and realization determine the payoff ...

[ ] SAVE marketing framework: instead of product, think Solution; instead of place, think Access: instead of price, think Value: instead of promotion, think Education ... the P's of marketing made better ... [Thank you, Christopher P Neck]

[ ] Fast or slow ... which way to go? ...

[ ] Cash: money that is immediately available ... [Thank you, Google Dictionary]

[ ] We can't control the weather ... but we can dress appropriately!

[ ] Customer needs, wants, and desires ... the pain-pleasure spectrum!

[ ] Key question for our venture: What percentage of the market do we plan to get over what period of time? ...

[ ] Learn from friends and family ...

[ ] Commanding leadership style ... "military" style leadership – probably the most often used, but the least often effective ... [Thank you, Daniel Goleman]

[ ] Skilled innovators and entrepreneurs are bold ...

[ ] Key question for our venture: What strengths do we have in our venture? ...

[ ] We can't just wait for opportunity to knock ... we have to go out and find it and bring it back with us, kicking and screaming if need be!

[ ] Sometimes old methods of dealing with things do work ...

[ ] I-nnovation are new things personally-based ...

[ ] Promote our venture with social media ...

[ ] Think slow ...

[ ] The reason Starbucks became such a sensation is that it's the new "third place" ... the old third places (the pub, the VFW hall, the country club) all had declined in appeal or importance ... Starbucks became that other place, between home and work/school ... [Thank you, Dale Dauten]

[ ] To live a creative life, we must lose our fear of being wrong! ... [Thank you, Joseph C Pearce]

[ ] Beware: Anyone bearing "free" gifts ...

[ ] Integrate data from multiple sources ...

[ ] Facts, opinions, fiction, or propaganda ... what is what we are hearing, seeing, reading? ...

[ ] Remember not only to say the right thing in the right place, but far more difficult still, to leave unsaid the wrong thing at the tempting moment ... [Thank you, Benjamin Franklin]

[ ] Might as well enjoy our present company ...

[ ] Success is never final and failure is seldom fatal ... unless the parachute doesn't open ...

[ ] Meditate ...

[ ] Budget: the amount of money needed or available for a purpose ...

[ ] Smell ... what's it look like? ...

[ ] Multi-tasking is dead ... it never worked and it never will ... intelligent people love to sing its praises because it gives them permission to avoid the much more challenging alternative: focusing on one thing ... [Thank you, Timothy Ferriss]

[ ] Doubt is the key to knowledge ...

[ ] Innovation: something new and better ...

[ ] Innovation is a mashup of many different areas, different specializations ...

[ ] A good business plan gives a clear sense of what the founders expect to accomplish in 3 to 7 years ...

[ ] Key question for our venture: What are the key assumptions underlying our objectives for the future? ...

[ ] A little knowledge is good, a lot is better ... but too much can overwhelm creativity and innovation ...

5280 TIPS for INNOVATORS and ENTREPRENEURS

[ ] Beware: scammers abound ...

[ ] A meeting is an event at which the minutes are kept and the hours are lost ...

[ ] What sunshine is to flowers, smiles are to people ...

[ ] Nurture innovation ...

[ ] Skilled innovators and entrepreneurs are able to observe trends ...

[ ] The going will get tough ... be tougher!

[ ] Skilled innovators and entrepreneurs welcome responsibility ...

[ ] Beware: don't let anyone take grandma's and grandpa's retirement savings money ...

[ ] Will this be important five years from now? ...

[ ] Don't use your teeth to open things ...

[ ] Be open to new ...

[ ] Distrust interested advice ... [Thank you, Aesop]

[ ] Exercise ... body, mind, ethics ...

[ ] Intelligence is not enough ... using it wisely is the key ...

[ ] Nothing is really work unless we would rather be doing something else ... [Thank you, J M Barrie]

[ ] Create a minimum viable product to start, a MAXIMUM VIABLE PRODUCT to grow ...

[ ] My definition of an expert in any field is a person who knows enough about what's really going on to be scared ... [Thank you, P J Plauger]

[ ] Wisdom often consists of knowing what to do next ... and what not to do next ...

[ ] There are risks and costs to a program of action, but they are far less than the long-range risks and costs of comfortable inaction ... [Thank you, John F Kennedy]

[ ] Few people think ... many have opinions ...

[ ] Be flexible ...

[ ] Anyone can have a good idea ... and everyone should!

[ ] Corporate entrepreneur credo: Be loyal and truthful to the sponsor ... [Thank you, Gifford Pinchot III]

[ ] Key question for our venture: Can we promote our venture with community involvement? ...

[ ] Seek the best ... rid the rest ...

[ ] Heavy or Light ... what should we focus on today? ...

[ ] Place: the regular or proper position of something ...

[ ] It's natural to be afraid of something we've never done before, but it's wise to not let that stop us ... [Thank you, Tom Hopkins]

[ ] Customer funding from fan-tastic customers ...

[ ] Each user interaction required on a website landing page is going to cost us 50% of the audience ... [Thank you, Bob Dumouchel]

[ ] There are two types of benefits: 1] objective ... fit, form, function, performance ... 2] subjective ... color, smell, branding ... we need to know which are most important to our customers ...

[ ] Every revolution was first a thought is one person's mind ... [Thank you, Ralph Waldo Emerson]

[ ] Potential venture legal issue: Issuing founder shares without vesting ... [Thank you, Connie Bagley]

[ ] Don't lie, cheat, or steal ...

[ ] Innovation is simply something new and better ... something: product, service, process, method, market ... new: not done before, at least for our target customers ... better: more benefits or a lower price than the competition ...

[ ] It could be a good opportunity if we can develop a significant value proposition ...

[ ] Skilled innovators and entrepreneurs are breaking the boundaries ...

[ ] Skilled innovators and entrepreneurs are independent in thinking ...

[ ] Vision: the ability to think about or plan the future with imagination or wisdom ...

[ ] Do not be afraid of resistance ...

[ ] The purpose of a business plan ... mitigate risk; optimize the odds of success; and chart the shortest path to becoming a healthy, stable venture ...

[ ] Be empathetic to personal problems ... Sometimes what happens outside of work can have a big affect on the quality of work produced. Be sensitive if colleagues have personal issues ... [Thank you, InsideCRM]

[ ] People always call it luck when we have acted more sensibly than they have ... [Thank you, B F Skinner]

[ ] There are exceptions to every rule, suggestion, recommendation ... the trick is knowing which are and aren't the exceptions ...

[ ] Action: the process of doing something ...

[ ] Get some help when we need it ... accountant, lawyer, consultant, domain experts ...

[ ] Feasibility Analysis: an evaluation and analysis of the potential of the proposed project which is based on extensive investigation and research to support the process of decision making ...

[ ] If we refuse to accept anything but the best, we very often get it ... [Thank you, W Somerset Maugham]

[ ] Look out to the future ...

[ ] Everything is important ... some things more than others, yes, but what is not important today may be top of the pile tomorrow ...

[ ] Innovators are often subjective thinkers ...

[ ] Competitors ... can't live with 'em, can't live without 'em!

[ ] Incorporate: to create a new corporation by making a legal filing with the Secretary of State of a given state ...

[ ] Stay professional, not personal ...

[ ] Have a little common sense ...

[ ] Be greedy when people are fearful ... be fearful when people are greedy! ... [Thank you, Warren Buffett]

[ ] Key question for our venture: Who are the target customers for this business venture? ...

[ ] Skilled innovators and entrepreneurs know how to organize ...

[ ] Skilled innovators and entrepreneurs are emotionally stable ...

[ ] Recognition can be more important than dollars ...

[ ] Network: ...

[ ] Don't start until we know how we want it to end ...

[ ] The Fuzzy Front-End is the weakest area of the innovation process ... the work is not structured; revenue expectations are uncertain; funding is usually variable; the work usually results in strengthening a concept, not achieving a planned milestone ... [Thank you, S Boyce]

[ ] Business plan competitions: they're a crap shoot ...

[ ] Successful companies not only create value, they also communicate their uniqueness to customers in credible ways ...

[ ] Key question for our venture: What other notable companies are in this industry? ...

[ ] Skilled innovators and entrepreneurs are able to escape perceptual sets and entrenchments ...

[ ] Inspiration, then perspiration ... it will take some work to make it better ...

[ ] Better have failed in the high aim ... than vulgarly in the low aim succeed ... [Thank you, Robert Browning]

[ ] Count to ten first ... then, and only then, get mad!

[ ] The quality of the wine is inversely proportional to the ferocity of the beast depicted on its label ... [Thank you, Neil Pendock]

[ ] If everything is under control, we're going too slow ... put the pedal to the metal and race to victory ... [Thank you, Mario Andretti]

[ ] Be ready to do business ... whenever our customers are ready to do business with us ... [Thank you, Susan Ward]

[ ] Be accessible ...

[ ] Innovation is like a Ferris Wheel ... it keeps going round and round ...

[ ] Intelligent people make mistakes, too ...

[ ] Maintaining our good character is easier than trying to regain it ...

[ ] Media: Bad news drives good news out of the media ... [Thank you, Lee Loevinger]

[ ] Enterprise: a project or venture, typically one that is difficult or requires effort, initiative, and resourcefulness ...

[ ] Promote our venture with envelope advertisement ...

[ ] We know what we should do, but do we do it? ...

[ ] There are always highs and lows ... get in low, get out high ...

[ ] The Jim Jindrick Critical Success Factor Rule of Thumb: Earn Profits Solving Customer Problems with Something New and Better than the Competition! there may not be a sure-fire formula for success in business, but there is a recipe and this is it ... the results of the recipe depend on the quality of the ingredients that go in and the skills of the cook to put them all together ...

[ ] The consumer is our boss, quality is our work, and value for money is our goal ... [Thank you, Mars Candy Company]

[ ] One gallon of water is needed to extinguish the heat generated by one pound of burning wood ...

[ ] Most active angel investor groups in the US ... Alliance of Angels, Central Texas Angel Network, Desert Angels, Houston Angel Network, Hyde Park Angels, Keiretsu Forum, Launchpad Venture Group, Maine Angels, New York Angels, Sandhill Angels, Tech Coast Angels, Wisconsin Investment Partners ... [Thank you, Angel Resource Institute]

[ ] Death is not the end ... but is an effective way to cut expenses ... [Thank you, Woody Allen]

[ ] Key question for our venture: What advertising will we be doing? ... how much will it cost? ... can we afford it? ...

[ ] If we lose the element of fun at work, we've lost everything ... [Thank you, William Hewlett]

[ ] Build long-term relationships with key suppliers and partners ... [Thank you, Walt Disney]

[ ] Choose our partners carefully ...

[ ] Key question for our venture: What is our primary NAICS number? ...

[ ] The future of work consists of learning a living ... [Thank you, Marshall McLuhan]

[ ] Wisdom means seeing implications and drawing conclusions ...

[ ] Frequency is the number of times a member of our target market is exposed during that time period ... [Thank you, William Bygrave,]

[ ] Expertise: expert skill or knowledge in a particular field ... an expert is a person who has made all the mistakes that can be made in a very narrow field ... [Thank you, Niels Bohr]

[ ] Ethics matter above all ... be honest and reliable in all of our business and personal relationships ... [Thank you, Karl Eller]

[ ] A new venture may be feasible if creating a solution is viable ...

[ ] The measure of success is not whether we have a tough problem to deal with, but whether it's the same problem we had last time ... [Thank you, John Foster Dulles]

[ ] Jim Jindrick Rule of Thumb: We need all the SPLUCK we can get ... SPLUCK (Skills, Passion, LUCK) is a trait commonly shared by most successful innovators and entrepreneurs ...

[ ] Courteous: ensure that our communication is friendly, open, and honest, regardless of what the message is about ... be empathetic and avoid passive-aggressive tones ...

[ ] Consistency requires us to be as ignorant today as we were a year ago!

[ ] Write down our goals ... put them in order ... make them a priority ...

[ ] We all have baggage ... some of us can carry it on and put it in the overhead bin, others need to check it below ...

[ ] Key question for our venture: Can we collaborate rather than compete? ...

[ ] Skilled innovators and entrepreneurs are unwilling to conform ...

[ ] Everyone can contribute something special ... and should ...

[ ] Assume innocence ... allow for mistakes ...

[ ] The nail that sticks up gets hammered down ...

[ ] Pride, greed, lust, envy, gluttony, anger, and sloth ... the Seven Deadly Sins ...

[ ] Past or Present or Future ... what should we focus on today? ...

[ ] Experience is a hard teacher ...

[ ] Discover creative solitude ... sometimes we just have to get away ...

[ ] Smart or Dumb ... what should we focus on today? ...

[ ] Tick-tock, darn that clock!

[ ] How we interpret the data is often more important than the data itself ...

[ ] A good habit is easier to learn than a bad habit is to break ...

[ ] Think for ourselves ...

[ ] Five types of people adopt new products or services, but do so at different times: "innovators" jump first, "early adopters" are close behind, "early majority" buy when they are comfortable with the newness, "late majority" follow the flow, and "laggards" come late to the game ... [Thank you, Everett Rogers]

[ ] Continuously improve our sales skills, learn from others, and stay open to new ideas ...

[ ] Promote our venture with newspaper advertising ...

[ ] While many things change, most things remain constant ... [Thank you, John Naisbitt]

[ ] Pay attention to small details; they are often sources of special opportunities ...

[ ] Act like what we want to be ...

[ ] Corporate entrepreneur credo: Be true to the goals, but be realistic about the ways to achieve them ... [Thank you, Gifford Pinchot III]

[ ] Seek out the opportunity in situations ...

[ ] Many entrepreneurs pick the worst industries for start-ups ... [Thank you, Scott Shane]

[ ] If work was a good thing, the rich would have it all and not let us do it ... [Thank you, Elmore Leonard]

[ ] Success is about growing others ...

[ ] Successful innovators and entrepreneurs are full of energy.

[ ] How to attract new customers: offer free returns and refunds if not satisfied ...

[ ] Primary Research: a collection of original primary data, often undertaken after the researcher has gained some insight into the issue by reviewing secondary research or by analyzing previously collected primary data ...

[ ] The first sentence acts as the headline for what is coming next ... lose the reader right away and the game is over ...

[ ] Skilled innovators and entrepreneurs are attracted to challenges ...

[ ] A good business plan financially justifies the means chosen to sell the products and services ... [Thank you, Medli]

[ ] Don't be afraid to try something new ... we might even like it!

[ ] Beat the snot outta 'em ... our competitors, that is, not our customers!

[ ] What's in it for me? ... Crass as that may be, it is how many (or perhaps even most) customers think. The burden is on us to pre-think how they think and do what we can to let them know how we've got what they need, want, and desire!

[ ] Successful teams maintain control despite extreme pressures ...

[ ] Better to pull up than push down ...

[ ] Don't be left behind ...

[ ] How to kill creativity: "Well, maybe next year ..."

[ ] Sometimes old methods of dealing with things don't work ... and sometimes the new ones don't either!

[ ] Focus on an industry where our team has prior experience with success ...

[ ] We've got to be very careful if we don't know where we're going 'cause we might not get there ... [Thank you, Yogi Berra]

[ ] It might be a company but it's not a business without customers ...

[ ] We are judged not by what we have but by what we do with what we have!

[ ] Stay optimistic ...

[ ] Mentor and be mentored ... collaborate, cooperate ...

[ ] Edit everything we write ...

[ ] Pain does not last forever ... usually ...

[ ] Don't stop praising or thanking ... it costs nothing but aids much value ... [Thank you, A L Williams]

[ ] Promote our venture with magazine advertising ...

[ ] Argue for our limitations and sure enough, they're ours ... [Thank you, Richard Bach]

[ ] We may have a fresh start any moment we choose, for this thing we call failure is not the falling down, but the staying down ... [Thank you, Mary Pickford]

[ ] If we want to grow, we'll need some food and water ...

[ ] Key question for our venture: What advantages does our competition have over us? ... Are they surmountable? ...

5280 TIPS for INNOVATORS and ENTREPRENEURS

[ ] Skilled innovators and entrepreneurs are good at maintaining interpersonal relations ...

[ ] Create crisp, concise, clear, compelling communications ...

[ ] Skilled innovators and entrepreneurs are able to fantasize.

[ ] Tip for creating a good venture plan: Provide three-year forward-looking profit-and-loss, balance sheet, and cash-flow objectives statements ...

[ ] Skilled innovators and entrepreneurs are able to keep options open ...

[ ] God has a sense of humor ... often at our expense!

[ ] Successful teams have a division of tasks that is clear and concise ...

[ ] Some business plans are just based on the Business Model Canvas ... while a reasonable starting point, it usually not deep enough ...

[ ] Reputation is what people say about us, character is what God knows about us ... [Thank you, Bobby Bowden]

[ ] When stocks are down, buy ... they'll go lower ... ignore that ... when stocks are up, sell ... they'll go higher ... ignore that ... apply this rule consistently and make money in the market ... [Thank you, John Rosevear]

[ ] Promote our venture with co-op advertising ...

[ ] Do or Don't ... do what is good, don't do what isn't ... it's that simple ...

[ ] In every decision and action, realize that innovation is critical to our success ... [Thank you, K A Zein]

[ ] Speak with the listener in mind ...

[ ] It wasn't raining when Noah built the arc ... [Thank you, Howard Ruff]

[ ] Anticipating behavior of our competitors can help us sharpen our focus and respond strategically when we are actually challenged ... [Thank you, Kenneth A Sawka]

[ ] An ounce of action is worth a ton of theory ...

[ ] To get along, go along ... [Thank you, Sam Rayburn]

[ ] Education cannot be taken away ...

[ ] Emotional or Rational ... what should we focus on today?

[ ] It's easier to get into something than get out of it ...

[ ] Key question for our venture: Would any prior employers of a team member have a potential claim to our venture's intellectual property? ...

[ ] A schedule defends from chaos and whim ... [Thank you, Annie Dillard]

[ ] Key question for our venture: What strategic opportunities exist in the market? ...

[ ] The Kiss of Death ... "We don't have to do anything new and better and different!" ...

[ ] Domain Knowledge: knowledge about a specific industry, technology and/or market, typically based on extensive experience in that industry or technology arena ...

[ ] Promote our venture with consumer magazines ...

[ ] Skilled innovators and entrepreneurs are imaginative ...

[ ] Corporate Entrepreneurship: the act of initiating new ventures or creating new value with an already established organization or company ...

[ ] Find out what we like doing best ... then get someone to pay us for doing it ...

[ ] Experience: the knowledge or skill acquired over a period of time, especially that gained in a particular profession by someone at work ...

[ ] Efficiency focuses on cost, effectiveness focuses on value ... [Thank you, Roger Kirkham]

[ ] Don't burn our bridges ... we might need them for retreat!

[ ] Common Mistake: lack of comparable business models ... [Thank you, Andrew Zacharakis]

[ ] It is easy to hold the fort when it's not being attacked ...

[ ] Dream with our eyes wide open ...

[ ] It could be a good opportunity if the problem is clear ...

[ ] Don't lose the big picture in the minutiae details ...

[ ] Red flag: a warning of danger or problem ...

[ ] Try really hard ... then try harder ...

[ ] Key question for our venture: Who don't we need in our venture? ... Who do we need? ... How do we balance the load?

[ ] Never give in, never give in, never, never, never ... [Thank you, Winston Churchill]

[ ] Always assume our competition is smarter than us ... often they are! ... [Thank you, Walter Rathenau]

[ ] Never continue in a job we don't enjoy ...

[ ] We must know more than the competition, but that's not always the case ... tread softly sometimes!

[ ] Do not feel lonely ... the entire universe is around us!

[ ] Innovators are good at synthesizing ...

[ ] Try to make someone happy every day ...

[ ] Do not meddle with a business we know nothing about ...

[ ] Successful innovators and entrepreneurs are continually refining their senses, especially sight, as the means to enliven experience ... [Thank you, Michael J Gelb]

[ ] Key question for our venture: What is the possibility that something unpleasant or unwelcome will happen? ...

[ ] Entrepreneurship creates a lot of wealth, but it is very unevenly distributed ... [Thank you, Scott Shane]

[ ] We cannot create experience ... we must undergo it! ... [Thank you, Albert Camus]

[ ] The entrepreneur always searches for change, responds to it, and exploits it as an opportunity ... [Thank you, Peter F Drucker]

[ ] Figures can lie ... it's all in the assumptions ... [Thank you, Louise Francesconi]

[ ] Conditions will never be perfect ...

[ ] Change: become or make different ...

[ ] Key question for our venture: What is the primary competition for our venture? ...

[ ] Tip for creating a good venture plan: Start with a clear, concise executive summary of your business ... [Thank you, Mary Crane]

[ ] Don't micromanage ... give them an assignment and let 'em go do it!

[ ] Don't take the wrong side of an argument just because our competitor has taken the right side ...

[ ] There is always more to know about everything ... [Thank you, Barbara Ann Kipfer]

[ ] Common bootstrapping strategy: work from home ...

[ ] If we can't measure it ... we can't control it!

[ ] Some regions, states, and even nations provide a better environment for fostering entrepreneurship than others ... [Thank you, William Bygrave]

[ ] R&D: research and development, typically a department in a venture responsible for new product development ...

[ ] People will meet the expectations that we set for them ...

[ ] Successful entrepreneurs have an ability to make good decisions ... [Thank you, Janet Kraus]

[ ] Ask lots of relevant questions ... even if it means asking some irrelevant ones along the way!

[ ] Product Launch: the orchestrated introduction of a new product (or version of a product) to the market ...

[ ] An executive summary is one page long ... two at the most ...

[ ] Sometimes it's like a bacon and egg breakfast ... the chicken is involved but the pig is committed ... are we the chicken or are we the pig? ...

[ ] The time to repair the roof is when the sun is shining ... [Thank you, John F Kennedy]

[ ] Do not do what is already done ... do something new and better ...

[ ] The P's of Marketing ... product, place, price, profit, promotion, position ...

[ ] We can go further when we know where we are going ... there is a fine middle between planning too much and planning too little

[ ] Many people would sooner die than think ... In fact, they do ... [Thank you, Bertrand Russell]

[ ] Get our act together ...

[ ] Promote our venture with membership in organizations ...

[ ] Single steps add up to a completed goal ...

[ ] Lack of money isn't the real problem ... lack of a good idea is! ... [Thank you, Ken Hakuta]

[ ] There is no past and there is no future ... there is only now!

[ ] Get ready, get set, go! ... [Thank you, Carlos Alsua]

[ ] Eliminate, elaborate ... What can we eliminate? Remove something? Eliminate waste? Reduce time? Reduce effort? Cut costs? ... "I can eliminate ... by ..." ...

[ ] If the phone doesn't ring, it's us ... If our customers aren't calling us, what are we doing or not doing that's wrong ... it's not them, it's us! ... [Thank you, Jimmy Buffett]

[ ] Entrepreneurship is a collection of methods and madness ... it is not just one thing, it's a composite of many things that together create a powerful force for creation, invention, and innovation ...

[ ] Organize the day in the morning ...

[ ] We have met the enemy, and he is us! ... [Thank you, Pogo]

[ ] Everything we hear is not true ... what is and isn't can make all the difference in the world!

[ ] Let's do it because we want to ...

[ ] Do things right ...

[ ] If people are offered a fact which goes against their beliefs, they will scrutinize it closely, and unless the evidence is overwhelming, they will refuse to believe it ... If, on the other hand, they are offered something which affords a reason for acting in accordance to their beliefs, they will accept it even on the slightest evidence. The origin of myths is explained in this way ... [Thank you, Bertrand Russell]

[ ] Entrepreneurs are often good at ordering things by priority ...

[ ] Thou shalt not kill ... tempting as it may sometime be!

[ ] Fool: ...

[ ] There are 10^{11} stars in the galaxy ... that used to be a huge number ... but it's only a hundred billion ... it's less than the national deficit! we used to call them astronomical numbers ... now we should call them economical numbers! ... [Thank you, Richard Feynman]

[ ] Innovation has a fuzzy front-end that needs an entrepreneurial awareness to focus potential and power ... [Thank you, Ken Smith]

[ ] The best value wins ... whoever delivers better benefits at a lower price wins the business ...

[ ] Straight or Curved ... what should we focus on today? ...

[ ] Never stop questioning ... even after we have an answer, especially after we think we have an answer, keep looking for other alternatives because our competitors will ... [Thank you, Albert Einstein]

[ ] Think 10 years rather than 10 minutes ... [Thank you, Warren Buffett]

[ ] Use secondary information that was collected by an independent research organization, not one with an axe to grind ...

[ ] Key question for our venture: How are they a threat to our venture? ...

[ ] Stick to standard conventional formats for our financial reports ...

[ ] Key question for our venture: What are the major opportunities in our industry? ...

[ ] Never promise more than we are willing to deliver ...

[ ] The only completely consistent people are dead ... [Thank you, Aldous Huxley]

[ ] The student should surpass the teacher ... (unless the teacher's name is Jim, in which case the student should take him out to lunch!)

[ ] Listen to the smarties in the party ...

[ ] Profit is a reward for doing a good job!

[ ] Affiliative leadership style ... emphasizes the importance of teamwork, and creates harmony in a group by connecting people to each other ... [Thank you, Daniel Goleman]

[ ] Write it down ... Capture all ideas, big or little, good or bad, fast or slow!

[ ] Skilled innovators and entrepreneurs are able to accept rejection ...

[ ] If it ain't broke, don't fix it ... instead, make it even better than it was before ...

[ ] Good enough never is ... we gotta be better so we don't get beat ... [Thank you, Debbie Field]

[ ] Success may stifle creativity by leading people to focus narrowly on existing solutions rather than exploring new ones ...

[ ] Time is the most valuable and scarce resource ...

[ ] It's easy to find leaders ... they have people following them ... [Thank you, Bill Gore]

[ ] How can we answer this Question: Is our venture in a growth industry? ...

[ ] Our brand is a pitch to our customers to do business with us ...

[ ] Do everything as if the customer were standing next to us ... we should not be ashamed of anything we do, including making a fair profit!

[ ] Let's do onto others as we would have them do onto us!

[ ] Use secondary information that is based on large sample sizes ...

[ ] Persist ... resist resting on our laurels!

[ ] We cannot be defeated if we just keep taking one breath after another ... [Thank you, Oprah Winfrey]

[ ] Do something nice ...

[ ] Time is limited ...

[ ] Plan or Do ... what should we focus on today? ...

[ ] No good deed goes unpunished ...

[ ] It could be a good opportunity if the market is significant.

[ ] Potential venture legal issue: Starting a business while employed by a potential competitor, or hiring employees without first checking their agreements with the current employer and their knowledge of trade secrets ... [Thank you, Connie Bagley]

[ ] Pick a battle big enough to matter but small enough to win ... [Thank you, Jonathan Kozol]

[ ] Small markets before large ones ...

[ ] Revenue is not predictable, so we must control our costs ... in general, make costs variable wherever we can ...

[ ] Facts are facts and will not disappear on account of our likes ... [Thank you, Jawaharlal Nehru]

[ ] Will this problem matter in 10 years? ... if not, is it worth addressing? ... [Thank you, Nelson Wang]

[ ] Guerilla marketing ... sneak in there where they least expect it!

[ ] When I started, I wanted a piece of the pie; now I want to make the pie ... [Thank you, Seton Claggett]

[ ] Communicate ... keep the channels open and flowing with information!

[ ] Hire the best, fire the rest! ... hire slow, fire fast ...

[ ] Character is what we are ... reputation is what others think we are ...

[ ] Protect our intellectual property ...

[ ] A person without a smiling face ought not to open a shop ... [Thank you, Linsay Craton]

[ ] It is better to ask some questions than to know all the answers ... [Thank you, James Thurber]

[ ] SWOTT it ... what are the Strengths, Weaknesses, Opportunities, Threats, and Trends? ... good to SWOTT the competition, our customers, ourselves!

[ ] It's not just "I can" ... it's "I will!" ...

[ ] Successful entrepreneurs have an ability to assemble and motivate a business team ... [Thank you, Lynda Applegate]

[ ] Entrepreneurial Myth: Many start-ups achieve the sales growth projections that equity investors are looking for ... not even close ... [Thank you, Scott Shane]

[ ] Nothing is as easy as it looks ...

[ ] A good business plan identifies significant risks and proposes rational contingencies ... [Thank you, FoodChange]

[ ] Stop the run, create turnovers, and eliminate big plays ... once we do that, we'll be fine ... [Thank you, Bradie James]

[ ] If we would persuade, we must appeal to interest rather than intellect ... [Thank you, Benjamin Franklin]

[ ] Skilled innovators and entrepreneurs are futuristic ... [Thank you, Kyle Cherrick]

[ ] Sometimes we see brands on the balance sheet ... sometimes we don't! ... [Thank you, Economist]

[ ] Successful teams have complementary skills and collaborate styles ...

[ ] Visualize success ... what do we see? ... what do we need to do to get there? ...

[ ] Take the bull by the horns ... don't let go 'cause that bull will rip us to pieces!

[ ] Be spontaneous and imaginative ...

[ ] Every path leads two ways ... [Thank you, Paul Fahring]

[ ] Legal, moral, and ethical ... what should we focus on today? ...

[ ] Limits must be tested ... high and low, up and down, top and bottom ...

[ ] Sing it loud for all to hear ... don't be shy about telling the world about what we have to offer! ... [Thank you, Buddy the Elf]

[ ] They may forget what we said, but they will never forget how we made them feel ... [Thank you, Carl W Buechner]

[ ] Total Addressable Market (TAM): the total potential market for a product or service, measured in dollars of revenue per year ...

[ ] What we (hopefully don't) have here is a failure to communicate ... [Thank you, Strother Martin]

[ ] If we see a bandwagon, it's too late ... [Thank you, James Goldsmith]

[ ] Show our customers we're there for them ...

[ ] Find our true passion ... What puts a smile on our face? What do we find easy? What sparks our creativity? What would we do for free? What do we like to talk about? What makes us unafraid of failure? What would we regret not having tried? ... [Thank you, Frederic Premji]

[ ] What sparks your creativity? ... [Thank you, Frederic Premji]

[ ] Promote our venture with print advertising ...

[ ] Can we lead? Can we follow? Can we support the team?

[ ] The markets will fluctuate ... [Thank you, J P Morgan]

[ ] Don't lie, especially to that person in the mirror ... if we tell the truth, we won't have to try to remember what we said before ...

[ ] Try not to make stupid mistakes; only very clever ones! John Peel ... [Thank you, John Peel]

[ ] Common cause of venture death: intellectual property issues ...

[ ] Most people who begin the process of starting a company fail to get one up and running ... [Thank you, Scott Shane]

[ ] Memory is more indelible than ink ... [Thank you, Anita Loos]

[ ] Serial Entrepreneur: someone who starts multiple businesses ... (as opposed to a cereal entrepreneur in the breakfast food business) ...

[ ] Give a name to all major projects; it gives everyone an easy way to refer to a common set of goals ... [Thank you, Bill Gates]

[ ] Key question for our venture: What are the key differentiated features of our products or services? ...

[ ] Time teaches us all things ...

[ ] If our short-term liabilities exceed our short-term assets, we are bankrupt ... [Thank you, Norm Brodsky]

[ ] Intrapreneurs are often in trouble because they act when they are supposed to wait ... [Thank you, Gifford Pinchot]

[ ] Treat customers as appreciating assets ...

[ ] Reach out and touch someone ... see how we can help them ...

[ ] The difference between genius and stupidity is that genius has its limits ... [Thank you, Albert Einstein]

[ ] Pretend we don't know anything ... then go out and learn.

[ ] Customers don't care about functions or specific activities that occur within our organization ... the end game is whether they are getting the right product at the right time at the right price ... [Thank you, Max Guinn]

[ ] Promote our venture with enthusiast magazines ...

[ ] Serendipity strikes when we may least expect it ... are we ready to catch it when it hits? ...

[ ] Have fun ... beats being miserable!

[ ] The trouble with doing something right the first time is that nobody appreciates how difficult it was ... [Thank you, Walt West]

[ ] Scale: the relative size or extent of something ... scaling a venture by expanding the customer base ... geographically, demographically, psychographically ...

[ ] Do small things well ...

[ ] Successful teams are full of energy ...

[ ] Experience teaches only the teachable ... [Thank you, Aldous Huxley]

[ ] How can we answer this Question: Is our venture scalable? ...

[ ] Set a good example ...

[ ] Venture Capital: capital invested in a project in which there is a substantial element of risk but the potential of a significant financial reward ...

[ ] Make eye contact ...

[ ] Some people can compress the most words into the smallest ideas ... [Thank you, Abraham Lincoln]

[ ] Use a round number when we are talking theoretically, and a hard number when we are presenting hard data ... theoretical: "Make $100,000 as a professional massage therapist." ... hard data: "Last year Henry earned $103,287.45 in his massage therapy practice." ... [Thank you, Ugur Akinci]

[ ] There is no dress rehearsal ... this is it ...

[ ] Strategy is all about winning ... what is "winning" to us? Different strokes for different folks ...

[ ] Key question for our venture: When is a business venture plan finished? ... A: Always and never ... a plan should always be ready to go, but a plan should also evolve over time ...

[ ] Skilled innovators and entrepreneurs are willing and able to make decisions ...

[ ] How can we answer this question: In our market space, are we the benefits-leader, the low-price-leader, or both? ... "both" is hard to do but hard to beat!

[ ] Prepare and someday our time will come ...

[ ] If we don't know what we good at, how will we know what we're good for? ...

[ ] Know when to cut our losses ... [Thank you, Warren Buffett]

[ ] How to kill creativity: "That's a dumb question ..."

[ ] Always shave a day off every deadline we're given ... [Thank you, John Darley]

[ ] It is amazing how much good we can do if we do not care who gets the credit ... one for all, all for one ... we are the team!

[ ] People tend to believe what they least understand ... [Thank you, P T Barnum]

[ ] We can never offer our customers too many benefits ... we should not assume we know which ones will be most important to them ...

[ ] We'll always find time to do the things we really want to do ... not always the things we need to do ...

[ ] Only entropy comes easy ...

[ ] Potential venture legal issue: Failing to make a timely Section 83(b) election ... [Thank you, Connie Bagley]

[ ] Direct or Scenic ... what should we focus on today? ...

[ ] Don't put all our eggs in one basket ... product, customer, supplier, et al ...

[ ] Make decisions not because they are easy, cheap, or popular ... make them because they are right!

[ ] Focus on markets that have enough potential to support our venture ...

[ ] Skilled innovators and entrepreneurs are productive ...

[ ] The best way to find out if we can trust somebody is to trust them ... [Thank you, Ernest Hemingway]

[ ] Gain or Loss ... what should we focus on today? ...

[ ] Engineer: a skillful creator of something ...

[ ] Keep our word, even to our enemies ...

[ ] Research, ideation, feasibility, vision, mission, goals, objectives, strategies, tactics, tasks, assignments ...

[ ] Promote our venture with customer newsletters ...

[ ] I'm OK, you're OK, we're OK ... that's a whole lot better than if one or all of us is not ... [Thank you, Thomas A Harris]

[ ] Key question for our venture: What is our public relations strategy? ...

[ ] We are judged by what we finish, not by what we start ...

[ ] No words ever spoken to us should change the way we feel about ourselves ... we are in control of our own destiny!

[ ] Don't ask for money before we know for what, where, and when it is going to used ... create a "use of funds" schedule so we have some idea what we need and how much it's going to cost ...

[ ] Key question for our venture: Do we have a good loyal customer base? ... how can we get some good loyal customers?

[ ] Keep an open mind ... and an open heart ...

[ ] Change our routines to shake things up a bit ...

[ ] What do you like to talk about? ... [Thank you, Frederic Premji]

[ ] Ask lots of questions, don't presume to know the answers.

[ ] Hire the best, then delegate ... let them do what we hired them to do!

[ ] B2G: abbreviation for a Business-to-Government relationship ...

[ ] We can know a lot about something, but not really understand it ... like gravity ... [Thank you, C F Kettering]

[ ] Skilled innovators and entrepreneurs are stimulated by variety ...

[ ] An ounce of prevention can save us from having to walk through a pound of manure ...

[ ] Focus on a few things, not many ...

[ ] Skilled innovators and entrepreneurs are proud of what they do ...

[ ] Key question for our venture: How can we research our competition? ... what do we really, really need to know about them? ...

[ ] Indirect price ...

[ ] Without a deadline, I wouldn't do nothing, baby ... [Thank you, Duke Ellington]

[ ] Business plan competitions: the best venture does not always win ...

[ ] There's no one side to anything ...

[ ] Time is the scarcest resource and must be carefully managed ... [Thank you, Peter F Drucker]

[ ] Engineering is the improvement of what is; innovation is the destruction of what is! ... [Thank you, Dick Morley]

[ ] Try to see our customer's point of view first ...

[ ] Ask "Why?" ... If that doesn't work, ask "Why not?" ...

[ ] Keep our desks neat ...

[ ] Exercise: List 10 things we could do better in our venture ...

[ ] Prototype: a first, typical or preliminary model of something, especially a machine, from which other forms are developed or copied ...

[ ] Understand the power of touch ... be it a great handshake, hug, or arm squeeze ...

[ ] If we run after two rabbits, we won't catch either ... We have to focus on our Plan A. We can't get distracted or we'll

misutilize our most valuable resource, time! ... [Thank you, Wile E Coyote]

[ ] Successful Innovators and entrepreneurs know how to focus on the idea today ... [Thank you, Patricia G Greene]

[ ] Picking a name for our venture, company, product, or service is one of the hardest things we'll ever do ... the name should be distinctive, instantly recognized, easy to remember, pleasant to see, pleasant to say, and easy to spell, not confusing itself and not be easily confused with other names ... there should be a connection between the name and the product, service, or business venture it represents ... the name should suggest what the business venture, product, or service does ... the name should be descriptive of the benefits offered by the product, service, or business venture ... the name should convey the proper image, fit customers expectations, and even reinforce customer expectations ... there should not be any negative connotations with the name ... the name should not be limiting ... the name should coordinate with other names used in the organization, work in all target markets, and be able to be legally protected.

[ ] Key question for our venture: What business are we in? ... what business should we be in? ...

[ ] A-class people hire A-class people ... B-class people hire C-class people ...

[ ] Venture Planning Checklist: A] Market / Industry Attractiveness: Problems to Be Addressed; Industry and Environment; Potential Competitive Advantages ... B] Product Market Fit: Prospective Customers; Potential Solutions ... C] Go To Market / Customer Acquisition Strategy; Marketing Strategies; Sales Strategies ... D] Operating Plan; Production Operations; Team ... E] Financial Viability; Financial Objectives; Funding Proposal ... F] Business Model: Business

Model Canvas; Status Timeline; Additional Venture Values; Scope and Scale ...

[ ] Cloudy or Sunny ... what's our disposition today? ...

[ ] Mistakes are opportunities to learn ...

[ ] Time is money ... [Thank you, Benjamin Franklin]

[ ] Everything we write is copyrighted ...

[ ] Efficiency is doing things right ... effectiveness is doing the right things ... [Thank you, Peter Drucker]

[ ] Sink or Swim ... what should we focus on today? ...

[ ] All the advice and wisdom cannot help us until we apply it!

[ ] Cash is king, and there is never enough ...

[ ] Promote our venture with national newspapers ...

[ ] Zero defects ... so we don't have to make it all over again!

[ ] If we're not criticized, we might not be doing much ...

[ ] Don't lose the substance by grasping at the shadow ...

[ ] The brand is the essence of the company ... [Thank you, Julie McHenry]

[ ] Promote our venture with buttons ...

[ ] I am always doing that which I can not do, in order that I may learn how to do it ... [Thank you, Pablo Picasso]

[ ] Show enthusiasm even when you don't feel like it ... it's a good habit to grow ...

[ ] We can't just ask customers what they want and then try to give it to them ... by the time we get it built, they'll want something else! ... [Thank you, Steve Jobs]

[ ] Customers get into a rut that makes them resistant to change ... [Thank you, Gary Gesme]

[ ] Heredity or environment? ... were we born to innovate or were we in the right place with the right people, or perhaps a combination? ...

[ ] Avoid jargon ...

[ ] Use the most recent data we can find ...

[ ] Faith can move mountains ... innovation and entrepreneurship can turn mountains into ski resorts ...

[ ] Sometimes push our luck ...

[ ] The future is something which everyone reaches at the rate of sixty minutes an hour, whatever they do, whoever they are ... [Thank you, C S Lewis]

[ ] Assume: making an ass out of u and me ...

[ ] The truth is powerful ... [Thank you, New York Times]

[ ] Stay on your toes ... follow your nose ...

[ ] People love to buy ... what people don't love is to be cheated or tricked ... [Thank you, Dean Rieck]

[ ] Six-word formula for success: think things through, then follow through ... [Thank you, Eddie Rickenbacker]

[ ] Prepare a list of questions before asking for advice ...

[ ] There is no knowledge that is not power ... [Thank you, Ralph Waldo Emerson]

[ ] Nascent Market: a very new, formative market in which vendors sell their products or services to early adopter customers ...

[ ] Courtesy and kindness never goes out of style ...

[ ] Skilled innovators and entrepreneurs are good decision makers ...

[ ] Make meetings 15 minutes shorter than needed ... [Thank you, Todd Adams]

[ ] Build a working prototype ... ia picture may be worth a thousand words, but a prototype is worth a thousand pictures.

[ ] Stand firm on our beliefs and principles ... [Thank you, Walt Disney]

[ ] Never tell people how to do things ... tell them what to do and let them surprise us with their ingenuity ... [Thank you, George S Patton]

[ ] Information is pretty thin stuff, unless mixed with experience ... [Thank you, Clarence Day]

[ ] Keep your head when those around you are losing theirs ...

[ ] Surf the big waves ...

[ ] Successful innovators and entrepreneurs have resilience ...

[ ] Don't run out of cash ... No cash, game over ...

[ ] Corporate entrepreneur credo: It is easier to ask for forgiveness than for permission ... [Thank you, Gifford Pinchot III]

[ ] Praise every improvement, even the small ones ...

[ ] Traits of leaders who are good at executing: achiever, arranger, believer, consistent, deliberate, disciplined, focused, responsible, and restorative ... [Thank you, Gallup]

[ ] Out of every 10 venture capital deals, two will fail, six will continue to go along, and the other two deals are where they make some money ... [Thank you, Stephen Lund]

[ ] Sometimes, when we reach for the stars, we fall short ... but we must pick ourselves up again and press on, despite the pain ... [Thank you, Ronald Reagan]

[ ] Reflection is a critical skill for innovators and entrepreneurs ... [Thank you, P G Greene]

[ ] Venture capital investments in the US by region ... Bay Area: 33% ... Southern California: 14% ... New England: 11% ... New York Metro: 9% ... Washington State & Potomac (tie): 4% ... Texas: 3% ... Research Triangle: 2% ... All Other US: 20% ... [Thank you, Dow Jones]

[ ] Don't carry grudges ... get on with life ...

[ ] Promote our venture by posting to social media ...

[ ] Tip for creating a good venture plan: Provide a detailed description of all revenue streams (product sales, advertising, services, licensing) and the company's cost structure (salaries, rent, inventory, maintenance) ...

[ ] My advice is free ... and worth every cent! ... [Thank you, James Arnold]

[ ] Costs of doing business ...

[ ] Businesses are dying and being created constantly ... this is a healthy process ... [Thank you, Andrew Corbett]

[ ] The whole ocean is made up of little drops ...

[ ] It's useless doing something efficient that shouldn't be done at all ... [Thank you, Peter F Drucker]

[ ] How can we answer this Question: Can we sell our products directly to consumers? ...

[ ] Curiosity killed the cat, profits from the new opportunity found and exploited bought a new cat ... a bigger, better cat at that!

[ ] Don't make a decision until all sides are heard ...

[ ] The power to decimate and destroy is a lot easier than the energy it takes to build ... [Thank you, Dan Rather]

[ ] A new venture may be feasible if it fills a need ...

[ ] Someone who thinks logically provides a nice contrast to the real world ... [Thank you, Lori Monserrate]

[ ] Everything is changing ... people are taking their comedians seriously and the politicians as a joke ... [Thank you, Will Rogers]

[ ] Instead of creating financial projections, create financial objectives ...

[ ] High achievers are magnets for work ...

[ ] Nothing happens until something is sold ...

[ ] Eat smaller portions ... chew longer before taking another bite ...

[ ] Exceed the minimum standards ... do more than expected.

[ ] Beware puffudery ... and fudduderry, too ...

[ ] Think about the problem in a new way ...

[ ] Learning and unlearning is critical in any path we choose to walk on ...

[ ] Take reasonable risks for reasonable reasons ...

[ ] Don't overstay our welcome ... it's like an over-attentive waiter. An attentive waiter is good, an over-attentive waiter not ...

[ ] Debt allows entrepreneurs to retain full ownership of the company, while equity entails giving ownership to outside investors ... [Thank you, Andrew Zacharakis]

[ ] Good marketing communications fits the target market, has an effective message, and is repeated ...

[ ] Be nimble, be quick, jump over the candlestick before the competition ... and be careful not to get our butt burned in the process!

[ ] Keep work about work ... [Thank you, InsideCRM]

[ ] Successful teams provide performance feedback to each other ...

[ ] Key question for our venture: Why is our team uniquely capable to execute our venture plan? ...

[ ] Simply elegant ... the ultimate design goal ...

[ ] Keep our venture simple ... the world is already complex ...

[ ] Improvisation is a group activity ... support the group to the end ...

[ ] If at first we don't succeed ... try, try again! And again. And again and again. ... [Thank you, William Edward Hickson]

[ ] Promote our venture on the radio ...

[ ] Tool or Weapon ... what should we focus on today? ...

[ ] Ads with people in them typically have a higher response rate than those without ... cute, friendly animals are good, too!

[ ] Every person is born with a talent ...

[ ] If someone is trying to bring us down, it means we're above them ...

[ ] Good questions outrank easy answers ... [Thank you, Paul A Samuelson]

[ ] Good cooks learn something new every day ... [Thank you, Julia Child]

[ ] Your opinion is no better than mine ... but if you have more data, knowledge, or expertise, bring it on!

[ ] Opportunity: a set of circumstances that makes it possible to do something ...

[ ] Value Equation: Value equals Benefits divided by Price (V = B/P) ...

[ ] Work hard but work smart ...

[ ] Skilled innovators and entrepreneurs are able to handle abstractness ...

[ ] Successful teams can handle pressure ...

[ ] Listen to music ... sing a song, play along ...

[ ] Pretty is great ... easy is better (referring to product benefits and features)!

[ ] Fight as if we are right, listen as if we are wrong ... [Thank you, Karl Weick]

[ ] Sharply differentiate our brand ...

[ ] Nobody cares ... Do it because we want to do it! ... [Thank you, Marris Bloomberg]

[ ] Apply the scientific method ... Ask a question; Do background research; Construct a hypothesis; Test the hypothesis by doing an experiment; Analyze the data fromt the experiment and draw a conclusion; Communicate the result; Decide what to do next (move on, start over, move over ...)

[ ] FFFF: abbreviation for Fit, Form, Function, Features ... four fundamentals of product design and development ...

[ ] Successful innovators and entrepreneurs can find a balance between science and art, logic and imagination ... [Thank you, Michael J Gelb]

[ ] A venture operations manual defines authority clearly and distributes responsibility ...

[ ] Happiness is a positive cash flow!

[ ] Nothing ventured, nothing gained ... nothing gained, nothing to venture in the future ...

[ ] Don't write a tome when a word or two will do ...

[ ] Make our own future ...

[ ] We won't get rich with just one big win ... we gotta keep playing' the game!

[ ] The one that listens is the one that understands ... [Thank you, Albert Einstein]

[ ] How can we answer this Question: What is our desired impact on the world? ... our part of the world? ...

[ ] Don't be a good starter but a bad finisher ...

[ ] Everybody is ignorant, only on different subjects ... [Thank you, Will Rogers]

[ ] When we make a mistake in front of our customers, it's a great opportunity to shine in their eyes when we make up for it ten-fold ...

[ ] How to attract new customers: offer current satisfied customers rewards for telling their friends ...

[ ] We can't know everything ... we won't know everything ... our best judgment will be the key ...

[ ] Speak with integrity ...

[ ] Strive for accuracy ...

[ ] Let others think it is theirs ...

[ ] Technology innovation and commercialization is inherently an iterative process where the innovator-entrepreneur learns from mistakes and builds on that learning ... [Thank you, Kathleen Allen]

[ ] There's no place like home ... [Thank you, Dorothy]

[ ] The best way to have a good idea is to have lots of ideas ... [Thank you, Linus Pauling]

[ ] If we don't know the answer, where can we find out? ... we'll never know everything, but that shouldn't stop us from trying ...

[ ] Wisdom is knowing where to look and what to overlook ...

[ ] Send a thank-you note ...

[ ] The food for thought is thinking ...

[ ] Know our audience ...

[ ] Successful teams share work expectations ...

[ ] The greatest challenge to any thinker is stating the problem in a way that will allow a solution ... [Thank you, Bertrand Russell]

[ ] Customer retention costs ...

[ ] Promote our venture on video displays in shopping malls.

[ ] Quidquid latine dictum sit, altum sonatur ... (Whatever is said in Latin sounds profound) ...

[ ] Don't let them scare us ... unless they're really big and ugly, then run away as fast as we can!

[ ] Time is more valuable than money ...

5280 TIPS for INNOVATORS and ENTREPRENEURS

[ ] Only the paranoid survive ... [Thank you, Andy Grove]

[ ] Promote our venture with hot air balloon ...

[ ] Try new things ...

[ ] Truths last forever ... doesn't make them easy to find ...

[ ] The show must go on ... our audience is waiting ... [Thank you, P T Barnum]

[ ] Pull: move steadily in a specified direction ...

[ ] Don't get cocky ...

[ ] Hofstadter's Law: It always takes longer than we expect, even when we take into account Hofstadter's Law ... [Thank you, Douglas Hofstadter]

[ ] The most unhappy customers are the greatest source of learning ... [Thank you, Bill Gates]

[ ] Be open to the new and different ...

[ ] The better value wins ...

[ ] Go for the low hanging fruit first ...

[ ] Early to bed, early to rise, work like hell and advertise ... [Thank you, Ted Turner]

[ ] Pricing strategies ... "Get big fast"; cost-based, competitive-pricing, perceived value ... [Thank you, William Bygrave]

[ ] If we don't want to see trees, stay out of the forest ...

[ ] Do or do not ... there is no try ... [Thank you, Yoda]

[ ] The idea doesn't have to be big ... it just has to change our part of the world ... glue that wouldn't stick very well wasn't such a big deal until it became the magic ingredient of 3M Post-it Notes ... [Thank you, Spencer Silver]

[ ] Become the moment ...

[ ] Be someone to somebody ...

[ ] The key to our long-term success is learning how to continually add value ... [Thank you, Andy Grove]

[ ] Don't dilute our efforts ... the easy things always seem to get in the way of the hard ...

[ ] Key question for our venture: How do our prices compare with the rest of my industry? ...

[ ] Entertain our customers to keep them focused on our products and services ...

[ ] Exercise your mind ...

[ ] There is a sucker born every minute ...

[ ] Key question for our venture: What have we learned from our competitors' strengths? ...

[ ] The best time to make friends is before we need them ...

[ ] The details are not the details ... the details make the design ... [Thank you, Charles Earnes]

[ ] Promote our venture with grand opening/anniversary celebrations ...

[ ] Skilled innovators and entrepreneurs are realistic ...

[ ] No happiness without action ... [Thank you, C Narvasa]

[ ] Key question for our venture: Is our venture, product, and/or service name distinctive? ...

[ ] The mind is not a storehouse to be filled but an instrument to be used ... [Thank you, John Gardner]

[ ] We are a combination of heredity and environment ... we can't change heredity but it's open season on environment ...

[ ] A good business plan presents evidence of the marketability of the products and services ... [Thank you, Mark Peterson]

[ ] Divide the number 100 by the forward speed of a storm to estimate the inches of rain the storm will deliver ... [Thank you, National Hurricane Center]

[ ] Skilled innovators and entrepreneurs are confident ...

[ ] If we discover we're on the wrong path, turn around ...

[ ] What is quickly done may take some time to undo ...

[ ] Times change and we with time ...

[ ] Pick a niche ...

[ ] Hats: used to refer to a particular role or occupation of someone who has more than one job ... what hats is she wearing, and for how long? ...

[ ] It could be a good opportunity if our team is passionate and persistent ...

[ ] We've all heard that a million monkeys banging on a million typewriters will eventually reproduce the works of Shakespeare ... now, thanks to the Internet, we know this is not true ... [Thank you, Robert Wilensky]

[ ] A phone directory is full of facts, but it doesn't illuminate.

[ ] Numbers run a business ... if we don't know how to read and interpret them, we're running blind ... [Thank you, Norm Brodsky]

[ ] Streamline our process of getting new products to market.

[ ] Alone we can do so little ... together we do so much! ... [Thank you, Helen Keller]

[ ] A good leader is also a good follower ... and knows when to do which ... [Thank you, Mat Friedman]

[ ] Elevator pitch content: tell them who we are, tell them what we do, tell them where we do what we do (geography of our markets), tell them when we do what we do, tell them why we do it (our mission, our venture goals), and how we do what we do (our "secret sauce" without revealing our secret ingredients) ...

[ ] Promote our venture with Internet ...

[ ] Cash ... there is never enough!

[ ] Promote our venture with telephone hold messages ...

[ ] Look out for the future ...

[ ] Parent - Adult - Child ... at what level are we communicating, both sides of the equation? ... [Thank you, Thomas A Harris]

[ ] Carry the spirit of the child with us forever ...

[ ] The eight C's of an effective elevator pitch: concise, clear, compelling, credible, conceptual, concrete, customized, consistent ... [Thank you, Chris O'Leary]

[ ] The FUD Factor: abbreviation for Fear, Uncertainty, and Doubt ... a method by which one vendor raises concerns in the mind of a prospective customer regarding certain qualities or capabilities of the vendor's competitors ...

[ ] Bad weather can ruin the best-laid plans ... we need to pay attention to the environments in which we operate to see how the wind blows in each ...

[ ] A gift to your enemy: forgiveness ... [Thank you, Oren Arnold]

[ ] Aim for excellence, not perfection ...

5280 TIPS for INNOVATORS and ENTREPRENEURS

[ ] Change is a challenge for the courageous ...

[ ] Know where the exits are located ...

[ ] Repeat what works, put to rest what doesn't ... [Thank you, Steve Wood]

[ ] Make sure it gets done ...

[ ] Basic resources: people, places, things, time, money ...

[ ] Don't bite off more than we can chew ... else, we could choke to death ... not a pleasant thought ...

[ ] It could be a good opportunity if our solution has better and sustainable benefits ...

[ ] Come to the point ... don't ramble ...

[ ] The experience of success may stifle creativity by leading people to focus narrowly on existing solutions rather than exploring new ones ... [Thank you, P G Audia]

[ ] The only difference between a problem and a solution is that people understand the solution ... [Thank you, Charles Kettering]

[ ] Study hard ... get smart ...

[ ] Product Development: the process of designing, creating or updating, marketing and providing a product to a target market ...

[ ] Save early, save often ... a dollar saved is like ten dollars earned!

[ ] Success is relative ... what does "success" mean to us?

[ ] Only those asleep make no mistakes ... [Thank you, Ingvar Kamprad]

[ ] A day without laughter is a day wasted ... [Thank you, Steve Martin]

[ ] We may have to go out of town to find funding for our venture ... look for investors that have an interest and knowledge in our industry ...

[ ] Skilled innovators and entrepreneurs are sociable ...

[ ] Effective leaders make the right things happen ... [Thank you, Roger Kirkham]

[ ] Promote our venture with signage at sporting events ...

[ ] Postmortems on defeats are never very useful unless they say something about the future ... [Thank you, James Reston]

[ ] WAG, TWAG, SWAG, Science ... Types of judgment: Wild Ass Guess, Tempered Wild Ass Guess, Scientific Wild Ass Guess, and Scientific Guess ...

[ ] Feel the music as well as hear it ...

[ ] If everything is coming our way, maybe we're in the wrong lane ... [Thank you, Mario Andretti]

[ ] Change brings opportunities ...

[ ] Nyuk nyuk nyuk! sometimes we just gotta nyuk! ... [Thank you, Curly Howard]

[ ] Any clown can complain, criticize, and condemn ... but it takes character and control to be compassionate and caring ... [Thank you, Dale Carnegie]

[ ] Write a resume for our venture ...

[ ] Key question for our venture: Where and how can we find funding for our venture? ...

[ ] The difference between a successful person and others is not a lack of strength, not a lack of knowledge, but rather a lack of will ... [Thank you, Vince Lombardi]

[ ] Key question for our venture: What companies are the industry leaders, and why? ...

[ ] Better: a more excellent or effective type or quality ...

[ ] There is no finish line ... [Thank you, Nike]

[ ] Change will come, ready or not ... be forewarned!

[ ] Catalog theory: test it out in the catalog, throw out those products that don't generate significant revenue, add new ones in their place ...

[ ] If we don't risk anything, we risk even more ... [Thank you, Erica Jong]

[ ] Skilled innovators and entrepreneurs are independent ...

[ ] Fake it 'til we make it ... [Thank you, Emre Toker]

[ ] We can learn anything we want ...

[ ] We will never forget our first love ... in life and in business!

[ ] Develop a hypothesis ... then test it to see if it is true or false ...

[ ] No risk, no reward ...

[ ] Winners never quit, quitters never win ... [Thank you, Vince Lombardi]

[ ] Make something significant ... even if it is something small.

[ ] Children are better observers than adults ... they have fewer preconceptions ...

[ ] Think first ... then act!

[ ] Customers buy for features and benefits ...

[ ] Any intelligent fool can make things bigger and more complex ... it takes a touch of genius and a lot of courage to move in the opposite direction ... [Thank you, Albert Einstein]

[ ] If you have to whisper it, better not say it ...

[ ] Gravity sucks ... energy blows! (Physics in Four!)

[ ] Innovation is the distinction between a leader and a follower ... [Thank you, Steve Jobs]

[ ] It's all about our service ... [Thank you, Bob Lusch]

[ ] Amateurs started Google, Apple, Microsoft, Facebook ... professionals built the Titanic ...

[ ] Promote our venture with reminder advertising ...

[ ] Every leader in charge of a P&L has to make innovation happen, even if the company lacks a culture of innovation ... [Thank you, A G Lafley]

[ ] A good management team is critical for success ... [Thank you, Joe Broschak]

[ ] Lead with or without the title ... [Thank you, Nelson Wang]

[ ] Common Mistake: not comparing ourselves to comparable organizations to see how we fare ...

[ ] If we can't say something good, just keep it to ourselves ...

[ ] If we aren't fired with enthusiasm, we'll be fired with enthusiasm ... [Thank you, Vince Lombardi]

[ ] Elevator Pitch: a short verbal summary used to quickly and simply define a venture, product, service, organization, or event, and its value proposition ...

[ ] See a world in a grain of sand and heaven in a wild flower ... [Thank you, William Blake]

[ ] Skilled innovators and entrepreneurs are able to communicate non-verbally ...

[ ] Executive Summary: a short document or section of a document that summarizes a longer report or proposal or a group of related reports in such a way that readers can rapidly become acquainted with a large body of material without having to read it all ...

[ ] Potential business model: Sell products retail or wholesale ...

[ ] Have we clearly defined our company and our target markets? ...

[ ] Most of what we fear won't happen ... some things we never thought of will!

[ ] Desire for our neighbors what we desire for ourselves ...

[ ] Common bootstrapping strategy: use low-cost crowd-sourcing ...

[ ] Successful teams trust each other ...

[ ] Remain cool, calm, and collected ... panic only if all else fails!

[ ] Business planning starts when we start thinking about our new venture ... [Thank you, Dan Kuz]

[ ] Skate to where the puck is going, not to where it's been ... [Thank you, Wayne Gretzky]

[ ] Get our hands dirty ... Sometimes we need to show that no one's above doing unattractive tasks ...

[ ] Innovation is the destruction of what is ... and replaced by what isn't ...

[ ] Alpha: an initial model of machinery, software, or other products carried out by a developer ...

[ ] There is no 'I' in TEAM ...

[ ] Freemium is not a business model ... it's a marketing strategy ... we can give away samples to get prospective customers to try, but if they don't buy, it's over ...

[ ] Innovators are usually good at nonverbal processing ...

[ ] Finish ... if not, why did we bother to start in the first place? ...

[ ] Achieving good performance is a journey, not a destination ... [Thank you, Robert Lorber]

[ ] What is well-planted will well-grow ...

[ ] What trends do we see for our industry in the future? ...

[ ] Never ask the witness a question if we don't already know the answer ... [Thank you, Trial Lawyers Everywhere]

[ ] Promote our venture with home parties ...

[ ] Do everything for the right reasons ...

[ ] Take the high road ... the low road will just get us full of mud ...

[ ] Education sets us free ...

[ ] Common cause of venture death: poor marketing ...

[ ] Meet our obligations ... do not lie, cheat, or steal ...

[ ] Life begins when we start to understand ...

[ ] A good read: Made to Stick (Chip Heath & Dan Heath) ...

[ ] Key question for our venture: What are potential benchmark ventures in our industry? ...

[ ] Skilled innovators and entrepreneurs are self-starting ...

[ ] Give our customers their money back ... if they are happy for any reason ...

[ ] Big changes need small starts ...

[ ] Startup: the action or process of setting something in motion ...

[ ] Don't look back, someone might be gaining on us ...

[ ] Customer funding ...

[ ] Compliment others ... and complement others ...

[ ] Profit: a financial gain, especially the difference between the amount earned and the amount spent in buying, operating, or producing something ...

[ ] Never offer our hen for sale on a rainy day ... [Thank you, Sophie Novy]

[ ] Some solutions are neither right nor wrong ...

[ ] Don't give in to whims ...

[ ] We are confronted with insurmountable opportunities ... [Thank you, Walt Kelly]

[ ] Cut our losses ...

[ ] Management means knowing the difference between cornering people and getting them in our corner ... [Thank you, Lee Iacocca]

[ ] Key question for our venture: What kind of market are we in? ...

[ ] We either find a way or make one ...

[ ] Plans are only good intentions ... unless they degenerate into work ... [Thank you, Peter F Drucker]

[ ] Fun: amusing, entertaining, or enjoyable ...

[ ] Create not criticize ...

[ ] Probably: with considerable certainty ... but still a chance it could go the other way ...

[ ] Act - Learn - Build ... do something, learn what does and doesn't work, do something better ... [Thank you, Christopher P Neck]

[ ] Make herstory ... a good herstory, not a bad one ...

[ ] The smallest gesture can mean much to those who may need a little lift in their lives ... [Thank you, Gordon B Hinckley]

[ ] Entrepreneurs are usually rational ...

[ ] A good business plan shows an appreciation of investor needs ... [Thank you, Justin Williams]

[ ] I will prepare and someday my chance will come ... [Thank you, Abraham Lincoln]

[ ] Don't let what we don't know get in the way of what we do know ...

[ ] It is easy to be smart after the fact ...

[ ] Entrepreneurs put something new and better to work ...

[ ] When it comes to branding our business, keep it simple ... besides conserving our time and our budget, simplicity will cement our brand in the mind of our prospects in the most expedient manner possible ... [Thank you, John Williams]

[ ] We don't know what we don't know ... why taking a little test first can help us learn ...

[ ] Skilled innovators and entrepreneurs are able to identify problems ...

[ ] Engineering: the branch of science and technology concerned with the design, building, and use of engines, machines, and structures ...

[ ] Look for what is missing ...

[ ] Paint a pretty picture, please ... show our venture to our customers in the very best light ...

[ ] There will always be resistance ...

[ ] All we need is love ... but a little chocolate now and then doesn't hurt ... and money ... [Thank you, Charles M Schulz]

[ ] If we think we're gonna get rich quick by starting a new venture, good luck! hate to break the news here, but it is going to take time, money, skill, passion, and a good dose of luck!

[ ] Promote our venture with packaging ...

[ ] A little spark can kindle a great fire ... but be careful: only you can prevent forest fires! ... [Thank you, Smokey the Bear]

[ ] Customer discovery, customer validation, customer building, company creation ... finding the customer comes before finding a solution ...

[ ] More facts, not fiction ... [Thank you, Michael Bassey Johnson]

[ ] Sometimes big companies buy little companies because they want what they got ... and sometimes big companies buy little companies because they want what they got gone!

[ ] Good industry research is critical to our success ...

[ ] Market Segmentation: the process of subdividing a market into distinct groups of customers with similar needs, such that a subset of the market ... [Thank you, Google Dictionary]

[ ] Common cause of venture death: poor timing ...

[ ] Focus on results ...

[ ] Do what we do best and stick with it ...

[ ] Don't argue with an idiot ... they'll drag us down to their level and beat us with experience ... [Thank you, G Rivera]

[ ] Risk without measurement is suicide ... analytics are a must ... [Thank you, Ian Lurie]

[ ] Be a You Betcha Buddy ... not a NoBody (someone who says "No" all the time!) ...

[ ] Just because someone says something doesn't make it true!

[ ] Do or Die ... if we don't do, we will die. We must continue to do something new and better ...

[ ] Be a good friend ...

[ ] Key question for our venture: What does our venture do?

[ ] There are lies, damn lies, and statistics ... [Thank you, Benjamin Disraeli]

[ ] Efficient: maximum productivity, minimum waste ...

[ ] Standard parts are not ... [Thank you, Gordon Strang]

[ ] Magic happens, but not very often ... when it does happen, put on a happy smile ...

[ ] Promote our venture with network TV advertising.

[ ] Don't over-analyze ... don't over-anything except maybe eggs for breakfast ...

[ ] Make it easy for first-time buyers ... they are doing something new and even if it is simple, it is still new to them.

[ ] When writing our business plan, avoid empty claims ... if we say something is so, back it up in the next sentence with a statistic or fact or quote from a knowledgeable source that supports the claim ... [Thank you, Kaye Vivian]

[ ] A good read: Blue Ocean Strategy (W Chan Kim & Renee Mauborgne ...

[ ] Everyone is in sales ... [Thank you, Harvey Mackay]

[ ] Key question for our venture: Is our venture, product, and/or service name easy to remember? ...

[ ] Pain: suffering or discomfort that may be an opportunity for a venture to solve ...

[ ] Key question for our venture: What is the venture's desired pre-money valuation? ...

[ ] Awkward or Comfortable ... how do we want our customers to feel when they work with us? ...

[ ] Zero in on our target ... then go for it!

[ ] Timeline: a graphic representation of the passage of time.

[ ] Love is the triumph of imagination over intelligence ... [Thank you, H L Mencken]

[ ] When writing our business plan, avoid amateurish financial projections ... spend some money and get an accountant to do these for us ... they'll help us think through the financial side of our venture, plus put them into a standard business format that a business person expects ... [Thank you, Kaye Vivian]

[ ] The longest journey begins with the first step ... [Thank you, Neil Armstrong]

[ ] Go ahead, make my day ... [Thank you, Clint Eastwood]

[ ] Start with customers that are really excited about what we have to offer them ...

[ ] Laughter helps us recover quicker ...

[ ] When products and services become largely indistinguishable, time becomes the only competitive advantage ... [Thank you, Andy Grove]

[ ] Invent just for the fun of it ...

[ ] Competitive Advantage: a condition or circumstance that puts a venture in a favorable or superior business position ...

[ ] The more we know, the less we fear ... the more we help our customers, the less they will be scared ...

[ ] Napping can dramatically increase learning, memory, awareness, and more ... [Thank you, HealthSpiritBody]

[ ] New ways of thinking about familiar things can release new energies and make all manner of things possible ... [Thank you, Charles Handy]

[ ] The happiness in the disagreeable work comes from getting it out of the way ...

[ ] Two things are infinite, the universe and human stupidity, but I'm not sure about the universe ... [Thank you, Albert Einstein]

[ ] Problem: a matter or situation regarded as unwelcome or harmful and needing to be dealt with and overcome ...

[ ] Read between the lines ...

[ ] Eighty / Twenty Rule of Thumb: 20% of our products generate 80% of our revenue ... [Thank you, Vilfredo Pareto]

[ ] Genius is the ability to do something that nobody thought could be done at all ...

[ ] Often times there is a large gap between what the entrepreneur believes is valuable and what the target customer perceives ... [Thank you, Andrew Zacharakis]

[ ] Sell solutions, not just products ... [Thank you, Klaus M Leisinger]

[ ] Science is facts ... just as houses are made of stones, so is science made of facts ... but a pile of stones is not a house and a collection of facts is not necessarily science ... [Thank you, Henri Poincare]

[ ] The least flexible component of any system is the user ... [Thank you, Jay Arthur]

[ ] My mind's made up, don't confuse me with facts ...

[ ] To be successful, the first thing to do is fall in love with our work ... [Thank you, Mary Lauretta]

[ ] Skilled innovators and entrepreneurs are sensitive to problems ...

[ ] Read a lot ...

[ ] Potential business model: Provide financing ...

[ ] If we can't beat 'em, confuse 'em ... apply this to how we might deal with our competition! ... [Thank you, Harry S Truman]

[ ] Team: two or more people working together ... it takes a team to raise a venture ...

[ ] Don't ask, don't get ... and don't ask for what we can't possibly get either ... [Thank you, Cliff Unger]

[ ] Extraordinary claims require extraordinary evidence ... if we want our customers, suppliers, employees, partners to

believe, let us always be upfront and honest ... [Thank you, Carl Sagan]

[ ] Answer trick questions with short answers ... [Thank you, Mary Elizabeth Bradford]

[ ] WAG, TWAG, SWAG, SWEAT, SWEET, or SCIENCE? ...

[ ] The pessimist complains about the wind ... the optimist expects it to change ... the realist adjusts the sails ... [Thank you, William Arthur Ward]

[ ] Hire a credible spokesperson ...

[ ] Never go grocery shopping when hungry ...

[ ] Serenade serendipity ...

[ ] When we we've made a mistake, fix it ...

[ ] Some people entertain ideas, others put them to work ... [Thank you, Maddy Truman]

[ ] Id or Ego ... what should we focus on today? ...

[ ] The best source of funding for our venture is revenue from sales of our products and services ...

[ ] Don't panic ... emotions should not replace rational thinking ...

[ ] We cannot make people care about something ... the decision to care is theirs ...

[ ] Mental Error: "Everyone in the world will want our product!" ... No, no, no, they will not ... some will, yes; more likely most will not ...

[ ] Believe we have no barriers ... but bring some big ladders, just in case!

[ ] Gross margins of 40% are a good benchmark that distinguishes more attractive from less attractive opportunities ... [Thank you, Andrew Corbett]

[ ] Do not believe everything we hear ...

[ ] Continue to grow and evolve ...

[ ] A complex system that works evolved from a simple system that worked ... [Thank you, John Gail]

[ ] Innovation is the best way to win ... it puts us ahead of the game ...

[ ] Combine ... What can we combine or bring together somehow? How about a blend, an alloy, an assortment, an ensemble? Combine units? Combine purposes? Combine appeals? Combine ideas? ... "I can bring together ... and ... to ..."

[ ] Skilled innovators and entrepreneurs are able to build on the strengths of others ...

[ ] Dare to innovate ... [Thank you, Sue Factor]

[ ] Help: make it easier to do something ...

[ ] Guidelines for creating financial objectives: Stay on the conservative side; Be honest in estimating what could be accomplished; Follow the industry norms; Model our numbers after a successful benchmark venture; Be consistent!

[ ] If we love what we do, it's not work ...

[ ] Successful teams listen to each other ...

[ ] The ability to learn and pivot faster than our competitors may be our only sustainable competitive advantage ... [Thank you, Arie De Geus]

[ ] The guiding principle is that we are writing a story, and all good stories have a theme ... a unifying thread that ties the

setting, characters, and plot together ... [Thank you, Andrew Corbett]

[ ] Successful innovators and entrepreneurs know how to absorb affordable losses ... [Thank you, Candida G Brush]

[ ] Fair is fair ...

[ ] There's always fleas; we've gotta concentrate on the dog ... [Thank you, Pepper Schwartz]

[ ] The necessity of producing is the enemy of the desire to create ... [Thank you, Raoul Vaneigem]

[ ] Put an old product in a new package ...

[ ] A good idea is surrounded by risk ...

[ ] 1 + 1 = 3 ... the effect of teamwork ... two together can do more than two apart ... [Thank you, Jonas Otter]

[ ] Conjoint Analysis: a statistical technique used in market research to determine how people value different features that make up an individual product or service ...

[ ] Focus on people their lives, their work, their dreams ... [Thank you, Google]

[ ] Promote our venture with personal letters ...

[ ] First Mover Advantage: the advantage gained by the initial ("first-moving") significant occupant of a market segment ...

[ ] Research & Development: work directed toward the creation, innovation, improvement, and introduction of products and processes ...

[ ] We only live once ... let's make the very best of it!

[ ] Types of expenses: Cost of Goods Sold, Operating Expenses, Interest Expense, Tax Expenses, Depreciation Expenses, Amortization Expenses ...

[ ] Needs or Wants or Desires ... what should we focus on today? ...

[ ] Common cause of venture death: inferior revenue model!

[ ] Ignorance never settles a question ... [Thank you, Benjamin Disraeli]

[ ] Enjoy ourselves ...

[ ] Promote our venture with Twitter ...

[ ] We've got a two-front war new product, new markets ...

[ ] If we run it up the flagpole and no one salutes, find a new flag ... or a new flagpole!

[ ] It all begins with an idea ...

[ ] Innovators are often good at music and art ... and musicians and artists are often innovative ...

[ ] A committee is like a cul-de-sac down which ideas are lured, then quietly strangled ... [Thank you, Barrett Cocks]

[ ] Take notes ... capture our thoughts, ideas, information, opportunities, leads, clues, hints, suggestions, recommendations, information ...

[ ] People like people who complement them ...

[ ] Timing is critical ... the same idea can have different fates ... [Thank you, Jerry Kaplan]

[ ] Excellerate or Accelerate ...

[ ] Exploration and ideation ... the earliest stages of venture development ...

[ ] How to kill creativity: "You're going to fail ..." ...

[ ] If we can't explain it simply, we don't understand it well enough ... [Thank you, Albert Einstein]

[ ] A little word of encouragement after a failure is worth more than a big heap of praise after a success ... [Thank you, Baseball Life]

[ ] Deliver a better value to a profitable niche market ... [Thank you, Michael Porter]

[ ] A business plan is a formal document that provides background and financial information about the venture, the goals and objectives and how the management team intends to reach them ... [Thank you, Webb Smith]

[ ] Make a difference to colleagues ... [Thank you, InsideCRM]

[ ] Don't get off the ladder before we reach the ground ...

[ ] Interact closely with customers ... [Thank you, S A Buckler]

[ ] Do what we do best, contract the rest ... focus on our core competencies first and foremost ...

[ ] Generalists and specialists, need 'em both!

[ ] How to retain customers: offer discounts for additional purchases ...

[ ] Sell, sell, sell ...

[ ] Avoid cliches and trite phrases ... [Thank you, Randy Accetta]

[ ] Someone else has already thought of it ... lucky for us, only 1 in 100 will act on it. That one outta be us!

[ ] Pictures or Paragraphs ... what should we focus on today?

[ ] Great Big City or Little Bitty Town ... what should we focus on today? ...

[ ] Play the hand that's dealt us ... but if we don't like the game, kick over the table!

[ ] Since Time is not a person we can overtake when he is gone, let us honor him with mirth and cheerfulness of heart while he is passing ... [Thank you, Johann Wolfgang von Goethe]

[ ] Hold our vision of success clearly in mind ...

[ ] Nothing great was ever achieved without enthusiasm ... [Thank you, Ralph Waldo Emerson]

[ ] To gain experience, we have to get out the building ...

[ ] We may delay, but time will not ... [Thank you, Benjamin Franklin]

[ ] How to improve our financial bottom line: change our target market ...

[ ] Questions? ...

[ ] Key question for our venture: Who owns our venture? ... what do they expect? ...

[ ] Make data-driven decisions ...

[ ] Glory is fleeting, but obscurity is forever! ... [Thank you, Napoleon Bonaparte]

[ ] Subcontract work and processes that are not our core competencies ...

[ ] To design something simple is very hard ... [Thank you, Rick Yngve]

[ ] Proactively seek new opportunities ...

[ ] Think of problems not as stumbling blocks but as stepping-stones ...

[ ] Be spontaneous ...

[ ] Key question for our venture: What is the likely exit for our venture – IPO or M&A? ... When do you see the exit happening? Who will be the likely acquirers? ...

[ ] Opinion is like a pendulum and obeys the same law ... if it goes past the center of gravity on one side, it must go a like distance on the other; and it is only after a certain time that it finds the true point at which it can remain at rest ... [Thank you, Arthur Schopenhauer]

[ ] Funding: the action or practice of providing money for a particular purpose ...

[ ] Rapid Prototype Venture: a process used to create a new venture in order to launch a new product or service concept in a short period of time ...

[ ] Key question for our venture: What can we let go? ...

[ ] When posting to a blog, think whether it is really something we would say face-to-face to a reasonable person who could beat us to a pulp without breaking a sweat ... if it would land us in a hospital in that situation, then it's probably not appropriate for us to post ... [Thank you, Mark Robarge]

[ ] Ready! Aim! Fire! ... in that order!

[ ] Be credible, be incredible, but don't be uncredible!

[ ] Problem Solving: finding solutions to difficult or complex situations ...

[ ] Web site for local business pattern information: www.census.gov/econ/cbp ...

[ ] Good results without good planning come from good luck, not good management ... [Thank you, David Jaquith]

[ ] Don't rock the boat ... sink it and start all over!

[ ] When writing our business plan, eliminate typos and misspelled words ... use the spell checker, hire an editor or have four people read the document from back to front, but get those errors out of there if we want to be taken seriously ... [Thank you, Kaye Vivian]

[ ] Develop the business around the people ... build it, don't buy it, and then be the best at what we do! ... [Thank you, Richard Branson]

[ ] The most important marketing tool is word-of-mouth ... good word-of-mouth comes from being great! ... [Thank you, Jay Conrad Levinson]

[ ] Value Proposition: an innovation, service, or feature intended to make a company or product attractive to customers ...

[ ] A good business plan provides a clear explanation of the one or two things the company does best ... [Thank you, Barry Weisband]

[ ] The good old days are gone ...

[ ] Don't invest in anything we don't understand ... it's called gambling and the odds are not in our favor ... [Thank you, Boyd Erman]

[ ] Don't make the day shorter by waking up late ... it's only 24 hours as it is ...

[ ] There will be ups, there will be downs ... the trick is to have more ups than downs ...

[ ] If we don't like change, we'll like irrelevance even less ... [Thank you, Jim Collins]

[ ] Components: a part or an element of a larger whole ... business plans are a collection of related components.

[ ] Use "talking headings"on slides to convey meaning ... stamp out generalities ... [Thank you, Randy Accetta]

[ ] Words or Numbers ... what should we focus on today? ...

[ ] Cultivate those who can teach us ...

[ ] Praise in public, criticize in private ...

[ ] Early-Stage: a new venture, typically one that is not yet financially stable and self-supporting, generally less than 5 years old ...

[ ] An imagination is a terrible thing to waste ...

[ ] By the time an opportunity is fully investigated, it may no longer exist! ... [Thank you, Amar Bhide]

[ ] Write so you can't be misunderstood ...

[ ] Common bootstrapping strategy: buy used ...

[ ] Get rid of the frivolous frills ...

[ ] Some ideas will last forever ... some will not ...

[ ] Anticipate what our competitors will do ... can we live with it? ...

[ ] Knowledge enables us to work more intelligently and effectively ...

[ ] Act quick on good ideas ...

[ ] Win, win, win, win, win ... everyone (customers, suppliers, employees, investors, management) has to win!

[ ] Key question for our venture: Is there a connection between our name and the product, service, or business venture it represents? ...

[ ] One for the money, two for the show, three to get ready, and four to go ...

[ ] Everything has a beginning, a middle, and an end ...

[ ] Stop wishing and wanting, start acting ...

[ ] Words and ideas can change this world ... [Thank you, Robin Williams]

[ ] The competition is a good source of ideas ...

[ ] All for one, one for all ... [Thank you, Alexandre Dumas]

[ ] Focus on markets where we have the best ability to sell and service ...

[ ] Don't sit down and wait for the opportunities to come ... get up and make them! ... [Thank you, C J Walker]

[ ] Don't get too greedy ... or we will get needy speedy ...

[ ] Hard and smart ... the best way to work! ... [Thank you, Bruce Rianda]

[ ] Dilute: finance/accounting term meaning to reduce a person's or entity's proportional (i.e., percentage) equity ownership, typically by issuing and selling new equity (stock) to other shareholders ...

[ ] Design for the world ... [Thank you, Google]

[ ] If we don't have a ruler, we can use a dollar bill ... it's six inches long, two bucks to the foot! ... [Thank you, Doug Clark]

[ ] Make history ... good history, not bad ...

[ ] Keep a voice recorder close at hand to capture information when writing it down is not convenient ...

[ ] Entrepreneurs have a knack for looking at the ordinary and seeing the extraordinary ... [Thank you, D G Mitton]

[ ] Imitation is the sincerest form of flattery ...

[ ] The way to greatness is paved with mistakes ... [Thank you, Stefan Antonowicz]

[ ] Promote our venture with a (famous) spokesperson ...

[ ] Branding mistake: lack of communication ... everyone in the company is a spokesperson and should be talking the same talk! ... [Thank you, Jarad Hull]

[ ] A company is considered "high tech" if 10% or more of its employees are engaged in R&D ...

[ ] Give something unexpected ... ie, hidden features in the software that come to light later ...

[ ] The greatest fault is to be conscious of none ...

[ ] Provide compelling information about each of the following in the executive summary ... Description of Opportunity ... Business Concept ... Industry Overview ... Target Market ... Competitive Advantage ... Business Model and Economics ... Team and Offering ... [Thank you, William Bygrave]

[ ] Key question for our venture: How can we define our marketing message?

[ ] Keep sentences to 23 or fewer words; short sentences enable us to deliver a clearer message and avoid getting lost in wordy rhetoric ... [Thank you, Michael Betrus]

[ ] List every potential market ...

[ ] Don't be timid ... don't be shy, take a look and find out why ...

[ ] Don't throw away the old pail until we're sure the new one holds water ...

[ ] I can see it now, a personal computer in every home ... [Thank you, Bill Gates]

[ ] A thank-you goes a long, long way ... (Once upon a time, I stayed with an organization way beyond what might have been normally expected because the general manager simply said, "Thank you, Jim. I appreciate you being here." Every week. Not gratuitous, either. He really did mean it!) ...

[ ] Not every source of venture funding is the right source for us ...

[ ] Promote our venture with trade journal advertising ...

[ ] Objective or Subjective ... objective is factual, subjective is opinionated ...

[ ] Skilled innovators and entrepreneurs are logical ...

[ ] When we fail, learn ...

[ ] Share or teach what we know ...

[ ] The truth is rarely simple ... [Thank you, New York Times]

[ ] We're drowning in information and starving for knowledge ... [Thank you, Rutherford D Rogers]

[ ] Constantly review developments to make sure that the benefits are what they were supposed to be ... [Thank you, William H Swanson]

[ ] Want: a strong wish for something ...

[ ] Make it easy for our customers to be evangelists for our venture ...

[ ] Create intellectual property that can act as significant barriers to our competition ...

[ ] It's all right letting ourselves go, as long as you can get ourselves back ...

[ ] An open ear and a closed mouth is a temporary substitute for wisdom ...

[ ] To lead people, walk behind them ... [Thank you, Lao-Tzu]

[ ] Think why we are saying no before we say no ...

[ ] A penny saved is ten pennies earned ... [Thank you, Benjamin Franklin]

[ ] The absence of alternatives clears the mind marvelously ... [Thank you, Henry Kissinger]

[ ] 80% of success is showing up, the other 20% is knowing what to do once we get there ... [Thank you, Woody Allen]

[ ] Batch our routine tasks and do them all at once ...

[ ] Love creates love ... creators love creators ...

[ ] Know thy customer ...

[ ] Empower all in our venture to do what is right ...

[ ] Idea: The most embryonic form of a new product or service. It often consists of a high-level view of the solution envisioned for the problem identified by the opportunity ... [Thank you, E Fisher]

[ ] Promote our venture with sales tools ...

[ ] Don't just do the easy stuff ... everyone does the easy, it's the hard that builds true value ...

[ ] We can't steal second base and keep our foot on first ... [Thank you, Kenny Lofton]

[ ] Do not condemn the judgment of another because it differs from our own ... we may both be wrong ...

[ ] Successful innovators and entrepreneurs have high levels of tenacity and courage ... [Thank you, Greg Vogt]

[ ] Our friends will flip-flop fast when we're facing failure ... cherish those that stick with us ...

[ ] Key question for our venture: What new ventures have recently entered our industry, and why? ...

[ ] Passion is perfect ...

[ ] Don't buy a cow if we just want a steak dinner ... [Thank you, Frank Novy]

[ ] Promote our ideas ... if we don't, who will? ...

[ ] Creative people embrace and leverage failures ... if that didn't work, why not and what if we try it this way instead ... [Thank you, Emma L Murray]

[ ] Celebrate little victories ...

[ ] Learn or Teach ... what should we focus on today? ...

[ ] To be extraordinary, either be the very best in one thing or really good in two ... [Thank you, Scott Adams]

[ ] The truth can't be manufactured ... [Thank you, New York Times]

[ ] Nobody likes a grump ... take it easy!

[ ] Due Diligence: the process employed by potential investors or their agents of investigating a business deal or the target of an investment or acquisition ...

[ ] Kiss of Death: something absolutely insurmountable that will stop us from reaching our goals and objectives ...

[ ] Find the right partnerships ...

[ ] It is no disgrace to fall down ... the disgrace is not getting up ...

[ ] Key question for our venture: How do we use financial statements in our venture? ...

[ ] Key question for our venture: What are our primary opportunities? ...

[ ] Pick a pertinent price point ...

[ ] ITO: abbreviation for Inputs-Transformation-Outputs, the concept of translating one set of elements (the inputs) into another (the outputs) ...

[ ] Key question for our venture: What motivates our venture founders? ...

[ ] Everything is more difficult than it appears ...

[ ] If we don't have any competition ... maybe there's no need for what we do!

[ ] Beware: cheaters ... unfortunately, there are a lot of them out there ...

[ ] We forget what we hear, we remember what we see, we know what we do!

[ ] Rapid Prototyping: a group of techniques used to quickly fabricate a scale model of a component or assembly ...

[ ] See excellence wherever it is ...

[ ] Reduce marketing costs by improving marketing quality ...

[ ] The only safe ship in a storm is leadership ... [Thank you, Faye Wattleton]

[ ] If it didn't work the first time, why do we think it will work the second? ... if we do the same thing over and over the same way why should we expect different results? ...

[ ] Maintain a good credit history ...

[ ] There is no garden without weeds ...

[ ] Hit 'em where they ain't ... go where our customers are and our competitors aren't ...

[ ] We are not meant to fly solo ... we're not meant fly at all, which is why we need an airplane and a good crew to go along!

[ ] There is no maybe ...

[ ] Promote our venture with rebates ...

[ ] There's no formula for success in business ... but there is a recipe: earn a profit solving customer problems with something new and better than the competition! Like any recipe, the results depend on the quality of the ingredients and the skills of the cook ...

[ ] Keep an Opportunity Journal ... Evernote.com is a great tool to capture ideas and information, and to find it again when it's needed ...

[ ] Financial Objectives: monetary goals for a venture ...

[ ] Junk accumulates to fill the space available for its storage ... [Thank you, Bruce O Boston]

[ ] Be fearless ...

[ ] Big picture or small details ... we need both ...

[ ] Define, gather, form, test, analyze, interpret, modify ...

[ ] Knowledge can be memorized ... wisdom must think things through ...

[ ] Customer Value Proposition positioning ... (1) Target group and need (2) Brand (3) Concept and (4) Point of difference ... [Thank you, William Bygrave]

[ ] Skilled innovators and entrepreneurs are original ...

[ ] Where there's money, there's mischief ...

[ ] Weird or Wonderful ... what should we focus on today? ...

[ ] Competitive Creativity: the process of innovation ...

[ ] The accomplish the impossible, we must attempt the absurd ... [Thank you, Miguel de Unamuno]

[ ] Parent approval is a powerful force ...

[ ] Alpha, beta, 1.0 (one point oh) ... terminology for the stages of product development ...

[ ] Our brand must make us immediately and positively distinguished from our competitors ...

[ ] Collaboration: the action of working together to produce or create something, or make something happen ...

[ ] Skilled innovators and entrepreneurs are willing to solve puzzles ...

[ ] We already have some very valuable assets: our capabilities, experiences, education, talents, and passion ...

[ ] Oh, a wise guy, eh? ... yes, hopefully, yes! ... [Thank you, Moe]

[ ] The closed mouth gathers no feet ...

[ ] Maintain a personal collection of potential opportunities and ideas ...

[ ] There's no such thing as being totally wrong ...

[ ] How can we answer this Question: Is the lifetime value of a customer significantly greater than the cost of customer acquisition? ...

[ ] A good attorney knows the law ... a great attorney knows the judge ... [Thank you, Paul Efron]

[ ] A good business plan provides evidence of customer acceptance of the venture's products and services ... [Thank you, Anita Bell]

[ ] Reality leaves a lot to the imagination ... [Thank you, John Lennon]

[ ] Our worst humiliation is someone else's entertainment ... [Thank you, Karen Crockett]

[ ] A spreadsheet program can double as a flat-file database to store data we collect from our field research ...

[ ] Pause and think ...

[ ] Avoid jargon, slang, and abbreviations ... CFATH HAND YOYO!

[ ] Key question for our venture: Who are our major competitors? ... what do we know about them now? What else do we need to know about them? ...

[ ] A good read: Eats, Shoots and Leaves (Lynne Truss) ... how could someone possibly write an innovative book about grammar? Lynne did ...

[ ] When our work speaks for itself, don't interrupt ... [Thank you, Henry Kaiser]

[ ] List 10 things we do that our customers don't like ... what are we going to do about it?

[ ] People say nothing is impossible ... but I do nothing every day! ... [Thank you, Theodor Rosyfelt]

[ ] If it's wrong, make it right ... if it's right, make it better ... [Thank you, James Arnold]

[ ] Don't fake it ... be authentic and credible with our marketing ... [Thank you, Richard Pachter]

[ ] Key question for our venture: How is our venture different and better than the competition? ...

[ ] Stay calm ...

[ ] Take advantage of fortuitous circumstances ...

[ ] There's always room for improvement ... [Thank you, Oscar De La Hoya]

[ ] Venture Capitalist: an organization or individual speculator who makes money available for innovative projects (especially in high technology) ...

[ ] Everyone has to win ...

[ ] Time or Money ... what should we focus on today? ...

[ ] We've got to know where we're going to see if we've arrived ...

[ ] Thought: ...

[ ] Some people think the same thought a thousand times ... others think a thousand different thoughts ...

[ ] Output: the amount of something produced ...

[ ] Develop a minimal, nominal, and optimal list of what is need to get this new venture up and running, and how much money is required for each category ...

[ ] Come darkness, we'll appreciate the light ...

[ ] The more we reason, the less we create ... [Thank you, Raymond Chandler]

[ ] We can't explain everything ... so let's not try ...

[ ] Hypothesis: a proposed explanation that is used as a starting point for further investigation, often made on the basis of limited evidence ...

[ ] The past was once the future ... now is now the past ...

[ ] Write our own personal script for success ... [Thank you, Bill Strickland]

[ ] Key question for our venture: Can we readily demonstrate our products or services? ...

[ ] At my lemonade stand I used to give the first glass away free and charge five dollars for the second glass ... the refill contained the antidote ... [Thank you, Emo Phillips]

[ ] Learn as much as we possibly can from our competition ... what works for them, what doesn't ...

[ ] There just might be a point when it's time for new executive leadership, with different skills and strengths ... ventures evolve and may need a new crew for a new ocean ... [Thank you, Terry Semel]

[ ] Nothing succeeds like success ... hard to get that taste out of our mouth ...

[ ] Key question for our venture: How big can our venture become? ...

[ ] Don't blindly follow our competition ... some of them are idiots!

[ ] This time, like all times, is a very good one, if we know what to do with it ... [Thank you, Ralph Waldo Emerson]

[ ] Beware: Pseudo-science can have a mesmerizing effect ...

[ ] Common cause of venture death: ignored customers ...

[ ] How to kill creativity: "That's not really creative ..."

[ ] Hang in there ... there's nowhere else to go right now ...

[ ] Make sure our customers can easily buy and use our products ...

[ ] The more, the merrier ... the more people in a poll, the more accurate the results ...

[ ] Find the emergency exits before the lights dim ...

[ ] Help ourselves by helping others ...

[ ] Sometimes the truth is not so simple ...

[ ] Promote our venture with local TV ...

[ ] Play has value ... if nothing else, it takes some of the stress off work ...

[ ] There is no such thing as instant experience ... [Thank you, J Robert Oppenheimer]

[ ] Time is a state of mind ... the faster the mind moves, the faster the time goes by!

[ ] Value innovation is a new way of thinking about executing strategy that results in the creation of a blue ocean and a break from the competition ... [Thank you, W Chan Kim]

[ ] We miss 100 percent of the shots we never take ... [Thank you, Wayne Gretzky]

[ ] Pleasure: satisfaction and enjoyment benefits delivered to customers ...

[ ] Promote our venture with trade fairs ...

[ ] Paint masterpieces ... even if they don't start or necessarily turn out that way ...

[ ] Be adaptable if we to be adoptable ... fit ever-changing customer needs, wants, and desires ...

[ ] Value: the Benefits versus the Price of something ...

[ ] Traits of leaders who are good at relationship building: adaptability, development, connectedness, empathy, harmony, inclusion, individualization, positivity, relating ... [Thank you, Gallup]

[ ] Rocket science follows the rules of physics, entrepreneurship follows the rules of thumb ...

[ ] Humor is to life what shock absorbers are to automobiles!

[ ] Make a list ... a list is a really good and simple tool for getting and keeping organized ...

[ ] It is better to suffer injustice than to do it ...

[ ] Key question for our venture: Do we have any regulatory risks? ... Like what? How are we going to deal with them? ...

[ ] Brevity is the soul of wit ... [Thank you, Henny Youngman]

[ ] Rocket science is 80% science and 20% judgment, entrepreneurship is 80% judgment and 20% science ...

[ ] A chicken doesn't stop scratching just because the worms are scarce ... we gotta keep looking for new customers! ... [Thank you, Sophie Novy]

[ ] Our minds can make things impossible ... or not!

[ ] A healthy business is worth about 5 times its EBITDA (a 5 price/earnings ratio) ... a growth company, an even higher price/earnings ratio ... perhaps 10, 15, 20 or more ... [Thank you, Bob Morrison]

[ ] We're number one! (Hertz) ... We try harder! (Avis) ...

[ ] We'll never run out of great ideas ...

[ ] Beware of dog ... dangerous old ??? ...

[ ] Success in business comes from a willingness to grind it out ... [Thank you, Guy Kawasaki]

[ ] 1.0: the first version.revision numbering for a new product ... (one point oh) ... "1" is the version number, "0" is the revision number ... if nothing major has changed but some small revision was made, only the revision number changes ... some customers are hesitant to buy the very first version of anything, so some companies start their version.revision number with something other than 1.0 (ie, 3.2) ... [Thank you, Gene Olson]

[ ] Winning isn't everything ... wanting to win is! ... [Thank you, Vince Lombardi]

[ ] Always add unique value ... [Thank you, Bill Blade]

[ ] Take charge of our own destiny ...

[ ] When we're down, everything falls on us ...

[ ] Word choice matters ...

[ ] Conventionality is the mother of dreariness ... [Thank you, C Benson]

[ ] Skilled innovators and entrepreneurs are ambitious ...

[ ] Clear, concise, precise ... a guide for all we do ...

[ ] For better or worse ... hopefully better, if we put our hearts and minds to making that happen!

[ ] No such thing as bad press ...

[ ] Link new technologies to old market needs ...

[ ] Key question for our venture: Who are the founders and key team members of our venture? ...

[ ] Benefits, baby, benefits! maybe we can have too many babies, but we can't ever have too many benefits!

[ ] Entrepreneurs are usually good at setting goals and objectives ... then meeting or exceeding them ...

[ ] Work with what we have ...

[ ] Be prepared for the unexpected ...

[ ] Key team members must have successful experience in our key industry ...

[ ] The tragedy of life doesn't lie in not reaching our goal ... the tragedy lies in having no goals to reach ... [Thank you, Benjamin Mays]

[ ] First deserve, then desire ...

[ ] Key question for our venture: What are the people that join our venture going to do? ...

[ ] Change is not made without inconvenience ... even from better to worse ... [Thank you, Richard Hooker]

[ ] How can we answer this Question: How many people do we need in our venture, the critical mass, in order to achieve our immediate goals and objectives? ...

[ ] Our most important competitive advantage is (or will be) our brand ...

[ ] A venture operations manual facilitates even-handed, consistent administration of personnel policies ...

[ ] Visionary leadership style ... most appropriate when an organization needs a new direction; where we need to go but not necessarily how ... [Thank you, Daniel Goleman]

[ ] Capital efficiency ...

[ ] Ideation: the process of forming ideas or concepts ...

[ ] Successful teams perform well in a chaotic environments!

[ ] Educate and train ...

[ ] The danger of being a first mover: we may get it wrong ...
[Thank you, William Bygrave,]

[ ] We need to work together ... there is no way to work apart
...

[ ] Promote our venture with direct mail ...

[ ] The best way to gather competitive information is through
network and trade shows ... [Thank you, William Bygrave]

[ ] Innovators usually have good imaginations ...

[ ] Most of our audience uses a search engine to find us ... all
the banners and viral marketing on earth won't come close to
results produced by a top 5 ranking for a relevant phrase ...
[Thank you, Ian Lurie]

[ ] The Internet is like a drug needle that goes right into the
bloodstream ... people download the precise point of view that
speaks to their own biases ... [Thank you, Thomas Friedman]

[ ] Skilled innovators and entrepreneurs expect success ...

[ ] The value of money lies in what we do with it ...

[ ] Anyone who stops learning is old, whether at twenty or
eighty; anyone who keeps learning stays young ... the greatest
thing in life is to keep our minds young ... [Thank you, Henry
Ford]

[ ] It is okay to cry ...

[ ] Every rule of thumb can be broken except this one ...
[Thank you, Roger von Oech]

[ ] Boil matters down to the simplest terms ...

[ ] Manpower, material, machinery, money, methods ... the
M's of manufacturing ...

[ ] Innovators are often emotional ...

[ ] Any fool can criticize, condemn, and complain ... and
most fools do! ... [Thank you, Benjamin Franklin]

[ ] Successful brands connect with the hearts and minds of
the customer ... they create an emotional connection! ...
[Thank you, Leslie Bromberg]

[ ] Earnings from sales to customers is our best source of
funding for our venture ...

[ ] Nothing is more effective than sincere, accurate praise ...
[Thank you, Bill Walsh]

[ ] Use PowerPoint (or Google Slides, or similar) as the
homebase for a business plan ... create a slide for each of the
major topics in the business plan ... that slide deck is the
master for any business plan presentation we may need to
make ... then use the "Speaker Notes" feature of PowerPoint to
write supporting sentences and paragraphs for each of the
slides ... when printing the slides, print them one to a page
with speaker notes shown ... voila, an instant business plan
complete with graphics (the slides themselves) ... further, the
"written" business plan and the "slide presentation" will be
"synced"!

[ ] Entrepreneurial Myth: Banks don't lend money to
start-ups ... actually, bank loans are the most common source
of funding for new ventures in the US ... [Thank you, Scott
Shane]

[ ] The one most responsive to change is the one that survives ... [Thank you, Charles Darwin]

[ ] If we don't have a sense of unity, it will be very hard for us to succeed together ... [Thank you, Barack Obama]

[ ] Timing: the choice, judgment, or control of when something should be done ...

[ ] The way to become boring is to say everything ...

[ ] Key question for our venture: How is our venture organization structured? ... is it optimal?

[ ] Quality: the degree of excellence of something ...

[ ] Walk the dog ... don't have dog? ... borrow one ... good exercise and good conversations ...

[ ] Promote our venture with per-order/per-inquiry ads ...

[ ] If we can't beat 'em, join 'em ...

[ ] Skilled innovators and entrepreneurs are rational ...

[ ] Shark Tank is a "reality" TV show, not necessarily "reality" entrepreneurship ... TV shows need drama, conflict, heros and villains and victims to attract an audience ... real life is a bit more mundane ...

[ ] List the attributes ...

[ ] Do not boast of a thing until it is done ...

[ ] Think different! ... [Thank you, Apple]

[ ] A new venture may be feasible if there are customers willing to pay for a solution ...

[ ] Key question for our venture: Is our name easily confused with other names? ...

5280 TIPS for INNOVATORS and ENTREPRENEURS

[ ] How can we answer this Question: How much funding is being raised for our venture right now? ... for how long will that hold us over? ...

[ ] Synthesis: arrange, assemble, collect, compose, construct, create, design, develop, formulate, manage, organize, plan, prepare, propose, set up, write ...

[ ] Promote our venture with business cards ...

[ ] Once we say something it's out of our control ...

[ ] The early bird gets the worm ...

[ ] Common bootstrapping strategy: borrow from friends ...

[ ] Focus first on a specific niche market ... after we capture the beachhead, we can move further ashore ...

[ ] Beware: experts from afar ...

[ ] Positive or Negative ... what should we focus on today? ...

[ ] Successful entrepreneurs have an ability to build networks ... [Thank you, Timothy Butler]

[ ] Define our own meaning of success ...

[ ] The longer a decision is left unmade, the greater the costs of implementing it ...

[ ] Praise in public, complain in private ...

[ ] Some things seem easy at first, but ... [you know the rest!]

[ ] Easy or Hard ... which one describes what we should be doing today? ...

[ ] Facts are stubborn things, but statistics are pliable ... [Thank you, Mark Twain]

[ ] The more things we plan to do, the more energy we will have to do them ... weird how that works ...

[ ] Grant: a type of funding typically provided by government agencies or non-profit foundations ... and typically for early-stage technology ventures, although not always ...

[ ] Focus on doing things that give us an unfair competitive advantage ...

[ ] If we fail at humor, at least no one is laughing at us ... [Thank you, A Whitney Brown]

[ ] What we see depends on what we look for ... [Thank you, John Lubbock]

[ ] Make it easy for prospective customers to get information about our venture ...

[ ] Promote our venture with brochures and pamphlets ...

[ ] Change happens ... with or without us!

[ ] Successful innovators and entrepreneurs know how to take small actions ... [Thank you, Candida G Brush]

[ ] Key question for our venture: How can we be a $50 million revenue venture in 5 years? ... Or, if we already are, how about $500 million in 5 years? ...

[ ] Even if we do not see it, we can still have faith that it is there ...

[ ] Key question for our venture: How many employees do we have? ... How many do we really need? ...

[ ] Value Proposition: a promise of value to be delivered and a belief from the customer that value will be experienced ...

[ ] Never judge people by appearance ... judge them by performance ...

[ ] Hook: something that catches the attention of prospective customers, journalists, listeners, and viewers ...

[ ] Change happens but ... sometimes it's good, sometimes it's not ...

[ ] Types of pricing strategies ... competition-led, customer-led, loss-leader, introductory offer, skimming, psychological, fair pricing, bundled pricing, value-based ...

[ ] Little things can mean a lot ...

[ ] An expert is someone who knows some of the worst mistakes that can be made is her field and how to avoid them ... [Thank you, Werner Karl Heisenberg]

[ ] Learners inherit the earth ... [Thank you, Eric Hoffer]

[ ] Better, faster, smaller, cheaper ... [Thank you, Intel]

[ ] Better to keep peace than to make peace ...

[ ] Customer needs are the basis of our business ... [Thank you, Mike Dell]

[ ] If we have to choose between paying customers and a fleshed-out business plan, choose the paying customers ...

[ ] You can tell a book by its cover ...

[ ] It could be a good opportunity if our team has or can learn the skills needed ...

[ ] No one can serve two masters ... not even a two-headed snake!

[ ] It pays to be obvious ... [Thank you, Isaac Asimov]

[ ] There is nothing so useless as doing efficiently that which should not be done at all ... [Thank you, Peter F Drucker]

[ ] All's well that ends well ... [Thank you, Bard of Avon]

[ ] Attributes of successful new venture founding team members ... Determination, resilience, tenacity, commitment, curiosity, work ethic, humanity ... [Thank you, Atish Davda]

[ ] Buy a bunch of cheap baseball hats ... Put a label on one hat for each of the work areas in our venture. Then, assign a hat (or likely, multiple hats!) to the individual that is responsible for each particular area, no area left without someone responsible. As we grow our venture, we hire new people to take on one of the multiple hats someone else has been wearing. Have a hat passing party to celebrate the growth of our venture ...

[ ] We can learn a lot from complaints ...

[ ] Be something to someone ...

[ ] Think of organizations and people who may have an interest in our success but aren't directly paid or rewarded for any success our business might realize, such as associations, the media and other organizations that sell to our customers ... [Thank you, Guy Kawasaki]

[ ] Make a difference ... even if it is little ...

[ ] Build an ecosystem of ideas ... [Thank you, 3M]

[ ] Successful teams provide mutual inspiration ...

[ ] Seek quality in all we do ...

[ ] Secondary research: the summary, collation and/or synthesis of existing research, data, and information ...

[ ] Charge for our work ... otherwise we will not be taken seriously ... [Thank you, E Aston]

[ ] Entrepreneurship is not reserved for startups ... Entrepreneurship is a lifelong skill that can be applied in most any and every environment ... [Thank you, Heidi M Neck]

[ ] Design: plan something with a specific purpose in mind ...

[ ] Successful entrepreneurs are collaborative ... [Thank you, Janet Kraus]

[ ] Key question for our venture: Are we sensitive to our customers' needs and requests? ...

[ ] Knowing isn't the same as doing ... [Thank you, Alan Webber]

[ ] When we all think alike, no one thinks very much ... [Thank you, Walter Lippman]

[ ] Don't kill the messenger who brings us bad news ... if the bird dies, so does the information that we may sorely need ...

[ ] Rome wasn't built in a day ...

[ ] Know when and how to cut our losses ...

[ ] Create a climate to grow innovation ...

[ ] Once a decision is reached, stop worrying ... go make it happen ...

[ ] Even when we have pains, we don't have to be a pain ...

[ ] Everyone is selling something ...

[ ] If all work is grunt work, work somewhere else ...

[ ] Prototyping, both products and services alike, is one strategy to test key assumptions about what a customer will value and be willing to buy ... we can use product brochures and product data sheet to solicit inputs from customers ... [Thank you, William Bygrave]

[ ] Focus on our customer's needs, wants, and desires ... [Thank you, Paul Graham]

[ ] Never get into fights with ugly people ... they have nothing to lose ... [Thank you, Robert M Gates]

[ ] Do what we love ... easier then to love what we do ...

[ ] Nature works 24 hours a day, 7 days a week, 365 days a year ... tirelessly finding ways to change our lives and loves ...

[ ] Key question for our venture: What are the principal risks to our venture? ...

[ ] Innovator and Entrepreneur: the two most important hats when creating a new business venture ...

[ ] Feedback is the breakfast of champions! Robert Lorber ...

[ ] We can automate the production of cars, but we can't automate the production of customers ... [Thank you, Walter Reuther]

[ ] No expectations, no failure ... isn't that a nice way to eliminate failure? Just eliminate any expectations and failure goes away, as does success!

[ ] A diamond was once a chunk of coal under pressure ...

[ ] Skilled innovators and entrepreneurs are action-oriented.

[ ] Always deliver our criticisms in private to minimize emotional fallout ... [Thank you, Kohn-O'Connell]

[ ] 20% of the products generate 80% of the revenue ... not atypical for many companies ... what is our ratio? ...

[ ] Education plus experience equals expertise ...

[ ] Watch for good deals ...

[ ] How much wood would a woodchuck chuck if a woodchuck could chuck wood? ... 700 pounds, give or take ...

[ ] Trust but verify ... trust what they say, but verify it is true.

[ ] TVM: (abbreviation for Time Value of Money) the principle that a certain currency amount of money today has a different buying power than the same currency amount of money in the future ...

[ ] Successful innovators and entrepreneurs are forever curious ...

[ ] The first mover advantage ends when the second mover steps in. The first mover has the first competitive advantage, the second mover must be better ...

[ ] Victory belongs to the most persevering ... [Thank you, Napoleon Bonaparte]

[ ] Make big things happen by paying attention to the small details ...

[ ] Specialist: a person who concentrates primarily on a particular subject or activity; a person highly skilled in a specific and restricted field ...

[ ] Promote our venture with thank-you letters ...

[ ] The main ingredient of stardom success is the rest of the team ... [Thank you, John Wooden]

[ ] Key question for our venture: How do we brand our business? ...

[ ] Build a demographic profile of our target customers ... age range, income levels, educational backgrounds, household characteristics, occupation, ethnicities ...

[ ] Key question for our venture: Why should users care about our products or services? ...

[ ] Spend our time solving problems, not worrying about them ...

[ ] When it is not necessary to make a decision, it is necessary not to make a decision ... [Thank you, Lord Falkland]

[ ] Look around ...

[ ] Make good eye contact ...

[ ] Sometimes we're the dog, sometimes we're the hydrant ...

[ ] Key question for our venture: How do we compare to our competitors? ...

[ ] Knowledge is not the same as understanding ...

[ ] Successful Innovators and entrepreneurs know how to best use the means at hand ... [Thank you, Patricia G Greene]

[ ] Don't take personal offense at criticisms from customers ... listen and learn ...

[ ] Short circuit opinions with facts ...

[ ] People remember images ...

[ ] Don't worry about people stealing our ideas ... if our ideas are any good, we'll have to ram them down people's throats (figuratively speaking, of course) ... [Thank you, Howard Aiken]

[ ] What I hear, I forget ... what I hear and see, I remember a little ... what I hear, see, and ask questions about or discuss with someone else, I begin to understand ... what I hear, see, discuss, and do, I acquire knowledge and skill ... what I teach to another, I master ... [Thank you, Mel Silberman]

[ ] Don't push unreasonable deadlines ... work smart and hard ...

[ ] Four key revenue drivers ... customers, frequency, selling process, price ...

[ ] No surprises ... [Thank you, Tom Larkin]

[ ] Nothing is worth doing unless the consequences may be serious ... [Thank you, George Bernard Shaw]

[ ] Skilled innovators and entrepreneurs are inventive ...

[ ] Life is what happens when we were making other plans ... [Thank you, John Lennon]

[ ] We can succeed at almost anything, if we have unlimited enthusiasm ... [Thank you, Charles M Schwab]

[ ] People are egocentric ...

[ ] Market Niche: a subset of the market on which a specific product, service, or venture is focused ... [Thank you, Google Dictionary]

[ ] Key question for our venture: What legal risks do we have? ...

[ ] Happiness is a state of mind ... not a destination ...

[ ] Happiness is when what we think, what we say, and what we do are in harmony ... [Thank you, Mahatma Gandhi]

[ ] Progress is our most important product ... [Thank you, General Electric]

[ ] How to retain customers: give them special treatment ...

[ ] Three PhD's do not make an MBA ...

[ ] Recognize the importance of transparency ... [Thank you, Nelson Wang]

[ ] Potential business model: Manufacture products ...

[ ] Charm is the quality in others that makes us more satisfied with ourselves ... [Thank you, Henri-Frederic Amiel]

[ ] Ban the word "projections" ... we're making "objectives" for our venture, objectives that we need to meet and make

happen ... projections have no responsibility attached to them ... objectives are our responsibility to make them happen ...

[ ] It takes 9 months to have a baby ... 9 women can't do it in one!

[ ] People, places, things, time, money ... need 'em all in our venture ...

[ ] Be direct with our communication ... beating around the bush only frustrates people ...

[ ] Innovators are usually good at instinctive thinking ...

[ ] Find a strategy that offers a high probability for success ... repeat it over and over ...

[ ] Greatness is in our heart ...

[ ] Strategies or Tactics ... what should we focus on today? ...

[ ] Life is a great big canvas ... let's throw all the paint on it we can ... [Thank you, Danny Kaye]

[ ] Customer NWD Profile: an outline that defines the Needs, Wants, and Desires a customer would like to receive from a product, service, or process ...

[ ] Entrepreneuring is hard work ...

[ ] A committee is a group of people who individually can do nothing but as a group decide that nothing can be done ... [Thank you, Fred Allen]

[ ] Inputs - Transformation - Outputs ... that's what every business does ... transforms customer orders into products and services ...

[ ] Mistake: an action or judgment that is misguided or wrong ...

[ ] Promote our venture with personal sales ...

[ ] Concept: a well-defined form, including both a written and visual description, that includes its primary features and customer benefits combined with a broad understanding of the technology needed ... [Thank you, G M Ajamian]

[ ] Stay true to our contracts ...

[ ] Mind our image ...

[ ] The shortest distance between two points is a line ...

[ ] Climb a ladder step by step ... and our venture is one big ladder ...

[ ] First discuss issues on which we're pretty sure we'll agree ... [Thank you, William N Yeomans]

[ ] If our plan depends on us suddenly being "discovered" by the world, our plan will probably fail ...

[ ] Key question for our venture: What does the future have in store for our venture? ... How do we know? ...

[ ] I am guided by the vision of what I believe this show can be ... [Thank you, Oprah Winfrey]

[ ] Types of primary research: discussions, brainstorming, interviews, focus groups, surveys, surveillance ...

[ ] Break down barriers ...

[ ] Goals should be specific, realistic, and measurable ... [Thank you, William G Dyer]

[ ] Commit to innovation ...

[ ] Have patience with all things ...

[ ] Learn from our mistakes ...

[ ] State the facts fully and accurately ... [Thank you, Joel Raphaelson]

[ ] All work and no play makes Jack a dull boy and Jill a rich widow ... [Thank you, Evan Esar]

[ ] Don't wait for inspiration to start something ... action always generates inspiration, inspiration seldom generates action ... [Thank you, Frank Tibolt]

[ ] Market market market ...

[ ] Talent is a key to success ...

[ ] Help our customers remember us ... what can we do that they won't forget? ...

[ ] Let the quality of our work speak on our behalf ...

[ ] Minimal Viable Product (mvp): version of a new product which allows a team to collect validated learning about customers with the relatively low effort. An mvp is often an alpha or beta version of the final product offered for sale ...

[ ] Post-Money Valuation: the value or nominal worth of an entire company immediately after a financing round ...

[ ] Companies must move away from a "command and control" structure and cultivate a true spirit of teamwork at all levels ... everyone in the company must adopt a managerial outlook and take responsibility for the quality of what they produce ... the enterprise must be steered by a clear set of objectives while giving everyone the autonomy to decide how to reach those results ... [Thank you, Peter F Drucker]

[ ] Challenge ourselves ...

[ ] If we don't like what we're hearing, respond with a question, even if it's just "Why are you saying that?" ... this is a pretty good "trick" ... don't get mad, make the other person work ... keep those questions coming ... we might even learn a thing or two! ... [Thank you, Mark McCormack]

[ ] Gross Income: Revenue minus the Cost of Goods Sold (COGS) ...

[ ] Company: a commercial business ...

[ ] New things become used things the very next day ... don't buy new if a good used is half the price ...

[ ] Priority: regarded as more important ...

[ ] Most people won't buy something until they've been exposed to the seller 5 or 6 times ... [Thank you, Terry Wygal]

[ ] Word-of-Mouth marketing: Giving people a reason to talk about our services, and making it easier for that conversation to take place ... [Thank you, William Bygrave]

[ ] Everyone meets the future ... if they don't, they're dead ...

[ ] Emerging markets are characterized by "stealth" competitors ... [Thank you, Andrew Corbett]

[ ] Be succinct ...

[ ] Key question for our venture: How do we market or plan to market our products or services? ...

[ ] There are two sides to every story ... one side is usually better than the other ...

[ ] Companies are not creative, people are ...

[ ] There are two ways of exerting one's strength: one is pushing down, the other is pulling up ... [Thank you, Booker T Washington]

[ ] Reduce production costs by improving product quality ...

[ ] IT (Information Technology) is not marketing ... don't make them run the web site, it's not fair to anyone ... [Thank you, Ian Lurie]

[ ] How to kill creativity: "It's impossible ..." ...

[ ] Use product sampling to gather primary research data ...

[ ] Continuous feedback ...

[ ] The devil is in the details ...

[ ] We tend to get what we expect ... [Thank you, Norman Vincent Peale]

[ ] Promote our venture with advertorials ...

[ ] Each new invention is eventually replaced by a newer invention ...

[ ] Two of ten venture capital deals will fail, six will continue to go along, and the remaining two are where the money is made ... [Thank you, Stephen Lund]

[ ] Concentrate on what we do best ...

[ ] Our education is not complete just because we're not in school ...

[ ] Keep expenses variable wherever possible ...

[ ] Don't throw anything away ... keep it safe until we need it!

[ ] A good business plan presents a clear explanation of why the venture concept is a significant opportunity ...

[ ] Try, and try again ... [Thank you, Avi Tal]

[ ] Understand what we really need to do to survive and thrive ...

[ ] Understand that when we're wrong, we're wrong ...

[ ] I didn't wanna say yes, but I couldn't say no ...

[ ] If we think we can or can't, either way we're right ... [Thank you, Henry Ford]

[ ] Business plan competitions: beware when prize donor is on the judging panel ...

[ ] Identify our biggest weakness ...

[ ] Borrow instead of buying things ...

[ ] Experience is a comb nature gives to men when they are bald ...

[ ] Common cause of venture death: lack of access to customers ...

[ ] Common bootstrapping strategy: take as little salary as possible ...

[ ] Don't overreact ... but don't underestimate ...

[ ] Come to our senses ... what do we see, hear, smell, feel, and taste? ...

[ ] Promote our venture with exterior building signs ...

[ ] Success breeds success, and envy ...

[ ] Deliver the right product at the right price to the right customers at the right time and right place ...

[ ] The problem is never how to get new innovative thoughts into our mind, but how to get old ones out ... [Thank you, Dee Hock]

[ ] Continually review new products and services and processes from our competitors ...

[ ] Innovating: creating something new, competitive creativity ...

[ ] Key question for our venture: What hats do we need to fill in our venture? ...

[ ] That which blossoms will also decay ...

[ ] Save a little good for later ... we may need it ...

[ ] Key question for our venture: Does our name convey the proper image? ...

[ ] Key question for our venture: What are the risks and the rewards for our venture? ... is it worth doing it, or is it more risky not to do it? ...

[ ] Be persistent ...

[ ] Never stop exploring ...

[ ] Memory feeds imagination ... imagination feeds inspiration ... inspiration feeds creativity ... creativity feeds invention ... invention feeds innovation ... [Thank you, Amy Tan]

[ ] There is nothing worse than a sharp image of a fuzzy concept ... [Thank you, Ansel Adams]

[ ] A good read: Four Steps to the Epiphany (Steven Gary Blank) ...

[ ] The crew will be productive if they feel empowered ... [Thank you, D Michael Abrashoff]

[ ] Buy some lottery tickets ... seriously! We know we're going to lose, right? But still, we could win, someone is going to win, why not us?! Similar thought process investors go through when reading our business plan ...

[ ] Corporate entrepreneur credo: Work underground as long as possible ... publicity triggers the corporate immune mechanism ... [Thank you, Gifford Pinchot III]

[ ] Common cause of venture death: lack of skill ...

[ ] We'll be nothing if we're not excited by what we're doing!

[ ] There are three different competitor groups we'll need to keep in mind when we develop a new idea ... primary,

secondary and tertiary ... the placement of a new product within each group is based on how often our business would compete with them and how we would tailor our messages when competing with each of these groups ... [Thank you, Guy Kawasaki]

[ ] Never interrupt our competitor when they're making a mistake ... [Thank you, Napoleon Bonaparte]

[ ] Common cause of venture death: bad location ...

[ ] We don't know what we don't know ... we gotta get out there and learn!

[ ] A/B Testing ... compare two versions of a single variable typically by testing a subject's response to variable A against variable B, and determining which of the two variables is more effective ...

[ ] There's usually some process by which a potentially great idea gets prostituted into something lacklustre, or by which the wrong idea gets put forward ... [Thank you, Clayton Christensen]

[ ] Unicorn: an early-stage company that has grown significantly in perceived market value, generally over $1 billion ...

[ ] Hot or Cold ... what should we focus on today? ...

[ ] Beware of analysis paralysis ... [Thank you, Rick Daniel]

[ ] Key question for our venture: What characteristics are we looking to bring into our venture? ...

[ ] It is nice to be important, but it's more important to be nice ...

[ ] Be good at accepting compliments ... be better at giving them!

[ ] Never invest in anything that eats or needs repainting ... [Thank you, Billy Rose]

[ ] The best way to understand business is to start one ... [Thank you, Kathryn McGlamery]

[ ] Seed financing: money invested to fund an early-stage company ...

[ ] Create customer profiles ...

[ ] Life is filled with compromise ...

[ ] Learning is not compulsory ... neither is survival ... [Thank you, W Edwards Deming]

[ ] Common cause of venture death: wrong team ...

[ ] Promote our venture with tie-ins with other products ...

[ ] Listening is the sincerest form of flattery ...

[ ] How to ruin a business plan: Make mistakes; Underestimate the competition; Overestimate sales objectives; Try to do too much at once; Use erroneous data; Make up numbers without supporting data; Lie ...

[ ] Do not be mice or the cat will eat us ...

[ ] Promote our venture with blog marketing ...

[ ] Work hard ... work smart and it's not hard work ...

[ ] Income: money received for work or through investments!

[ ] Dollars or Cents ... sometimes it's better to make a lot of cents than just a few dollars ...

[ ] There is only today ... yesterday is gone, tomorrow may not come ...

[ ] Sleep on it ... the brain works in mysterious ways at night!

[ ] Competition or collaboration ... can current competitors change into competent collaborators? ...

[ ] Simple: easily understood or done ...

[ ] Somethings borrowed ... somethings new!

[ ] Them or Us ... what should we focus on today? ...

[ ] To get rich quick, buy a lottery ticket ...

[ ] Those who cannot remember the past are condemned to repeat it ... [Thank you, George Santayana]

[ ] Character: distinctive nature of something ... [Thank you, Google Dictionary]

[ ] Entrepreneurs are often good at symbolisms ...

[ ] Work expands to fill the available time ... We need to set time limits or the work may never be completed ... [Thank you, C Northcote Parkinson]

[ ] Launch: introduce a new venture, product, or service to the public or target market for the first time ...

[ ] Storyboarding is a easy form of prototyping ... high level view of high-level thinking ...

[ ] Wear hats in our venture ... we'll each have multiple hats at first ... as our venture matures, we'll pass some hats to new colleagues ...

[ ] Use credit cards wisely ...

[ ] Change can be cruel ... and sometimes kind, but usually cruel ...

[ ] Be purposeful, passionate, and persistent ...

[ ] If a wine says "Serve well chilled" on the label, it's a crummy wine ... what do we have on our label that our

customers might not be interpreting quite the way we wanted? ... [Thank you, Mari Stull]

[ ] We aren't gonna do what we don't like to do ... so we better be doing something we like to do ...

[ ] Rocket science has finite variables, entrepreneurship has infinite variables ...

[ ] Use what we have ... if we don't use it, do we need it? If we don't need it, why do we have it? ...

[ ] Genius simplifies the complex ...

[ ] How much burn will occur until our venture gets to profitability? ...

[ ] A pessimist has no motor, an optimist has no brakes ... [Thank you, Patrick Marcus]

[ ] Talk doesn't cook rice ...

[ ] Assure our products can be built efficiently in quantity ...

[ ] Our venture identity includes our name, logo, tagline, color scheme, product design, packaging, and decor ...

[ ] Recommended reading ... Entrepreneurship: A Real-world Approach (Rhonda Abrams) ...

[ ] Make the positives overweigh the negatives ...

[ ] Promote our venture with STEAM ... STEAM is short for Science, Technology, Engineering, Arts, and Math ... a movement in our schools these days to promote those disciplines to students ... is there some way we can promote STEAM with our venture? ...

[ ] Try to learn something about everything, and everything about something ... [Thank you, Thomas H Huxley]

[ ] A good business plan describes the manufacturing and/or service delivery processes and associated costs in appropriate detail ...

[ ] Knowledge is finite ... ignorance infinite ... [Thank you, Ryne Handelman]

[ ] A venture operations manual establishes a comprehensive source of company policies and procedures ...

[ ] Experience cuts costs ... the more we do something, the better we get ...

[ ] Creative people experiment and iterate ... yes, no, yes, no, maybe, maybe not ... wow! ... [Thank you, Emma L Murray]

[ ] Silly things do cease to be silly if they are done by sensible people in an imprudent way ... [Thank you, Jane Austen]

[ ] Do everything as if our customers are standing by our side ... we will not be embossed by our business practices ...

[ ] How to retain customers: keep them happy ...

[ ] Be open to suggestions ...

[ ] Much of what we see and hear becomes irrelevant after a week ...

[ ] Users are more productive with the mouse when they have less distance to travel and a larger target to click on to do their task ... [Thank you, Paul Fitts]

[ ] A venture operations manual promotes continuity in management style throughout the organization ...

[ ] Our learning has just begun again ...

[ ] A key marketing objective is to generate leads ... and lots of them! Leads to new customers!

[ ] Promote our venture with programs and yearbooks ...

[ ] Anger is a brief madness ... but it can do damage that lasts forever ...

[ ] The only way to make it cheaper is to make it better ... [Thank you, W Edwards Deming]

[ ] Be the best at what we do ... nobody else be better! ... [Thank you, Richard Branson]

[ ] More than three or four people leading the venture and the communication channels start to become too complex ...

[ ] Get voted onto the team every day ...

[ ] Skilled innovators and entrepreneurs are able to go beyond logical expectations ...

[ ] Art can free the soul ...

[ ] See our vulnerabilities so we can guard them from attack!

[ ] A venture plan serves as an alignment tool for a new business venture ... [Thank you, Tom Byers]

[ ] Common bootstrapping strategy: network wherever and whenever possible ...

[ ] Bread and water can so easily be toast and tea ... [Thank you, Kathy Hatch]

[ ] Define the terms ...

[ ] Our ability to change can change the world ...

[ ] Left alone, muddy water will gradually become clear ...

[ ] Talk is cheap ... action is valuable ...

[ ] People like people who compliment them ...

[ ] Of all the words of mice and men, the saddest are "It might have been." ... [Thank you, Kurt Vonnegut]

[ ] Business: an organization focused on the work that has to be done to profitably solve customer problems better than the competition ...

[ ] The old mantra was to make the brand irreplaceable ... that's not enough today ... now the brand has to be irresistible! ... [Thank you, Kevin Roberts]

[ ] If it sounds too good to be true, it probably is ... [Thank you, M Reeves]

[ ] Rub them against our teeth ... a real pearl will grate ... [Thank you, Tom Parker]

[ ] People influence people ... [Thank you, Robert F Mager]

[ ] It doesn't matter if a cat is black or white so long as it catches mice ... [Thank you, Deng Xiaoping]

[ ] Be proactive, not reactive ...

[ ] Don't just talk, act ...

[ ] It takes twenty attaboys to make up for one oh-shit! Corollary: The attaboys are a lot harder to come by, too!

[ ] Watch, listen, learn ... practice, understand ...

[ ] Keep our eyes on the road ahead ...

[ ] Search Engine Optimization (SEO): making changes or adjustments to a website with the intent of improving its search engine rankings ...

[ ] Branding mistake: no focus ... [Thank you, Jarad Hull]

[ ] Some people see things as they are and say "Why?" ... I dream things that never were and say "Why not?!" ... [Thank you, George Bernard Shaw]

[ ] To invent, we need a good imagination and a pile of junk ... [Thank you, Thomas Alva Edison]

[ ] Types of revenue models ... unit sales, advertising, data, intermediation, licensing, franchising, subscription, professional, utility and usage ...

[ ] Listen before speaking ...

[ ] Word of mouth doesn't just happen ... it happens because 1] we are amazingly better than everyone else, or 2] we are amazingly worse than everyone else!

[ ] Income Statement: a financial document that gives operating results for a specific period; it typically ...

[ ] Not all accidents are bad ... the smoke detector was discovered "by accident"! ... [Thank you, Cindy Pearsall]

[ ] Search others for their virtues, ourself for our vices ... [Thank you, R Buckminster Fuller]

[ ] We can do things quicker than we think ...

[ ] Pique the interest of the reader ...

[ ] Where there is creativity, there exists a chance of conflict ... [Thank you, Thomas Quick]

[ ] The vast majority of patents don't make any money ... the inventions simply aren't better than the existing alternatives! ... [Thank you, IEEE Spectrum]

[ ] Never underestimate the power of a happy customer ... [Thank you, Ian Lurie]

[ ] Be the best in the world ... if not the world, our community!

[ ] No one is above the law ... hard to run a business from a jail cell!

[ ] Procrastination is opportunity's natural assassin ... [Thank you, Victor Kiam]

[ ] It takes understanding to create desire ... make it easy for our customers to understand ...

[ ] It is better to be first in the mind than to be first in the marketplace ... [Thank you, Jack Trout]

[ ] Innovator's Dilemma: if we create something new our something old may be obsolete ... what impact might that have on our venture in the short and long run? ... [Thank you, Clayton M Christensen]

[ ] Industry Map: a visual and/or written representation of all players in an industry ...

[ ] Few things are impossible to diligence and skill ... [Thank you, Samuel Johnson]

[ ] Have a stock of promotion items that we can use as giveaways at our tradeshow booth ... [Thank you, Susan Ward]

[ ] Common Mistake: "We don't have to talk to our customers, we already know what they want!" ...

[ ] Catalog: a publication containing details and often photographs of items for sale ... [Thank you, Google Dictionary]

[ ] A person makes a name, not a name the person ... [Thank you, Barbara Ann Kipfer]

[ ] Drive as we would have others drive ...

[ ] Write a haiku ...

[ ] Offer incentives to stimulate ideas ... the best incentive is "thank you" ...

[ ] Write thank-you notes ... build our network of people who have helped us in the past and hopefully in the future, too ...

[ ] It's important that we like who we work with, and they like us ... trust and be trusted ...

[ ] Focus on niche markets ...

[ ] Bear down!

[ ] Assignments: a task given to someone as part of a job ...

[ ] The truth is necessary ... [Thank you, New York Times]

[ ] Help when it's needed is the best kind of help ...

[ ] Successful entrepreneurs have an ability to identify high-potential business opportunities ... [Thank you, Lynda Applegate]

[ ] Environment: the setting or conditions in which a particular activity is carried out ...

[ ] Whenever we fall, let's pick something up ... [Thank you, Oswald Avery]

[ ] Promote our venture with door-to-door canvassing ...

[ ] Successful innovators and entrepreneurs have an insatiably curious approach to life and an unrelenting quest for continuous learning ... [Thank you, Michael J Gelb]

[ ] How to retain customers: keep innovating ...

[ ] Don't be wasteful ...

[ ] Cents or sense ... if we don't have many cents, we will have to have a lot of sense ...

[ ] Don't make everything work ... some things just need to sit there ...

[ ] Think of our new idea in terms of its product/service features, the benefits to customers, the personality of our company, what key messages we'll be relaying, and the core

promises we'll be making to customers ... [Thank you, Guy Kawasaki]

[ ] How to kill creativity: "The rules are ..."

[ ] Every tale can be told in different ways ...

[ ] Apply all we've got to the project at hand ...

[ ] Complex scientific equations can be approximated within an order of magnitude using only calculations performed within the space available on the back of an envelope ... [Thank you, Enrico Fermi]

[ ] Customer problems range from unpalatable pain to passionate pleasure ...

[ ] Types of business plans ... back of a napkin, sketches, business model canvas, business brief, feasibility study, pitch deck, formal written business plan ... [Thank you, Heidi M Neck]

[ ] Promote our venture with signs towed by airplanes ...

[ ] Key question for our venture: What are our core competencies? ...

[ ] Eighty percent of sales comes from twenty percent of the clients ...

[ ] If the fans don't wanna come out to the ballpark, no one can stop 'em ... [Thank you, Yogi Berra]

[ ] Let's get our team all psyched up and ready to go ...

[ ] 1.61803398875 ... the Golden Mean, the Golden Section, or the Golden Ratio ... an expression that describes what is generally considered to be the universally perfect proportions in sciences such as architecture and anatomy ... two quantities are considered to be in a perfect golden ratio if the

larger quantity is approximately 1.61803398875 times the smaller one ...

[ ] Cream always rises to the top ...

[ ] Be accurate and correct ...

[ ] When it is dark, we can see the stars ... [Thank you, Ralph Waldo Emerson]

[ ] There is a fortune at the end of the rainbow ... it's getting to the end that's hard ...

[ ] Explain things simply ...

[ ] Sweat Equity: ownership earned by the entrepreneur in lieu of taking a salary ...

[ ] Some things don't have a particular order to follow ...

[ ] The conventional view saves us from the painful job of thinking ... [Thank you, John Kenneth Galbraith]

[ ] Doing is more valuable than thinking about doing ...

[ ] Most patents do not make money ... only about 2% are "winners" ... these are the 2% of patents that are not only inventive but also innovative ... they are both new and better than what is already out there ... [Thank you, IEEE Spectrum]

[ ] Beware of false profits ... "cooking the books" is not a sustainable business practice not to mention illegal, immoral, and unethical!

[ ] Experience the luxury of doing good ...

[ ] We have brains in our head, we have feet in our shoes, we can steer ourselves any direction we choose, we're on our own, and we know what we know, and we are the ones who'll decide where we go ... [Thank you, Theodor Seuss Geisel]

[ ] Market valuation factors ... market conditions, competition, market opportunity, value added, market comparables ...

[ ] Look for the critical success factors ... [Thank you, Amar Gupta]

[ ] A mind is a terrible thing to waste ... [Thank you, UNCF]

[ ] Continually identify new technology solutions ...

[ ] Nothing is impossible for the person who doesn't have to do it themself ...

[ ] Communications must have AIDA ... AIDA is an acronym for Attention, Interest, Desire, Action ... every ad or promotional activity should have these four elements ...

[ ] Got SPLUCK? ... Skills, Passion, LUCK ... the most successful innovators and entrepreneurs have the right balance of all three!

[ ] See us first at the finish line ...

[ ] Avoid offering unsolicited advice ...

[ ] All our dreams can come true, if we have the courage to pursue them! ... [Thank you, Walt Disney]

[ ] Start by copying the best-of-the-best competitor, then do it better than them ...

[ ] If we can dream it, we can do it ... [Thank you, Walt Disney]

[ ] Complete: all the parts ... not likely our venture plan will ever be complete, but don't let that stop us from going forward!

[ ] Easy to see, hard to do ...

[ ] First things first ... set priorities, then do them top to bottom, not the other way around (quite common ... lower priority items are easier than higher priority so often get done first) ...

[ ] Treat others like we want to be treated ...

[ ] Mental Error: "We're going to make a ton of money!" ... In pennies, a ton of money is $3,632.02. That's not too bad. A ton of hundred dollar bills is $90,800,000. Now that's a bit more challenging. It's also a pretty broad spectrum and pretty vague!

[ ] If we haven't found something strange during the day, it hasn't been much of a day ... [Thank you, John A Wheeler]

[ ] Don't rule out quitting ... if the glove don't fit, maybe we shoulda quit and find something more comfortable to wear? ... there may well come a time when we have to cut our losses and move on with life ... don't make a rash decision! ... [Thank you, Mike Birbiglia]

[ ] Key question for our venture: What is the planned use of proceeds from this round? ...

[ ] If they're reading, they're not listening ... that's why we should keep the number of words on our slide presentations to a minimum ...

[ ] Watch our thoughts; they become words ... watch our words; they become actions ... watch our actions; they become habits ... watch our habits; they become character ... watch our character; it becomes our destiny ... [Thank you, Frank Outlaw]

[ ] Consistency is the last refuge of the unimaginative ... [Thank you, Oscar Wilde]

[ ] No great thing is created suddenly ... [Thank you, Epictetus]

[ ] Wisdom is knowledge in action ... [Thank you, Austin Sams]

[ ] Planes or Trains or Automobiles ... what should we focus on today? ...

[ ] Growth: the process of increasing in size ...

[ ] When all aspects of our organization are aligned with our brand ... amazing things can happen! ... [Thank you, Leslie Bromberg]

[ ] Simple, short, sweet, and clear ... for all our communications ...

[ ] Analysis: detailed examination of the elements or structure of something, typically as a basis for discussion or interpretation ... [Thank you, Google Dictionary]

[ ] Make the competition irrelevant ...

[ ] Give the credit where it is due ... [Thank you, Joann MacMaster]

[ ] A venture operations manual reduces the number of emotional decisions, encouraging a businesslike climate of objectivity ...

[ ] Promote our venture with place mats ...

[ ] Have good manners ... [Thank you, Danila Rajski]

[ ] Ask for help ... identify good consultants, mentors, advisors, and collaborative partners that we can lean on now and then ...

[ ] Generalist: a person competent in several different fields or activities ...

[ ] The sale is not final until the check clears the bank ... and even then, the customer could still come back for a refund!

[ ] Potential business model: aggregate or distribute information ...

[ ] Our e-mail address is our personal brand, so keep it professional and simple ... [Thank you, Kevin Tofel]

[ ] The creative instinct is an enormous super energy which no single life can consume ... [Thank you, Pearl Buck]

[ ] Successful innovators and entrepreneurs are committed to success ...

[ ] Making a great presentation: Use visuals (slides) sparingly ... a rule of thumb is one visual for every one to two minutes of presentation time ... fifteen minute presentation means fifteen slides ... [Thank you, Ian McKenzie]

[ ] The truth has no agenda ... [Thank you, New York Times]

[ ] We do not merely want to be considered just the best of the best ... we want to be the only ones who do what we do! ... [Thank you, Jerry Garcia]

[ ] Angel investors commonly say they are wrong 9 times out of 10 ... the standard angel investor folklore is that 1 investment out of 10 will "make it big", 2 or 3 will be "living dead", and the other 6 or 7 will fail ...

[ ] Contingency Plan: an alternative course of action to follow if our primary path to success isn't leading us there ...

[ ] Comme ci comme ça ... like this like that ...

[ ] What we anticipate seldom occurs; what we least expect usually happens ... [Thank you, Benjamin Disraeli]

[ ] Key question for our venture: How can we build our business concept? ...

[ ] Learn "best practices" from firms that operate both inside and outside our industry ... [Thank you, William Bygrave]

[ ] Have people stand during meetings ... tends to keep things on track, short, sweet, to the point ... [Thank you, Todd Adams]

[ ] Is it a right-brain creative meeting, or a left-brain analytical meeting, or a meeting just to convey information? ... don't mix them up or we'll all get confused ...

[ ] How can we answer this Question: How will our venture attract and retain talent? ...

[ ] Key question for our venture: Who are our indirect competitors? ... what do we know about them now? What else do we need to know about them? ...

[ ] Dreams can become realities if we put our minds to work!

[ ] A real entrepreneur is somebody who has no safety net underneath them ... [Thank you, Henry Kravis]

[ ] Entrepreneurs are often objective thinkers ...

[ ] Need: something that is a necessity as opposed to a preferred want or desire ...

[ ] There is only now ... the past is just a memory, the future but a dream ...

[ ] Formula: a method, statement, or procedure for achieving something ... there are few magic formulas with business ventures, but there are benchmarks from which we can learn what does and doesn't work ...

[ ] Initial Public Offering (IPO): a corporation's first offer to sell stock to the public ...

[ ] We win more sales by energizing our current customers than by trying to capture new ones ... [Thank you, John McCain]

[ ] Skilled innovators and entrepreneurs are able to juxtaposition two or more incongruities ...

[ ] Empathy is a critical skill for innovators and entrepreneurs ... [Thank you, P G Greene]

[ ] Leadership is getting someone to do what they don't want to do in order to achieve what they want to achieve ...

[ ] Time is the longest distance between two points ... [Thank you, Tennessee Williams]

[ ] Some of the world's greatest feats were accomplished by people not smart enough to know they were impossible ... [Thank you, Doug Larson]

[ ] Out of the mouths of babes come great truths ...

[ ] How to improve our financial bottom line: hone our operational model to become more efficient ...

[ ] Prospect: short for Prospective Customer ...

[ ] When we have a brilliant idea, instead of making others think it is ours, why not let them cook and stir the idea themselves? ... [Thank you, Dale Carnegie]

[ ] Key question for our venture: How do we define a market need? ...

[ ] I do not think there is any thrill that can go through the human heart like that felt by the inventor as she sees some creation of the brain unfolding to success ... such emotions make a person forget food, sleep, friends, love, everything ... [Thank you, Nikola Tesla]

[ ] Lost opportunities cannot be recalled ... except in our minds, and that can be painful ...

[ ] A venture plan is ready when the investors are willing to put up the money to launch ... get the investors involved early in the creation of the plan!

[ ] Drive our dreams ...

[ ] A mistake is food for creativity ...

[ ] Set up a realistic budget ...

[ ] If we're are wrong, do it with style and grace ...

[ ] Forward or Backward ... what should we focus on today?

[ ] Bill of Material (BoM): a list of the raw materials, sub-assemblies, intermediate assemblies, sub-components, parts and the quantities of each needed to manufacture an end product ... [Thank you, Google Dictionary]

[ ] Be bold enough to make stuff that's small but great ... [Thank you, Mike Birbiglia]

[ ] Decision: the action or process of deciding something or of resolving a question ...

[ ] The future is not what will happen ... the future is what is happening! ... [Thank you, C K Prahalad]

[ ] Ask around ...

[ ] If the climate is cold, move somewhere warm ... if the customers just aren't heating up, let's try somewhere else ...

[ ] Damn the torpedoes, full speed ahead ... [Thank you, David Glasgow Farragut]

[ ] Potential venture legal issue: Failing to incorporate early enough ... [Thank you, Connie Bagley]

[ ] Take it all as it comes ...

[ ] Innovation and entrepreneurship are more art than science ...

[ ] Skilled innovators and entrepreneurs are able to think logically ...

[ ] Some questions have no answers ... some answers have more questions ...

[ ] Every exit is an entry somewhere else ... [Thank you, Tom Stoppard]

[ ] What does it mean to "make it"? ... if we don't know what that means, how will we know if we're there? ...

[ ] Eat less, exercise more ... [Thank you, James Arnold]

[ ] Speak when we're angry and we'll make the best speech we'll ever regret ... [Thank you, L J Peter]

[ ] Promote our venture with print on the box/container ...

[ ] Miracles multiply with sharing ...

[ ] All marketing has a message ... what's ours? ...

[ ] Strive for value ...

[ ] Strategic Position: the orientation of a venture in relation to the environment, in particular, the competition ...

[ ] It is better to bend than to break ...

[ ] Doing is learning ... doing it badly is still learning, but the lessons are much harder and more painful ... [Thank you, Gina Trapani]

[ ] Holy Cow: something that gets attention, or something that cannot be touched ...

[ ] If we have just one wish, make it an idea ...

[ ] The M's of Operations: money, machinery, manpower, mission, messages, material, methods ... [Thank you, Buck Crouch]

[ ] Hook readers right away with the executive summary, otherwise it is unlikely that they will read any other part of the plan ... [Thank you, Andrew Corbett]

[ ] Substitute ... What can we substitute? ... what can be used instead? ... who else instead? ... what other ingredients? ... what other material? ... what other process? ... what other power? ... what other place? ... what other approach? ... what other sounds? ... what other forces? ... "Instead of ... I can ..."

[ ] Promote our venture with drive-time radio ...

[ ] Identify our biggest opportunity ... apply ample resources!

[ ] Focus first on building customer loyalty ...

[ ] Successful teams collaborate ...

[ ] Describe the types and strengths of complementary relationships between companies in this industry ...

[ ] Quality is never an accident ... it is always the result of high intention, sincere effort, intelligent direction and skillful execution; it represents the wise choice of many alternatives, the cumulative experience of many masters of craftsmanship ... [Thank you, Rhoberta Shaler]

[ ] Promote our venture with postcards ...

[ ] An artist does not know when she is going to paint a masterpiece ... (As for Jim, I know I'm going to paint a messterpiece!) ...

[ ] How can we answer this Question: Should we donate our products? ...

[ ] Don't be a rubber stamp ... think!

[ ] Key question for our venture: What are the key metrics that our management team focuses on? ...

[ ] Don't tell 'em, show 'em!

[ ] Experiment: a procedure undertaken to make a discovery, test a hypothesis, or demonstrate a known fact ...

[ ] The future is what we make it ...

[ ] Promote our venture with loudspeaker announcements ...

[ ] Key question for our venture: What weaknesses do we need to strengthen in our venture? ... how are we going to do that? ...

[ ] How can we answer this Question: Can we license our products? ...

[ ] The best success comes after failure ...

[ ] The cure for boredom is curiosity ... there's no cure for curiosity ... [Thank you, Dorothy Parker]

[ ] Distribution: the act of distributing, or moving goods (products) to market for ultimate sale to end-user customers.

[ ] It's one thing to talk of bulls, it's another to be in the bullring ...

[ ] Use focus groups to gather primary research data ...

[ ] Stable Venture: an organization that has become financially self-sustaining and no longer requiring survival investment ...

[ ] Plant yellow flags where needed ... this might not work out like we thought!

[ ] Laggard: the last group of potential customers to adopt a new technology or innovation in the technology adoption life cycle ...

[ ] The rate at which angel-backed companies go public or get acquired is about 1 to 1.5 percent ... [Thank you, Scott Shane]

[ ] Bad news drives good news out of the media ... [Thank you, Lee Loevinger]

[ ] How to improve our financial bottom line: change our business model ...

[ ] A rotting fish begins to stink at the head ... [Thank you, Racine Salmon-a-Rama]

[ ] We are here now ... where is it we want to be tomorrow? ...

[ ] Character is what we have left when we've lost everything else ... [Thank you, Evan Esar]

[ ] There's idea creativity, material creativity, spontaneous creativity, event creativity, organizational creativity, relationship creativity, inner creativity, productivity creativity ... how can we not find somewhere to be creative some more ... [Thank you, William C Miller]

[ ] How to kill creativity: "We tried that and it didn't work ..."

[ ] Do background research first ...

[ ] Skilled innovators and entrepreneurs are objective in their approach to interpersonal relationships ...

[ ] Allow time for random exploration ...

[ ] Use a good mind in good ways ...

[ ] Social Responsibility: an obligation to act in ways that benefit society at large ...

[ ] Accounting: the action or process of keeping financial records ... [Thank you, Google Dictionary]

[ ] To act is easy, to listen is hard, to understand even harder!

[ ] Think of intuition as rapid cognition or condensed reasoning that takes advantage of our brain's built-in shortcuts ... [Thank you, Carlin Flora]

[ ] The truth is sometimes hard to accept ...

[ ] "I'm tryin' to think, but nothin' happens!" ... there are those days, eh? ...

[ ] Be careful not to be led astray by the needs, wants, and desires of just one customer ... some customers can be quite persuasive ... make sure their needs, wants, and desires are representative of the majority of our key customers ...

[ ] Identify the pros and the cons ... the ups and the downs, the rights and the lefts, the starts and the stops ...

[ ] We can cope with difficult situations ... we've done it before, we can do it again ... just hang in there, hard as it may be ...

[ ] Good communication is as stimulating as black coffee ... and just as hard to sleep after ... [Thank you, Anne Morrow]

[ ] The role of the Board of Advisors is to offer a source of expert guidance and feedback to the lead entrepreneur ... [Thank you, Andrew Corbett]

[ ] The more brains we use, the less material we need ...

[ ] Create a psychographic profile of our target market: characteristics based on attitudes, values, lifestyles, desires, business styles, and behavioral characteristics ... [Thank you, Rhonda Abrams]

[ ] The secret of success is doing something we love ...

[ ] Desire: strong feeling of wanting to have something that is not absolutely needed ...

[ ] Get our team all psyched up and ready to go ...

[ ] Venture building is more art than science ...

[ ] The right answer to the wrong problem is very difficult to fix ... [Thank you, Peter F Drucker]

[ ] Make a model ... if the model works, make some more ...

[ ] If it's a good idea today, will it be a good idea tomorrow? ... odds are, yes ... [Thank you, Warren Buffett]

[ ] Persuade by example ...

[ ] The truth is seldom simple ...

[ ] Do not overwork a willing horse ...

[ ] Typical new venture startup expenses: materials and supplies, equipment, facilities, labor, fees ...

[ ] Review the venture marketing and sales plan quarterly ... not too often but not too long between either. If everything is pretty much on track, that's great. If it's not, why not and what do we need to do to "course correct"? ...

[ ] Listen and learn ...

[ ] The harder we work, the luckier we'll get ... [Thank you, Gary Player]

[ ] Skilled innovators and entrepreneurs are not willing to give up ...

[ ] Beware of false prophet prophets ...

[ ] Skilled innovators and entrepreneurs ask questions, and lots of them ...

[ ] Behind every great fortune lies a great crime ... [Thank you, Mario Puzo]

[ ] To Know or Understand ... what should we focus on today? ...

[ ] Like an epidemic, change so often happens quickly and unexpectedly ... [Thank you, Malcolm Gladwell]

[ ] Entrepreneurial Mindset: the ability to recognize opportunities for innovation and enterprise ...

[ ] Promote our venture with discount premium booklets ...

[ ] Modify, minimize, magnify ... can we modify our product, service, or process in some way? ... change meaning, color, motion, sound, smell, form, shape? ... other changes? ... how can we 'minify': what can we remove? make smaller? condense? miniaturize? lower? shorter? lighter? omit? streamline? split up? understate? ... how can we magnify: what can we add? more time? greater frequency? stronger? higher? longer? thicker? extra value? plus ingredient? duplicate? multiply? exaggerate? ... "I can modify/minimize/magnify.. in this way ... to ..."

[ ] Write the executive summary after we have gained a good understanding of the business by working through all the other sections ... [Thank you, Andrew Zacharakis]

[ ] Focus on making an impact ...

[ ] Form: the visible shape or configuration of something ...

[ ] Branding mistake: trying too hard ... we want our customer to notice us but not be intimidated! ... [Thank you, Jarad Hull]

[ ] Accident: an incident that happens unexpectedly and unintentionally ... accidents aren't always bad things ... many great discoveries were made by accident ...

[ ] Beware: "investors" that want money to introduce us to other "investors" ...

[ ] Investor: an individual or organization that commits capital to a venture in order to gain financial returns ...

[ ] Culture is incredibly difficult to change ... do it right at the start ...

[ ] Customer Funding: a business arrangement between a venture and its customer wherein the customer agrees to provide the venture with some level of up-front funding in advance of delivery of the product or service ... many successful businesses are begun by making a sale first, they finding ways to deliver the goods ...

[ ] So many people, so many opinions ... there is nobody else like us and it is a mistake to think they are ...

[ ] It's hard to take an interest in work we don't like ... [Thank you, Francis Bacon]

[ ] Denial is not a river in Egypt ... [Thank you, Al Franken]

[ ] Skilled innovators and entrepreneurs are healthy ...

[ ] Keep it simple, stupid ... [Thank you, Seymour Cray]

[ ] Write with the reader in mind ... [Thank you, William N Yeoman]

[ ] If it looks right, it's right ... if it don't, it ain't! ... [Thank you, David Rogers]

[ ] Team time together ... take a little break and get to know each other better ...

[ ] How to kill creativity: "It's never been done before ..."

[ ] I cannot say whether things will get better if we change ... what I can say is they must change if they are to get better ... [Thank you, Georg C Lichtenberg]

[ ] Assume risk in exchange for profit ...

[ ] How to attract new customers: use a famous spokesperson to tell our story ...

[ ] When we succeed, be further inspired ... [Thank you, Reid Wilson]

[ ] Starting to do something is the hardest part of doing something ...

[ ] Always be better ... better is better than best ... someone else may think they are the best, but we're better ... best is stationary, better is moving ahead ...

[ ] Stay hungry, stay foolish ... [Thank you, Steve Jobs]

[ ] How to kill creativity: "We don't have money ..."

[ ] Task and assignments ... who is going to do what, when, where, why and how?

[ ] Reinvent ourselves, or risk becoming obsolete ...

[ ] Experience is that marvelous thing that enables us to recognize a mistake when we make it again ... [Thank you, Franklin P Jones]

[ ] Corporate entrepreneur credo: Be thoroughly engaged, take ownership, and persevere ... [Thank you, Gifford Pinchot III]

[ ] Don't burn the bridges behind us ... we might need them to get out later ...

[ ] It's never a shame when we admit we don't know something, and often a shame when we assume that we do ... [Thank you, Eric Zom]

[ ] Promote our venture with envelope stuffers ...

[ ] Be prudent and careful for the future because that's the only place in time we can go ...

[ ] People think in terms of people ... the primary function of the brain is to deal with social interactions ... feature people through names, personal pronouns, quotes, testimonials, stories, photos of satisfied customers, et al in our advertising ... [Thank you, Dean Rieck]

[ ] Wise people learn when they can ... fools when they must ... [Thank you, Arthur Wellesley]

[ ] A good business plan provides a rational explanation of why the investor should trust the management team to do what they say they are going to do ... [Thank you, University of Wisconsin Colleagues]

[ ] Put lots of money into the marketing budget ...

[ ] Beware of multiple-meaning words ... when someone says "Wow!", it's not necessarily a good thing ...

[ ] The is no great success without great commitment ...

[ ] "Th-th-th-that's all folks!" ... [Thank you, Porky Pig]

Thank You

I am not a natural-born writer. It's taken a fair bit of time to compile, write, and edit this book. I've done my best to say "thank you" to those that have loaned me a bit of their wisdom, their thoughts, their encouragement ... knowingly or not. Many of the people named in this book I have never met (Albert Einstein, for example)! For some, I may well have missed or misplaced credits, and I deeply apologize. For others, I cannot say thank you enough for all your help, tips, tools, rules of thumb, checklists, encouragement, support, feedback, and critiques. Again, thank you!

By the way, just in case you're wondering, I do know what an ellipsis is... (no space after a word, three periods in a row, then a space). Other than the one in the previous sentence, I don't think I used an ellipsis in this entire book. However, I did extensively use the "pauseandthink" ... (a space after a word, three dots, and another space). I used the pauseandthink wherever I wanted the reader to ... yep, pause for a little bit and think about what they had just read, and how they could use what they read in their own life. I'd like to think I invented the pauseandthink ... why not? Why shouldn't I get to invent a new punctuation mark? (This IS a book about innovation, after all!) ... If you'd like to use my pauseandthink, go ahead and do so. I just ask that you give me a little credit (but no blame, please!) when someone asks you about it ...

Finally ... Save Swing Jazz, Pelicans, and Oxford Commas!

Dedication

For Nancy with a Laughing Face ...

About the Author ...

Jim Jindrick has 30+ years experience in high-tech research and development, product engineering, operations and manufacturing, international marketing, and new business development. He's launched internal corporate ventures, spin-off companies, and independent startups.

Products and ventures his teams created generated over a billion dollars in lifetime revenue to date. Jim received some 35 U.S. and international patents for innovations in automotive test and diagnostic equipment, smart-grid electric power distribution automation devices, and personal computer instrumentation and data acquisition systems.

Jim was a Mentor-in-Residence for the McGuire Entrepreneurship Center in the Eller College of Management at the University of Arizona. He had the privilege of collaborating with over a thousand brilliant students creating over two hundred new venture plans. Jim was named an Eller Entrepreneurial Fellow, was an entrepreneur-in-residence at the University of Oregon, and a Moot Corp Fellow at the University of Texas.

A guest speaker for a variety of entrepreneurship and innovation events, workshops, university classes and programs, companies, and professional organizations, Jim is an advisor, consultant, mentor, and director for new venture startup and development clients throughout the world.

Jim is an IEEE Life Member. He also has an FCC General Radiotelephone Operator License and an amateur (ham) radio license. While a student at the University of Wisconsin, he supported himself working as an announcer, news reporter, and engineer for several radio and television stations in Milwaukee, Madison, and Racine.

Contact the author: Jim.528otips.com

Your Notes ...